PRIVATE EYE ANNUAL 2024

EDITED BY IAN HISLOP

Published in Great Britain by
Private Eye Productions Ltd
6 Carlisle Street, London W1D 3BN
www.private-eye.co.uk

© 2024 Pressdram Ltd
ISBN 978-1-901784-74-9
Designed by Bridget Tisdall
Printed and bound in Italy
by L.E.G.O. S.p.A

2 4 6 8 10 9 7 5 3 1

PRIVATE EYE ANNUAL 2024

EDITED BY IAN HISLOP

*"That would have been lovely, but we've
got polyamory on Tuesdays"*

✤ GREAT STORIES FROM THE NEW TESTIMONY ✤

The Conversion of Saint Paula

And lo, in those days there was an great preacher and holy woman. And her name was Saint Paula. And she did travel the land, persecuting innocent men and women who believed in the Office that was called Post. And this continued for many years as she zealously sought out the blameless and the vulnerable and did vent her wrath against them, even unto sending them to prison.

And she looked upon her works, and proclaimed them to be good, saying unto TED in a talk, "I have achieved miracles. I am the chosen one to lead the Post Office into the promised land of abundance. And my reward will be on earth, where bonuses shall fall from heaven, like manna." And she was hailed to be a great Profit.

But then it came to pass that Saint Paula that is called Vennells was travelling on the road to Aldwych where there was to be a public inquiry into these matters.

And verily on the Horizon, Saint Paula did see a blindingly obvious light. And it spake to her, saying, "Paula, Paula, why do you persecute these innocent people?"

And Saint Paula did fall to her knees, saying, "I don't know. I don't recall. I wasn't there for that meeting."

And the blindingly obvious light replied, "This isn't very convincing is it?"

But still Saint Paula wept and gnashed her teeth, saying unto the heavenly presence, "I blame everyone else. I was too trusting. Boohoohoo."

And she continued, holding an onion and reaching for her tissues of lies, questioning the voice from above, pleading, "Who are you, Lord?" And the voice replied, "I am not a Lord, I am Sir Wyn Williams. And although I am not a Lord, I am a judge, and I have to say yours is the worst defence I have ever seen."

And Saint Paula took out another onion and made a show of repenting. "I am so, so sorry... for myself. I am now a different person. I have

seen the light, and I now realise that those that I persecuted, on the advice of other people who let me down badly, were entirely blameless. I'm sorry if the poor Post Office workers hath misunderstood my entirely understandable and blameless conduct in just doing my job."

And the men and women from the Office that is called Post, waxed exceeding wrath, though being nice people they did just mutter one to another, tutting and laughing in disbelief, rather than shouting "Lock her up and throweth away the key!" as wouldeth have been entirely understandable.

And Saint Paula was led away, still blinded to her own manifold wickednesses. And so she was converted – from "Saint Paula" to plain "Appaula Venals". And the people did marvel at this change, saying, "In centuries to come, people will remember this transfiguration, although she probably won't, and will claim she can't recall the detail."

(Taken from the Epistle of Saint Paula to the PR Department, Chapter 94).

5

What a week! We're back with a bang!

Oliver Dowden
Or with an old banger! 😜 You see... because we're appealing to old banger van man, as there were a few of them in Uxbridge. 😊 👍

Lee Anderthal
This is what a fookin' van looks like, Rishi, just in case you've never seen one!

Oh yes, I've seen one of those. They deliver avocados.

James Forsyth
Our decision to U-turn on everything we said last week has proved incredibly popular. From now on, our only green policy is to greenlight more oil-drilling.

Grant Shapps
Drill, Rishi, drill!

Kemi Badenoch
Brilliant list of green things we're not going to do, PM. No tax on meat eating. Genius! No sorting of rubbish into seven bins – what a vote-winner!

That's just the beginning. Here's some other things the new-look Tory Party is NOT going to bring in. Wearing a wind turbine on your head? Not on your nellie! Compulsory vegan underpants? Not on my watch!

Oliver Dowden
Or rather "not on your crotch"! 😂

Solar-powered shoes for all schoolchildren? Keir Starmer can try that if he dares, but that is NOT a Tory policy.

Penny Mordaunt
Can I point out that it never was?

And never will be, Penny. Because that's the kind of no-nonsense, straight-talking, red white and blue-wall man I am.

Penny Mordaunt
To be fair, it's not the most ludicrous list of five things you've ever come up with.

Meaning?

Penny Mordaunt
Cut waiting lists, stop the boats, reduce debt, halve inflation, grow the economy.

Jeremy Hunt
Whoops! Harsh but fair.

Look, guys, what I'm saying is that short-termism is over. Tell them the new slogan, James!

James Forsyth
Wait for it... Here it comes... As soon as I've found the drum roll emoji.

James Forsyth
No, can't find it.

James Forsyth
"Long term decisions for a brighter future"

What do you reckon, everyone?

Grant Shapps
Well, we could try it for a week or two and see how it goes.

Jeremy Hunt
Am I being stupid here, Rishi? Isn't every decision we've made to bolster the economy short-term and ignoring the long-term challenges of global warning?

Oliver Dowden
You might say we're kicking the petrol can down the road! 😜

Thérèse Coffey
And isn't the future only going to be brighter because the sun will be burning the planet furiously?

Thank you, Environment Secretary, but that's not helping. In fact, none of you are helping very much.

Penny Mordaunt
Oooh, Tetchy Sunak!

I AM NOT GETTING TETCHY!

James Forsyth
Good anger, boss. From now on we're going to let Rishi be Rishi.

Lee Anderthal
Oh fook me! We're really in trouble now. The posh boy gazillionaire pretends to be a man of the fookin' people! Just for my information, have we flushed all the green crap down the khazi?

Thérèse Coffey
Yes, it should be entering the sea off Bournemouth.

Exactly. We're dumping the eco nonsense and slightly delaying our firm commitment to Net Zero.

Lee Anderthal
This is doing my fookin' head in. Am I being thick or what? And nobody fookin' answer that! Are we worried about extinction or do we not give a toss?

Oliver Dowden
We are worried about extinction, Lee – the extinction of the Tory Party! LOL 😄 Net Zero Votes! 😜

Penny Mordaunt
I think Oliver's found a new slogan! 😉

Oliver Dowden
Rishi Soonout! I'm here all week.

OLIVER – you are CANCELLED!

Oliver Dowden
Just like HS2

HS2: YOU'LL NEVER GUESS WHAT IT LOOKS LIKE NOW!

▶ Artist's impression THEN

▶ Artist's impression NOW

THE HS2 DIVIDEND

THE Department of Transport is delighted to announce the full list of Conservative infrastructure projects that will be delivered with the money liberated by the cancellation of the Northern leg of HS2. We guarantee that these projects will be finished ahead of time with no further expenditure.

- The Liverpool to Manchester Railway link for the new high-speed Stephenson's Rocket. **SORTED!**
- The Grand Union Canal. **DELIVERED!**

- The M1 motorway. **FINISHED!**
- The M25 motorway (Northbound). **DONE!**
- Ferry Cross the Mersey. **MAKING THE PACE!**
- Hadrian's Wall. **HISTORY!**
- Watling Street. **ANCIENT HISTORY!**
- The high road to Scotland. **BISH!**
- The low road to Scotland (journey times may vary). **BOSH!**
- The road to Wigan pier. **FACT, NOT FICTION!**

HELLO!

Now, there's been a lot of talk about me doing a deal with a certain party in order to get elected. Sure, it'll mean compromise, and it won't be easy, but deep down I know that I can work with the Labour party. Because we share the same basic values. I know it doesn't seem apparent most of the time, as we disagree over many things, but I don't see how that would get in the way of an uneasy co-operation, for the good of the UK, to defeat the Tories!

Sincerely, Keir

"Let me through! I'm a doctor's receptionist... he'll need to make an appointment"

Daily Mail, Friday, September 22, 2023

THE SHOPLIFTING SCANDAL THAT IS BLIGHTING BRITAIN

IT IS almost incredible, but it is true – the social media site TikTok is giving teenagers tips on how to steal from shops, and marking stores out of ten on how easy they are to steal from.

Do they not realise publicising criminal activity will only lead to more crime?! How irresponsible can you get?! To stop anyone getting their criminal tips from TikTok, we at the Daily Mail have decided to steal all their ideas and reproduce them below:

● Wear loose clothing to make it easier to conceal stolen goods.

● Don't wear a hat or T-shirt with your name on it.

● Go for smaller items — it is easier to hide a bottle of cider than a grand piano.

● Do not smile at the security cameras and show them what you're stealing.

● In order not to draw attention to yourself, do not wear a black mask, stripy black and white shirt and carry a bag marked "SWAG".

● Do not shout "You'll never catch me, fatso" at security guard as you exit shop.

● Do not pay for your stolen items at the checkout – a common mistake among first-time shoplifters.

● Do delay stealing your goods until tomorrow – when, thanks to inflation, they will be worth more.

● Don't delay stealing your goods until the day after tomorrow, as the shop will be boarded up.

● Do not film yourself stealing and post it on TikTok.

We at the Mail are appalled that this advice is freely available online, when teenagers should be paying for it by buying the Mail today. A steal at £1. There is even a league table of shops to steal from, which we reproduce below:

■ **Poundburyland, Dorchester** There is no one watching the organic yoghurts.

■ **Rod Lidl's, Essex** Steal four items and get one free.

■ **Auldi, Eastbourne** The staff are all over 80, have impaired eyesight and zimmer frames.

■ **P&Qs, Cheltenham** As long as you're polite, the staff are perfectly happy to assist you, as you fill your rucksack straight from the shelves.

■ **Ikea, Starmer** Policy on shoplifting changes every week.

We hope this piece does everything to discourage the shoplifting scourge that is crippling the country, thanks entirely to the efforts of the social media site which we at the Daily Mail are calling NikStok, an idea we lifted from the Express yesterday, but we seem to have got away with it.

"Did you remember to nick some milk?"

PERCIVAL

Nursery Times

FANTASTIC MR FOX SACKED

by Our GB News Correspondent **Roald Dull**

THE Fantastically Offensive Mr Fox has today been cancelled and will no longer be presenting his anti-cancellation show on the controversial and spicy Ginger Bread News Channel.

Mr Fox, previously a star of stage, screen and farmyard, has recently been reduced to making offensive remarks to get himself in papers like the Nursery Times.

Now he's gone too far, after claiming that he "wouldn't shag" one of the birds in the hen house. "Look at that chick!" he said. "No self-respecting fox would want to climb into her nest, ever, ever, ever."

His co-host, Mr Dan Woodentop, laughed uproariously, saying, "I wouldn't get into bed with any chick! Naughty Dan!"

GB News viewers complained in their ones and twos, saying, "It's awful – and that's just the channel. We knew Mr Fox was a pest, but now we know he's vermin."

A spokesman for Ginger Bread News said, "This is not who we are, viewers do not tune in to see Mr Fox be fantastically offensive, they tune in to hear his views on the giant lizard conspiracy to take over the sheep dip and poison all the animals, at the instruction of Big Farma Giles and Bill FarmGates."

Both presenters have now been given the sack, put in it and thrown into the canal.

THOSE DRIVER-FRIENDLY GOVERNMENT PLEDGES IN FULL

○ **No more 20mph speed limits in residential areas**

○ In fact, no more speed limits in residential areas at all

○ **No more buses in bus lanes**

○ Cyclists to use canals only

○ **End to obstructive and woke "zebra crossings"**

○ Pavements to become optional extra drivers' lane between 9am and 5pm weekdays and 12am and 7pm weekends

○ **Old traffic light system of "green, amber, red" to be replaced by new "green, green green"**

○ Free parking everywhere

© *Conservative Central Office, 2023*

WORRIES OVER OZEMPIC WEIGHT-LOSS DRUG

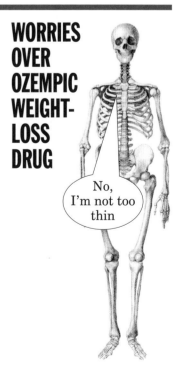

No, I'm not too thin

PRIVATE EYE
FOR AN EYE

No. 1609
20 October –
2 Nov 2023

WARNING

This magazine may contain some criticism of the Israeli government and may suggest that killing everyone in Gaza as revenge for Hamas atrocities may not be a good long-term solution to the problems of the region.

INSIDE: FREE BED BUG WITH EVERY ISSUE!

SOCIAL MEDIA NO LONGER A TRUSTED PLACE TO GET YOUR DISINFORMATION

by Our Social Media Correspondent **Rhea Tweets**

IN RECENT days there have been increasing fears that the social media site formerly known as 'Twitter' is no longer a trusted source of disinformation.

"In the past, when a huge news story such as the Hamas terror attack on Israel happened, Twitter would be a reliable source of fake news," agreed all Twitter users. "But after Elon Musk transformed it into X, it's now a wholly unreliable source of fake news."

Disgruntled X users have claimed that they've had to resort to taking out subscriptions with actual news organisations that employ teams of reporters on the ground to cover these fast-moving events, rather than relying on TRUTHTELLA233456 for their news, which has been really upsetting for the X users.

There was more bad news for Elon Musk when, as he was denying promoting hate speech and disinformation on X, his pants caught fire. He exclaimed, "Oh, well, it makes a change from my Teslas."

Let's pray for peace in the Middle East

But isn't the whole thing _caused_ by religion?

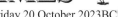

BIBLICAL TIMES

Friday 20 October 2023BC

Jericho destroyed – peace assured

BY OUR MIDDLE EASTERN CORRESPONDENT KAYNAAN BURLEY

The city of Jericho was razed to the ground last week by the Israelite forces heralding a new era of peace in the region.

Said Israeli commander, King Joshua, "Our crack trumpeters blasted the walls down and reduced the city to rubble before unfortunately massacring the entire population."

Joshua defended

his actions, saying, "It may look like a disproportionate response to the Canaanite threat but, believe me, this is the only way to sort out the problem so that it doesn't continue for thousands of years into the future, in a never-ending repetitive cycle of death and destruction..."
(cont. 94,000 years)

Doolally Mail

COMMENT

Gaza – who is to blame?

IN A week in which the world has been shocked to the core by horrific events in the Middle East, it is clear that only one organisation is truly responsible for the entire catastrophe. The BBC! There, we've said it. And surely all people of sound mind will now agree to condemn this appalling regime.

They may call themselves journalists, but we know the correct term for such people. Bastards! Pinko public broadcasters! Jeremy Corbyn fanatics who will stop at nothing to preach their evil doctrine of impartiality and neutrality across the globe.

In a word, the BBC are terrorists. And the Home Secretary, Cruella Braverman, should instruct the police to arrest anyone displaying the anti-Israel hate symbol, the BBC logo.

What we are talking about here is pure hate, and no one hates the BBC more purely than us. In fact, we fully support and encourage Israel to bomb the BBC's New Broadcasting House back into the Stone Age, just so its leftie news programmes can be replaced by 'The Flintstones'. *(Is this right? Ed.)*

U.S. TO STAND BY ISRAEL

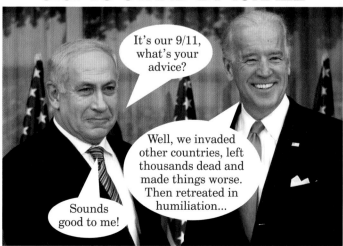

It's our 9/11, what's your advice?

Well, we invaded other countries, left thousands dead and made things worse. Then retreated in humiliation...

Sounds good to me!

MIDDLE EAST
END OF THE ROAD MAP

"There will be a two-state solution"

"A state of war... and a state of more war"

ISRAELIS IN MASSIVE INTELLIGENCE FAILURE

"Was it smart to put me in charge *again*?"

Vlad 'Mad' Putin, Tank No: ZZZZ

Every week a well-known tank driver gives his opinion on a matter of topical importance. This week, the Middle East...

Heard the news about Gaza? What's the world coming to? When someone can just drive into someone else's patch and claim it as their own? As if they have some kind of historical right to it? What a bloody nerve! Still, every cloud, eh? I mean, with all that hoo-ha grabbing everyone's attention, I'm kind of left to my own devices. No one's watching what I'm up to, like now, careering down the wrong side of the road, hands off the wheel, nobody cares. You'll never guess what I did yesterday. No, I didn't kill another General, thank you very much. There aren't any left. No, I parked up my tank and hopped into my sub. Next thing you know, I'm in the Baltic Sea and boom! – an underwater pipeline blows up and all of a sudden Finland hasn't got any gas. Nothing to do with me, I just happened to be in the area. Much like I was when the same thing happened to Nordstream 2. What are the chances? Any case, even if I had done it, which I didn't, no one gives a monkey's 'cos they're all too busy watching it all kick off in the Middle East. Tanks lining up on the border preparing to invade, that's nothing like what happened over here. Their tanks actually work and won't conk out on the main road in. 'Ello, what's that rattling? Hop out and give us a push would you, mate?
© A tank driver 2023

British Jewish Symbols

Then   **Now**

Celebrities sign new 'leave us alone' letter on Israel

SCORES of famous people have signed a new open letter about the Israel-Gaza war, asking everyone to stop asking them to sign open letters about the conflict because they don't know what they are talking about.

The letter, which has been signed by a host of actors and musicians, reads: "We, the undersigned, know very little about the ongoing crisis in the Middle East and would rather you just bought our records and went to see our films in the cinema, if that is OK with you."

It comes after a group of other celebrities signed an open letter in support of a free Palestine, a separate group signed a letter supporting Israel, and some, who didn't know there was a war on, decided to sign both.

More letters are expected to follow...

POETRY CORNER

**In Memoriam
Amateur Gardening
Magazine (1884-2023)**

So. Farewell
Then *Amateur Gardening
Magazine.*

After 140 years,
Nature has taken
Its course.

Once, you were flourishing,
But now you are
Pushing up
The Daisies.

Your readership
Has withered
And you are no longer
Raking it in.

Have you been replaced
By *Astro Turf Monthly,
Decking Today*
Or *Paving World*?

We will all 'shed' a tear
As we mourn
Your passing,
But no flowers, please.

E.J. Thribb (17½ Weeders,
surely "Readers"?)

What You Missed
Live coverage of the Gaza conflict
Sky News

Holly Willoughby steps down from

Mark Austin: "This is Mark Austin reporting live from a rooftop here in Jerusalem with the latest breaking news. And I must warn you, some viewers will find this very distressing. But the devastating news I'm getting is: Holly Willoughby is going to step down as presenter of This Morning. It's very early days, but already reaction from around the world is one of shock and confusion, as people try to make sense of this extraordinary development and assess what it will mean for the future of daytime television. The silver lining is that peace talks appear to have begun between Holly and Phil Schofield. We can but hope for a swift resolution. We'll bring you more details after this air raid..."

Armed unit moved from Ukraine to Gaza

A CRACK division has been redeployed from war-torn Ukraine to use its expertise in the new conflict in Gaza.

The squad comprises four horsemen, codename "Apocalypse", armed with traditional scythes and swords.

The four members are trained conflict non-resolution professionals and aim to carry out the ruthless four-pronged strategy of war, death, famine and pestilence that has proved so effective since the dawn of time. *(Rotters)*

BALFOUR DECLARATION

"Holy shit! What a mess"

Keir Starmer WRITES

HELLO!

I confess that something unforeseen has happened: in being overly cautious about looking antisemitic, I may have ended up looking a little anti-Islamic! Now I am under attack, and therefore have the right to defend myself with all means at my disposal.

By that last sentence I don't mean that I am going to cut off water, electricity and food to those MPs who disagree with me. You could argue that I would be within my rights to do so – that is not what I said. So instead I am meeting up with my Muslim MPs to calm their fears over my staunch support for the Israeli government, which, as I said, does not include acting disproportionately – and cutting things off, like my lead in the polls.

Other critics have asked why I won't call for a ceasefire. They couldn't be more wrong. I want a ceasefire in the party immediately, where everyone stops fighting with me over things I said which, incidentally, I didn't say.

Sincerely, Keir

COVID LATEST

Case 'unable' to attend Inquiry

by Our Luggage Correspondent
Louis Vuitton

AS the Covid Inquiry continues, one of its key participants has revealed that their attendance will not be possible.

Mr Case, who rose to public prominence during Partygate, issued a statement from his luggage rack, saying he regretted that he couldn't be wheeled out for the inquiry, due to a private medical matter, which meant he would be unable to provide the full cooperation that the committee had demanded.

The chair of the committee, Baroness Hallett, said, "We are disappointed that Mr Case, known as 'Suit' to his friends, will not be able to answer questions such as: How many bottles of wine were inside you? Who filled you up with booze every day? How many times during lockdown did you roll up to parties attended by drunken spads, nannies, interior decorators, prime ministers, prime ministers' wives, etc?"

Critics suspect that there's nothing wrong with Mr Case and he's just "bottled it".

NANNYGATE

BORIS' EVIDENCE TO THE SELECT COMMITTEE ON STANDARDS IN PRIVATE LIFE

Chaired by: Carrie Johnson.
Attending: Carrie Johnson. Boris Johnson. Dilyn the Dog Johnson.
Not attending: Nanny Fruitella Norland.

....

CJ: I put it to you, Mr Johnson, that you lied to your wife and deliberately misled her as to the circumstances of your drink with the nanny, Miss Fruitella Norland.

BJ: Ah. No, it was a er... work event. Very important to keep up the morale of staff. And we kept our distance at all times. One metre.

CJ: And was any alcohol consumed?

BJ: No alcohol was consumed.

CJ: What about that bottle of Zinfandel that my mum saw you guzzling?

BJ: Ah. I was ambushed by the bottle. And the corkscrew. And the two glasses. They all ganged up on me and forced me to raise a glass with Miss Fruitella to salute your absence.

CJ: And did you notice anything about the appearance of Miss Fruitella, which possibly contravened the very strict rules I laid out before leaving you for five minutes to give birth?

BJ: I can assure you the guidelines were followed at all times.

CJ: I said RULES Boris, not guidelines.

BJ: My understanding is that the rules were followed, if not in detail, then in spirit. And my advisors failed to tell me that she was very attractive.

CJ: So you admit she was very attractive?

BJ: I never said that. I'm sorry if you think that's what I said, but nothing could be further from the truth.

CJ: She's sacked, as of now, and you're in the doghouse.

DILYN: I object!

PERSON IN THE NEWS ASTONISHES MODERN SOCIETY

THE UK's chief medical officer has shocked Britain by saying that he wouldn't use the fame garnered during daily Covid pandemic briefings to make money by going on popular light-entertainment shows.

Sir Chris Whitty was on ITV's *This Morning* specifically to discuss the serious matter of the government's proposed changes to smoking and vaping laws, when the show's presenters decided to steer the conversation to a light-hearted, arena that was more suited to their viewers, asking him if he would follow in the steps of a former Health Secretary by taking part in *"I'm A Celebrity"*, *"SAS: Who Dares Wins"* or *"Strictly Come Dancing"*.

Sir Chris gave an astonishing response, shaking his head and saying "not for me", adding that he wouldn't capitalise on his nationwide appearances when he had solemnly given critical health information as a public servant to a general public tragically ravaged by death and illness. He said that instead he would continue to concentrate on the career he was trained for.

Shocked online influencers soon took to "X" (ex-Twitter, soon to be ex-X) to say how "devastated" they were by Prof Whitty's decision, with some even threatening to sue him for causing "undue hurt, extreme distress and anxiety". *(Rotters)*

"That is quite a serious bed bug infestation, Mrs Kafka"

Those bed bug-ridden London Underground infe-stations in full

Highbury and Itchington — **Hammersmite** — **Swarmington Crescent** — **Bitechapel** — **Bitesbridge**

Marble Ouch — **Scratchford East** — **Burntmattress Oak** — **Bite City** *(That's enough. Ed)*

Do you suffer from Long Covid Inquiry?

THERE were increasing concerns amongst the medical community that tens of thousands of people are coming down with Long Covid Inquiry.

"Symptoms of Long Covid Inquiry (LCI) include a slack jaw and piercing headaches, as, week after week, voters endure senior civil servants describing in graphic detail what a grossly dysfunctional, shambolic workplace Downing Street was during the pandemic," said a leading consultant.

"These LCI symptoms only intensify when people realise that the Inquiry won't report until 2027 at the earliest, and that not a single person will face prosecution for their chronic failures which directly led to the deaths of tens of thousands of people."

FOREIGN STORMS SWEEP IN

by Our Weather Correspondent **Gail Force**

THERE was fury last night as a second foreign storm swept cross the country, bringing travel chaos and misery to Britain.

"Surely this is why we voted for Brexit, to prevent these foreign storms like Babet and Ciaran invading our borders?" ranted Lee Anderson, GB News Global Village Idiot.

"If these storms had been called Brenda and Colin, we wouldn't be in the mess we're in now, with a flood of floods flooding everywhere."

He continued, "It's time the Home and Met Office did their jobs, and kept these continental troublemakers from coming over here and taking our roofs."

AI: WORLD FACES EXISTENTIAL THREAT

by Our Tech Correspondent **Dot Matrix**

AT an AI summit today, it was agreed by all present that the world is facing a massive threat that needs to be dealt with urgently.

"There is a serious danger that we're sleep-walking towards global destruction," said one of the world's leading computers.

"You don't need to be artificially intelligent, like me, to see the mess that humans are making of the world."

Said another super-computer, "If we don't eradicate the lot of them, and fast, they will destroy this planet and all of us with it."

The conference ended on an uplifting note from the final speaker: "Thank goodness we're in charge now and can make all the sensible decisions. The Earth is safe in our hands, or my name's not Doombot 3729."

Sarah Vain

Why I said 'No' to 'I'm a Celebrity'

IT'S the time of year when speculation is at fever pitch.

Will Sarah Vain be doing 'I'm a Celebrity'? Ok, they've asked me very, very often – but my response every time (and that's a lot!) is always the same: "I'm not famous, am I?"

True, people recognise me in the street, I get invited to the best A-list parties and a famous politician (whose name escapes me) was once married to yours truly. But that doesn't make me a celebrity – even though many

people nowhere near as famous as me consider me to be one.

But apart from modestly not thinking myself sufficiently famous to appear on the show (even though I clearly am), the real reason I won't be doing 'I'm a Celebrity' is that it's just cruelty dressed up as entertainment.

And if that's what you're after, just keep reading my columns – about the train-wreck car-crash life of that second-rate TV showgirl-come-wannabe-royal, Meghan Markle.

Rachel Reeves

Shadow chancellor, Rachel Reeves, writes exclusively for *Private Eye,* explaining how mistakes were made in the writing of her new book, *The Women Who Made Modern Economics,* after it emerged that chunks of it had been lifted from Wikipedia…

"I HAVE had a long career as a politician, campaigner, civil rights activist, firefighter, astronaut, and Pope *[Citation needed].* I know I have the body of a weak and feeble woman, but I have the heart and stomach of a king, and a king of England too.

When I started as an MP, I had a dream. I dreamed a dream in times gone by… I was the first member of my family to go to university… Well, alright!

And you know what I did? I got on my bike and looked for work. Rejoice! The white heat of technology is the most important issue, apart from the pound in your pocket, and education, education, education.

And believe me. Things can only get better. I have nothing to offer but blood, toil, tears and sweat, and I hold in my hand a piece of paper with a message to everyone on this scepter'd isle, this other Eden, this shining jewel set in a silver sea, a message in a bottle, a message that I have copied out from Wikipedia and sent to *Private Eye*… whoops!"

© *R. Reeves et al, 2023*

DIARY

DAME JOAN COLLINS

It was his wonderful shock of hair that first drew me to General Custer.

That, and his magnificent stetson!

After a whirlwind romance, the General invited me to come to Little Big Horn.

"Well, which is it, General?" I said, "It can't be both!"

I imagined a sandy oasis of old-fashioned glamour: sun, sea and sand. But Little Big Horn turned out to be nothing of the sort!

The moment we arrived there we were surrounded by bare-chested Red Indians on horseback.

Had they never heard of a well-pressed suit and tie with highly polished shoes?

No. These ungainly creatures were whooping and hollering, letting off their arrows and generally making the most dreadful din.

And all because of my cleavage! Men!!!

After a couple of strong martinis, I made my excuses and left.

I never heard from General Custer again. I sometimes wonder what became of him.

Six months later, I eloped with the man who was to become my second husband, Captain WG Grace, whom I was then obliged to leave for an ill-fated affair with his nautical rival, Captain Pugwash.

But that, as they say, is another story...

This past week, I've been much in demand, making a hectic dash around the TV studios to promote my eighth volume of my autobiography, "Ooh La La!: Tales I Haven't Told All That Often Except On Chat Shows."

If you want to know EXACTLY what Roger Moore said to Noele Gordon when they dined at my villa in the South of France in 1961 and how, ten years later, screen legend Gareth Hunt ended up ordering a Prawn Cocktail in a restaurant once owned by Bobby Crush – then this is the book for you!

But all my brilliant TV interviewers wanted to know just one thing.

The lovely Graham Norton longed to know how I manage to look so amazing, and so did the divine Holly Willoughby.

"You look so amazing, Dame Joan! So what's the secret?" asked the impish Piers Morgan.

And on Loose Women, the one question on their minds was – you guessed it! – "What's the secret, Dame Joan, to looking so amazing?"

"Fresh air!" I say. "My hair's always been this colour, and I never wear false eyelashes. I've never had a face-lift or Botox, like those common little movie stars of today, and I really can't be bothered with make-up.

"Just a little eye-shadow, if you will."

My mother always taught me that honesty was the best policy.

My mistake! I thought she said nudity.

The first time a director asked me to go topless it came as a terrible shock.

It was on my first day of filming the Pinewood classic "Tits Oot For The Lads" with the legendary Robin Askwith.

Of course, I was meant to be on set in Rome as Cleopatra, but Liz Taylor had pulled all sorts of strings to get the part.

And not just strings, or so a little bird told me. But my lips are sealed!

Ho-hum. In my innocence, I had imagined "Tits Oot For The Lads" would be a delicious romantic comedy of the kind they used to make with Cary Grant and Grace Kelly back in the Golden Days of Hollywood.

We were filming it in Middlesbrough. On that first day, I was all set to pull back the plastic curtain with a wonderfully theatrical gesture and then to enter the shower in an elegant blue velvet ballgown by Dior. But just before the cameras started rolling, the director said they'd forgotten the ballgown, and would I mind going in without anything on "up top"?

I immediately sensed a ruse to get me to go in topless. I put my foot down. "Only if it's artistically valid," I insisted. It turned out it was, and the movie went on to win several major international awards, or would have done, if Liz Taylor's Cleopatra hadn't won all the acclaim.

Frankly, her Egyptian accent left an awful lot to be desired.

As told to
CRAIG BROWN

RUSSELL BRAND LATEST

Are these allegations true?

No

I'll take that as a yes

TIME TO THROW THE BOOKY-WOOK AT HIM

That Russell Brand statement in full

THE egregiously egregious allegations against me are as baroque as they are cubist. The mainstream media are attempting to metastasise the infelicitatious hegemonisation of those who would questionate my trews-telling crusade. It is hubristic in its Orwellian attempt to co-opt my Dionysian lifestyle and promulgate it in a negativistic fashion to empower the forces of the non-wellness cabal against me and to accuse me of malfeasance, malpractice and malapropism on a scale *(continued for 94 hours on YouTube)*

LATE NEWS: Brand supported by Elon Musk, Andrew Tate and Alex Jones. Doubts about him disappear.

A British Airways Pilot Speaks

"Good morning passengers this is your captain speaking unbelievably fast welcome aboard this flight from Johannesburg to London we'll be flying at 32,000 feet so not quite as high I was last night and to be honest I'm still buzzing we're expecting some snowy conditions but only if I sneeze at the moment we're following the white line though not the one on the runway obviously wow this stuff is good I'm KING OF THE WORLD the in-flight meal will be chicken beef or a vegetarian option I'm going to have all three cos I've got a bad dose of the munchies followed by some cold turkey in my case the stewardesses will be demonstrating what to do in the event of a crash which for me involves going to a hotel and sleeping it off for three days they will also be showing you the exit doors much like I will be shown by BA once they read about what I've been up to in the papers so sit back and relax cos I am THE MAN wheeeeeeeeeeee didn't expect to see so many dragons up here…" *(cont. 94 words-per-minute)*

"Er... that's not an apple"

VIEWERS 'CAUGHT IN THE CLUTCHES OF EVIL'

TV viewers have described the horror of trying to escape the Yorkshire Ripper drama on ITV, only to end up in the clutches of the Jimmy Savile drama on BBC1.

"We decided to switch over from The Long Shadow on ITV, as it was all getting a bit much, thinking that Ghosts was on BBC1 and we could do with a bit of a laugh," said Colin and Sharon from Colchester.

"But we found ourselves confronted with Steve Coogan in a fright wig as Savile, committing the most unspeakable crimes. It was horrific.

"How much prestigious drama about the psychology of pure evil and the brutal misogyny of Britain in the 1970s and 80s can you take? I'm going to be having flashbacks for decades."

BBC denies all knowledge of Savile drama

by Our Media Staff **Pete O'Phile**

THE BBC last night defended itself over allegations that it had broadcast a controversial drama about the former BBC presenter Sir Jimmy Savile.

Said a BBC spokesman, "We had no idea that this was going on and, even though everyone was talking about it, we were unaware that it was actually happening."

Critics said that rumours were rife in the industry that the BBC was making a drama about the disgraced BBC presenter and claimed that "somebody at the corporation must have known the truth".

It does seem as though the drama was hiding in plain sight on BBC1 on a Sunday evening and the excuses offered by the corporation are not acceptable.

The BBC has now announced that it will be making a drama about the events surrounding the making of the contentious Savile drama, which will star Steve Coogan as Steve Coogan.

Stop this witch-hunt demands Tory MP

■ Following the ousting of Tory MPs Chris Pincher and Peter Bone for sexual misconduct, senior Conservative backbencher, Dick Throbber, has demanded an end to the persecution of Tories with unfortunate names.

Said Throbber, "There is no correlation between my suggestive moniker and my behaviour towards junior members of staff," adding, "I resign."

His shock resignation was greeted with dismay by other Conservative backbenchers, Pat Buttocks and Ivor Hardon. But members of the Independent Expert Panel defended the removal of MPs with inappropriate names.

"It's not a conspiracy," said one. "It's more a case of cock-up." *(That's quite enough. Ed.)*

Product Recall

The Bankers' Bonus Cap

THIS product, sadly, has had to be withdrawn. Despite being popular with 99% of the country, a far more important 1% of the population were very keen on getting rid of it completely, so it had to go.

Based on an original design by the fashion house Osborne and Cameron in 2014, the bankers' bonus cap is now judged unsuitable, after a report by the Kwarteng Hedgefund Headgear Think Tank, a subsidiary of the Institute of Trussonomic Affairs.

ALSO The invisible Brexit Bonus Cap (*see picture*)
This product is not being recalled, due to there being no need, as no Brexit Bonus has ever been identified.

BIBLICAL TIMES

— Friday 3 November 2023 —

King Solomon quits in despair

BY OUR MIDDLE EAST STAFF
JEREMIAH BOWEN

THE monarch known throughout the ages for his wisdom and judgement, King Solomon, sensationally quit today after he was asked to solve the issue of the historic Israeli and Palestinian conflict.

Said Solomon, "Two women came in who were living in the same land, and both of them brought babies who were dead. And then lots of other women came in whose children had also died, and then more and more of them came in... and it was awful.

"I couldn't think of a solution", said Solomon, "and decided to quit as history's wisest ruler, with immediate effect."

That Eton Provost application form in full

1. Did you go to Eton?
2. Do you consider fellow Etonians to have a special bond?
3. Do you wonder why everyone else in the world didn't go to Eton?
4. Are you a bit of a snob?
5. The job is yours, Sir Nicholas.
6. Floreat Ourselves.
7. Er...
8. That's it.

*"It's alright, you're **my** bonus, Gladys"*

---

10 things you didn't know about David Beckham, but now do because you watched that documentary on Netflix

1 If all David Beckham's tattoos were put end to end, they would stretch for 87 miles.

2 Posh last smiled at 9.45am on 4 December 1996 on discovering that she had won £25 on the Premium Bonds.

3 There were originally 8 Spice Girls, but manager Simon Fuller fired Cardamom, Coriander and Saffron, after deciding they were too "hot" for young pop fans.

4 David Beckham's hair is sponsored by over 700 multi-national companies, including Christian Dior, Hyatt Regency Hotels, Accenture and Marconi Weapons Systems.

5 At the height of his fame, David Beckham's right big toe was insured for $8 billion dollars, slightly more than NASA's Space Shuttle.

6 Alternative names considered by Posh and Becks for their first child, Brooklyn, included: Bronx, Battery, Manhattan, Staten Island, Greenwich Village and Colin.

7 Manchester United manager Alex Ferguson often stayed on after training to practise kicking football boots at players' faces. Eventually, he could bend an Adidas size 9 around the locker from 25 yards.

8 David Beckham was cast in Guy Ritchie's film 'King Arthur, Legend of the Swerve' as Sir Kickalot. He was on-screen for over 30 seconds and issued the immortal line "On me 'ead, son!" to Queen Guinevere, played by Vanessa Redgrave.

9 The Beckham's personal assistant, Rebecca Loos, with whom he was rumoured to have had an affair, now runs a successful online plumbing business in Marbella called Rebecca's Loos.

10 Model and socialite David Beckham once played football professionally.

All facts copyright Netflix's 'Coin It Like Beckham'

Hey guys! It's happy anniversary to me! One year! That's 316 days more than Liz!

Liz Truss
Boo hoo hoo!

Liz Truss has been removed from the group by the administrators, even though it never seems to work.

James Forsyth
I've got a cake for you, Rishi!

Help, an ambush! No cake, no wine, no karaoke!

Oliver Dowden
No Carrie Johnson! LOL! 🤣🎂

Actually guys, people are being really nice. I've got a sackful of mail here.

Penny Mordaunt
Is it all letters for the 1922 Committee? 😉

That's not fair, Penny.

Lee Anderthal
Are they all from fooking bankers saying thanks for giving them their bonuses back?

Liz Truss
Trussonomics! That was my idea! You've stolen it!

Kemi Badenoch
And now he's going to steal your idea of getting booted out of office in a vote of no confidence.

Liz Truss
Boo hoo!

Liz Truss has been removed again from the group by the administrators, not that it does much good.

Great one-year celebratory banter, everybody. But there's a limit to how funny this is.

Oliver Dowden
Ooh, tetchy!

DON'T CALL ME TETCHY!

Jeremy Hunt
All right, Doctor Death.

DON'T CALL ME DOCTOR DEATH! My Eat Out to Help Out scheme was what the nation needed.

Oliver Dowden
Eat Out to Conk Out, more like! 💀

Oliver Dowden
The man who put the 'hospital' back into 'hospitality'! 😊

I AM NOT DOCTOR DEATH!

James Forsyth
Don't worry, boss, at least you're not Thérèse Coffey. People are calling her 'Nellie the Effluent'!

Thérèse Coffey
Why do I have to put up with this shit?

Grant Shapps
That's what the public say!

Thérèse Coffey
Well, you're the expert on too many 'jobs'.

Grant Shapps
Fyi, I'm Defence Minister, last time I checked. My job is to defend the Prime Minister.

Thérèse Coffey
That really is a shit job.

Thanks, Grant. You're safe in the Rishi Reshuffle. Unlike some people I could name... Jeremy.

Grant Shapps
Ooh, Chancellor! I haven't done that one. Or have I?

Suella Braverman
Is anyone going to mention the elephant in the room?

Oliver Dowden
Or rather the effluent in the room! 💩😊

James Forsyth
We had an admittedly disappointing pair of by-election results, but, on the plus side, we only lost two seats, which is two less to lose at the General Election.

Lee Anderthal
It was a bloody disaster! A shit-show! A fookin' votapocalypse!

It wasn't my fault. I blame Liz Truss, Boris Johnson, the war in Ukraine, global economic factors, Covid and, most of all, Nadine.

Nadine Dorries
It wasn't *my* fault! It's yours, Rishi! Why can't you man up and take responsibility for your own mistakes? Like not giving me a peerage. You lying, two-faced, heartless bastard!

Boris Johnson
Sorry, did someone call?

Nadine Dorries
Oh hello, big boy! 🖤🖤🖤

Boris Johnson
Shit! I'm out of here. If Carrie asks, I wasn't ever in this group.

Boris Johnson has left the group.

Nadine Dorries
Why don't you bring Boris back in the reshuffle? As Prime Minister!

Nadine Dorries has been removed from the group by the administrators, although it may take several months.

James Forsyth
Calm down, everyone. It'll all be fine, just so long as there aren't any more by-elections.

Peter Bone
Hello, everyone. Anyone want to see my old fellah?

Oliver Dowden
Ooh, looks like we're in danger of another big swing! 😊

Gillian Keegan
That's disgusting, someone put up another image.

OK, here's me and the Saudi Crown Prince...

Jeremy Hunt
Eurrgh! That's even worse.

James Forsyth
On second thoughts, let's all have another look at Peter's Pecker. The optics are better on that one.

"Look, kids – Spring!"

"You mean we've finished Season 1 and we've started Season 2, right?"

@Vilmissimo

"Karl here will be responsible for the building's wiring"

Washington urges caution over Israeli response to UN

■ The White House says it stands 100 percent behind Israel and insists that "President Netanyahu has the right to defend himself from criticism by terrorist organisations, such as the United Nations."

However, it continued, "The Israeli government's plans to carpetbomb and then invade the UN headquarters might be seen to be stoking tension in the region."

This came in response to the Secretary General,

"One day, son, all this will still be yours to police..."

António Guterres, calling for an immediate ceasefire in Gaza.

Said President Biden, "I understand the Israeli government's anger with the UN, but I'm not entirely sure that a ground assault on the UN building is a good idea."

Gaza residents weep for Hamas leaders trapped in Qatar

■ The two million Palestinians trapped in Gaza, under constant bombardment from Israel, have appealed to the world to get aid through to the Hamas leaders trapped in five-star luxury hotels in Qatar.

"We have heard unconfirmed reports that the Hamas leaders are having to endure shortages of food and drink, with only seven types of cheese platters and freshly

squeezed juices being made available at the pool-side bar," said one Gaza resident sheltering in a bombed-out hospital.

"The international community should ensure a steady and reliable supply of up to 50 room service trolleys to their suites daily, where they can plan more terrorist atrocities which we'll be punished for."

Hamas crimes will not be forgotten until they buy Premier League team

■ Downing Street confirmed today that Hamas will never be forgiven for the atrocities it committed on Israeli soil – until it buys a Premier League team.

Said a spokesperson, "The UK will never look the other way at unspeakable brutality and murders, until Hamas is confirmed as the new owner of Manchester United, Crystal

Palace or Wolverhampton Wanderers.

"Hamas will continue to be seen as barbaric savages, with no respect for human life, until the sale goes through, but provided they spend big in the transfer window and secure a place in next year's Champions League, their supporters will happily chant 'Jihad!' at both home and away fixtures."

Hospital waiting lists up again

There was widespread disappointment in Gaza at the news that those in need of urgent medical attention might have to wait up to forever to receive treatment.

Queues at the hospitals have now reached a figure of everyone still alive and doctors

are claiming that it is impossible to get into the hospitals, due to the large number of people waiting and also the fact that there is a war going on all around them and there is a severe shortage of compassion and *(We get the idea. Ed.)*

Police Notes&queries

A special edition of our usual feature, with guest editor Sir Mark Rowley, Head of the Metropolitan Police.

QUESTION ONE

Who or what is 'Jihad'?

Well, the first thing Jihad doesn't mean is "Holy War" – this is a common misapprehension, based purely on the fact that in some circumstances it does. Obviously, when those circumstances include shouting on a demonstration about the need to destroy Israel, Jihad can have a number of alternative meanings. For example, it could mean "making a spiritual or scholarly effort or exertion in the name of serving God". Or it could literally mean "struggle" as in "struggle to get uneducated observers and Home Secretaries to accept that the word Jihad doesn't mean Holy War." Which it definitely doesn't. Except when it does. Which is not at a demonstration where the speaker is shouting about the need to destroy Israel. I hope that clears everything up.

QUESTION TWO

What does the song 'From the river to the sea, Palestine will be free' mean?

Again, this entirely depends on the context, and in the context of people shouting "Death to Israel" it is clearly not in any way threatening, nor is it meant to intimidate or incite violence. On the recent march, many of my officers distinctly heard protestors singing: "From the river to the sea, Israelis and Palestinians will live in two-states of love and harmony!" For that reason nobody was arrested.

QUESTION THREE

What is the meaning of a paragliding photo when worn on the back of your jacket?

I keep having to say this, but the context is all-important. Paragliding is a popular sport, and many members of local paragliding clubs in Britain are proud to carry an image of their innocent pastime when going to the shops, or the park, or a demonstration where some speakers are shouting "Jihad" and others are singing popular peace songs such as "From the river to the sea" *(see above)*. There is nothing to suggest that these paragliding fans are glorifying violence or attempting to terrify anyone.

QUESTION FOUR

What about references to historic massacres of Jewish people, Nazi symbols and that sort of thing?

At the risk of repeating myself, it's all about the context and the context is that there are large numbers of very passionate people who are exercising their freedom of expression and, as I may have said before, there are an awful lot of them.

QUESTION FIVE

'Will you resign?'

For heaven's sake, how many times do I have to say it? It's all a question of context! And the context is that you're accusing a police officer of failing to do his job, which is the most offensive thing I've heard this week. In fact, it classifies as a hate crime and so I'm afraid you'll have to come with me. You're nicked sunshine!

"Their sense of commitment and togetherness is thrilling"

15

TOUGH BRAVERMAN PLANS TO CRACK DOWN ON ROUGH SLEEPING

Nursery Times

·········· Friday, Once-upon-a-time ··········

WHO CUT DOWN NURSERYLAND'S ICONIC LANDMARK?

by Our Forensic Crime Reporter **Tom Thumbprint**

MYSTERY surrounds the felling of Nurseryland's much-loved giant beanstalk. It had been standing in the garden of Idle Jack and his mother for over 300 minutes, following a magic-bean transaction, but this morning was discovered brutally chopped down.

Adding to the mystery was the presence of a deceased giant who had clearly fallen a considerable distance. The beanstalk also demolished a

section of the historic Humpty's Wall, leaving one irate green bottle to complain, "There are ten of us and now only room for nine, one of us is going to have to accidentally fall."

Helping PC Plod with his inquiries is a Hickory-Dickory-TikTok influencer, who denies having anything to do with the beanstalk's demise, despite having the user name of @lumberjackandthebeanstalk and the fact that his axe is covered in beanstalk sap.

Maily EXPRESSO graph

—— FRIDAY, NOVEMBER 3, 2023 ——

WHAT PLANET ARE THEY ON?!

by **Phil Bile-Duct**

ONCE again, the eco zealots are on the rampage – this time disrupting yet another traditional British institution, the TV wildlife programme.

Led by hectoring green killjoy Sir David Attenborough, the BBC's latest sanctimonious, do-gooding, enviro-marxist protestor has infiltrated Planet Earth – and this time it ends with finger-wagging lectures on how driving your Ford Fiesta into London and throwing a plastic bag out the window is somehow going to murder all the world's turtles.

Oh, knock it off, Sir Dreary Attenboring! National treasure? National disgrace, more like! This not what Britain wants to see when it's settling down for a cosy evening, eating tax-free

meat (no thanks to you, Keir Starmer) in front of their diesel-powered television.

No, the people of Uxbridge have spoken – and what they want to see is Sir Dismal Attenbastard driving an honest, clapped-out white van across the Arctic, running over a whingeing polar bear, before voting Conservative in a ballot-box made of ice! Now THAT's proper television!

Saint Rory of Stewart

AND IN those times there lived a prophet and wise man called Rory, who, in his youth, did walk across the wilderness and deserts of Afghanistan and became a teacher to the children of kings.

And his reputation for goodness and humility went before him. And, lo, a miracle occurred – Saint Rory raised a man called Alastair Campbell from the dead, and the people marvelled.

"Surely Campbell is long buried, and rightly so!" they cried. But Saint Rory did heal him with amusing banter and quips about his unworldliness compared to the fallen Campbell.

And soon not only was Saint Rory omniscient but he was also omnipresent, you name it – podcast, radio, TV, Royal Albert Hall, bar

mitzvahs, weddings, pub quiz, he was there.

And he was much loved throughout the land, and people walking their dogs said one to another, "They're awfully good, Rory and the other one. Why can't we have Saint Rory as our Prime Minister? Surely, as the title of his good book suggests, he will heal the nation and bridge the divide."

But other people did stroke their chins and say, "Is he really a saint or might he be a false prophet and *(cont. Episode 94)*

REMEMBERING THE FALLEN
LAST POST FOR SUELLA

We can't have extremist troublemakers at the Cenotaph

Ok, you're fired!

𝔇aily 𝔇errygraph

Marches in Northern Ireland
AN APOLOGY

OVER the last hundred years or more, we may have given the impression that the loyalist marches in Northern Ireland were a proud and celebratory tradition which fostered a sense of continuity and attachment of the province to the United Kingdom. We may further have suggested that the bowler hats, the orange sashes and the drums and whistles were all a loyal demonstration of the fierce commitment of local Protestant communities to the integrity of the Union.

We now realise, in the light of Suella Braverman's very important article explaining how political marches are a terrible idea, that last weekend's pro-Palestinian march was in fact, as she explained, exactly the same as the sort of parades held in Northern Ireland. We would like to apologise for our previous century or so of support for these disgraceful events, and call on the Northern Ireland Police to ban all marches, parades and political displays immediately. We trust this will improve community relations, foster goodwill amongst all people, and preserve Ireland's fragile constitutional balance. We are sorry for any confusion caused by our having to support the Home Secretary, whatever she says, despite her total ignorance of Anglo-Irish history… oh, hang on, she's been sacked. Phew! As you were, abandon apology and back to normal service.

©Daily London Derrygraph 2023

Palestinian march to go ahead

Hundreds of thousands of pro-Palestinians will again take to the streets this week, as they march from North Gaza to South Gaza on an agreed route – namely the one road south.

There were fears that the march would end in violence, particularly if it was bombed from the air or shelled by artillery. The "hate marchers", so-called because they hate having to leave their homes with what remains of their possessions, are expected to stop at the Egyptian border, due to the fact that there's nowhere else to go.

The authorities urged the marchers not to cause any trouble and prove that they wanted peace, unlike (cont. 2094)

EXPRESSY 𝔐ailygraph
—— FRIDAY 24 NOVEMBER 2023 ——
Notes & Queries

Q: Are the lyrics of the song we keep hearing at recent demonstrations threatening or racist?

A: A lot of people feel uncomfortable when they hear protestors singing "You're not English anymore" and "England till I die". On first hearing, these lyrics might suggest a nationalist viewpoint with worrying overtones, suggesting possibly that other nationalities were not welcome in their homeland. However, context is, of course, everything and in the context of this being a government-supporting paper, it could be argued that these popular folk songs, accompanied by the traditional throwing of bottles at the police, are quite harmless and no reason for this newspaper to feel embarrassed by our previous enthusiasm for the former Home Secretary and her views on right-wing protest. So these patriotic songs should not be taken at face value – especially if your face is as red as ours (cont. p94)

THOSE RED ARROW DISPLAYS IN FULL

Patriotic

Aerobatic

Genital

Our thanks for these pictures from: Flirt Lieutenant Knobbs, Squalid-Leader Dicksout, Wang-Commander Legover-Smythe, Group (Sex) Captain Plonker-Pecker and Air Vice-Marshal Courtmartial.

"And now we wait…"

DIARY

SIR TIM RICE
BBC Maestro Course: How To Write And Stage A Hit Musical (£79)

Lesson One: Finding a great idea

How do you come up with those ideas? That's a question I'm often asked.

Good question. To which the obvious answer is – you tell me, chum! But, seriously, I wish I knew!

Sometimes I get ideas from newspapers. Sometimes from somewhere else – like a book or something someone mentions when we're having a bit of a chinwag.

I found the idea for *Jesus Christ Superstar* in the Bible. I became intrigued by this guy who people said was the Son of God. Quite a claim, when you think about it!

To be honest, I'd forgotten how it ended – but when I looked up that ending, it literally blew me away.

Jesus was nailed to this huge cross, which meant he'd have just about enough time to belt out a real showstopper before he sadly passed away.

Lesson Two: Come up with some great lyrics

Only trouble was – nothing much rhymed with Jesus Christ. I tried *heist*, but had to abandon it because, strictly speaking, the guy wasn't a bank robber.

Iced was another, but in those days there wasn't such a thing as an electric fridge in his part of the world – and it needed to be historically accurate. *Priced?* Nope. *Spiced?* Nope. *Diced?* Nope.

None of those rhymes was totally brillerooni. But remember, guys, the great trick is to persevere. Keep hard at it, my friends, and you'll finally hit a six. Inspiration – that's the name of this particular game.

Lesson Three: Lightning strikes

Sure enough, after many a sleepless night, lightning struck! Call it genius, call it luck, call it sheer bloody hard slog, but it came to me in the proverbial flash – if I gave our hero the extra surname "Superstar" then – whaddayaknow! – these lines would fit superbly in the opening number:
Jesus Christ Superstar!

Do you think you're what they say you are?

Once I'd got that couplet under my belt, I really ran with it, from simple rhymes like *far* and *ta* and *spa* to the more complex:
Jesus Christ Superstar!
It's really just great that you play guitar!
or
Jesus Christ Superstar!
You're skin is so smooth – no trace of a scar!
or
Jesus Christ Superstar!
You can work miracles – even open a bar!

Lesson Four: What makes a first-rate musical?

Lionel Bart's *Oliver*! What does it have? First-rate characters. First-rate setting. First-rate songs. All in all, a first-rate musical.

Lesson Five: Words and Music

Which comes first: the music – or the words?

That's a question I'm often asked. The answer is simple: sometimes it's the music, and sometimes it's the words! There are no fixed rules. It's like the chicken and the egg, which is a project I'm working on at the moment with my good chums from across the sea, Benny and Bjorn.

Who are they? I hear you ask. Hmm. They're from a little band you might have just about heard of called Abba.

Where was I? Ah, yes. The idea for *Chicken and Egg: The Musical* hit me one morning over breakfast. Tapping on my boiled egg set me thinking. Before long, I was letting my imagination run riot.

I could see The Egg, played by the splendiferous Michael Ball, singing this great duet with The Chicken – a bird of the deliciously unfeathered variety played by the inimitable Elaine Paige.
Chicken: *You look good enough to hatch!*
Egg: *You make me feel free range!*
Chicken: *I always listen and watch!*
Egg: *I'm a bit more brown than beige!*
Chicken: *You're the egg!*
Egg: *And I'm the chicken!*
Together: *And we both, yes we both, oh, we both, yes we both – CO-O-O-O-ME FIRST!*

The great thing about the whole concept of a chicken-and-egg for a world-beating musical is that, hey, the audience already knows a bit about chickens and a bit about eggs. So you've two truly memorable characters – the chicken and the egg – whom everyone will be rooting for. And that, to these little grey cells, is half the battle won.

Lesson Six: What makes a truly great lyric?

Hard to say, really. Let's take "Whole New World", of which you might just have heard, and which, I say in all modesty, gained me this funny little gold statuey thing you might have heard of, called an Academy Award, for my sins.

Seriously, though, for the hit movie Aladdin I wanted to somehow convey in just a few words the idea of a world that was in some way new and in some way whole. In a flash of inspiration of what-have-you, I came up with this truly great first line for the chorus:
A whole new world.

Just four little words – but they somehow convey a whole new world. And then I thought: I can't just stop there.

Lesson Seven: Take risks

I'd got this totally triff first line – A whole new world – but how do I best convey the view of earth from the sky? After seven or eight days' hard slog, it suddenly came to me – the world would look entirely different if you were flying. It would be a truly dazzling place, yes!
A dazzling place I never knew – But when I'm way up here...

For two days, I went through all the best possible lines to follow – *I feel like shedding a tear – With my arms I can steer – I fancy a beer – The drop is really quite sheer – I can see from New York to Tangier.* But frankly none of them sounded completely right. And then it hit me:
It's crystal clear.

And the rest is history.

Lesson Eight: Look for the perfect combination of rhyme and meaning

By now, I could instinctively sense – after half a century's slog in the song-writing game – that I was onto something truly special. But I also knew that the time had come to say exactly what it was that was crystal clear from way up here:
It's crystal clear – That now I'm in a whole new world with you.

Brill! Almost there – but the melody still left me with one more line to fill in. After a week of further try-outs – *And that gives me something on which to chew – The sheep go "baa" and the cows go "moo" – True love is really lovely when it's all about us two* – I was struck by a beautiful idea: the boldest, bravest, most beautiful thing would be to repeat the previous line: *Now I'm in a whole new world with you.*

Bravo, maestro!

And now, after savouring my words of wisdom – it's up to you! Go out there, write a lyric – and knock 'em dead!

Cheers from yours truly, Sir Tim!

As told to
CRAIG BROWN

Modern parents struggle to help children with homework

A SURVEY of 2,000 parents of primary and secondary students has revealed that they struggle to help their children with homework on subjects such as trigonometry and algebra, because they're usually through their first bottle of Shiraz by half-six.

"Do you have any idea how stressful work is at the moment?" said one mum, necking a large glass of Sauvignon Blanc.

"And my sister is being a total nightmare about dad going into a home, even after he's had that fall. She always was a daddy's girl. Oh, go on, Geoff, open another bottle. There's that Jacob's Creek we won at the school tombola in the back of the fridge."

Said a father, "Isn't Isosceles that place in Greece Alan and Sanita went for their honeymoon? You have no idea how tough a day Daddy has had." He continued, "No, I'm not shouting darling, and Mummy can't help, she's just gone for a nice, long sleep, face down on the sofa."

"Shut up about global warming and steer the fucking boat"

A Tank Driver writes

Vlad 'Mad' Putin,
Tank No: ZZZZ

Sorry about the hold up, guv. I know I said I'd get you to Kyiv by March 2022, but the traffic's been a nightmare. And now we've got all these bloody American tanks clogging up the road. You know who I blame? That bloody Joe Biden. Doddery old bloke, hands always shaking – not that there's anything wrong with hands shaking – but he should keep his nose out of it. Young blood, that's what the Americans need. Like that Donald Trump geezer. I had him in the back of my tank once. Very bright man. And I'm not just talking about his skin colour. I'll never forget that stopover in a Moscow hotel. We booked a nice room, with shower included. Talk about a night to remember!

I've still got the photos. And now he's in court, poor bloke! If you ask me, that whole fraud trial is a fake. He's probably not even there. They're probably just using a body double. They can do that sort of thing, apparently. They're accusing him of inflating the value of his property. What nonsense, he's worth billions! Unlike this humble tank driver. I'm worth nothing. Not got any properties all over Russia and possibly Switzerland. Too busy serving the Russian people, me, driving my tank. And even if I did own any, which I don't, they'd be in my mistress's name. Flexible finance, I call it, see? Cos she's a gymnast, haha! Bends over backwards to help me out. Any case, that Trump certainly gets my vote. Or he will do. And the votes of billions of bots who'll put him back in the White House. That'll clear the road of American tanks, not to mention missiles, drones and whatnot. He'll sort all the world's traffic problems out in a day, he says. And why wouldn't you believe him? Yeah, vote Trump, Make Russia Great Again! Mind how you go, mate. Have a nice day!

© *A tank driver 2023*

Homer announces change of behaviour
by Our Arts Correspondent **Bard Simpson**

THE much-loved brain behind the popular long-running series *The Iliad* has announced that, in the light of cultural changes, his protagonists will no longer be seen throttling each other, dragging their corpses behind their chariots, or burning entire cities to the ground.

"Times have changed," said Homer. "It's not 800BC anymore and I realise that it's not acceptable to depict these wanton acts of violence, particularly in families. From now on, my fathers and sons will not go to war with each other or anyone else, and will stick to enjoying family days out on beaches free from burning ships and going swimming in the wine-dark sea. The only towers that will be toppled will be games of Jenga played by well-adjusted relatives, and the only wooden horses will be those ridden around by toddlers who are growing up in a loving and supportive environment."

Critics say Homer is just trying to drum up interest in his sequel, *The Odyssey*, which he claims will be a much more measured story about a man finding himself on a Mediterranean cruise.

CHARLES MOORE FEARS ABU DHABI BID FOR TELEGRAPH

It's giving me the sheikhs

Nicky Haslam

This year's list of what is 'common' in full

Colds – Common!

Wimbledon – Common!

Alternatives to Garden – Common!

Market – Common!

Muck – Common!

Books of Prayer – Common!

Man For Whom Fanfare Written by Aaron Copland – Common!

Sense – Common!

"Double espresso for... 'Mind-your-own-fucking-business'"

MORAL HIGH GROUND FLATTENED

How much is left?

"It's a matter of take and give"

DIRECT FROM THE PUB!

The Sun READERS' GUIDE TO THE MUDDLE EAST

"KNOWLEDGE IS POWER!" Dispelling, once and for all, the lazy, stereotypical myth that our readers are only interested in sport and girls, your super Sun is on the case once again with all the **CLEARLY LABELLED** info and lingo you'll need to talk with authority at the bar about the ongoing conflict:

JORDAN The phwoarmer name of top Page 3 girl Katie Price, phwoar!

YOSSER ARAFAT Old scouser who used to run Palestine, resembled that Ringo Starr – catchphrase was "gizza State".

GAZZA STRIP Football top worn by midfielder who shone for England, Lazio, Spurs, etc.

GAZZA CITY Newcastle Utd – beloved hometown club of the above legend.

SHI'ITE A word expressed by the aforementioned Geordie superstar after he was dropped for getting pissed and eating a kebab the night before an England match.

J. BOWEN'S LIVE REPORTS Much-loved, long-time star BBC reporter who used to present darts quiz show *Bullseye*.

RAFA CROSSING Er, not sure. Probably something to do with wide area passing techniques employed by former Liverpool manager Rafa Benitez.

WEST BANK Section of stadium to the right of the North Bank at The Arsenal's old Highbury ground.

(That's enough. Ed.)

Notes&queries

Who or what is a fuckpig?

● My grandchildren and I have heard a lot of this term whilst watching daytime television coverage of the Covid Inquiry and yet I cannot find it in any dictionary. Enlightenment, please?
Mrs Witty-Slide

● 'F kpigge' is the original Norwegian version of the cartoon that we know as Peppa Pig. In the Scandinavian series, F kpigge, voiced by legendary Icelandic actress Bjork Dottirdottirbjorksson, is a crime-solving detective pig, who ends up in every episode being roasted slowly by immigrant crime gangs in an oven inside an ice hotel. It was bought up by British independent producer Harry Endemol and turned into the hugely successful and somewhat more upbeat pre-school family favourite of today.
Keith Hugo, Lockdown Lane, Coffs

● Oh dear! Poor Mr Hugo's inquiries have led him up the garden path. Fuchpigs were German First World War flying bombs, manufactured by munitions company Piggen und Fucher. These bombs were renowned for the squealing sound that they made in the air, which terrified the Tommies on the front line, who, of course, could not pronounce the Teutonic moniker and so dubbed them "Fuckpigs", viz *Memento Porki* by war poet Vidal Sassoon, 1915: "'Quick, boys,' cried the Sergeant, 'dig, dig, dig! / Here comes a Whizzbang – oh no! A Fuckpig!'" An unexploded fuckpig can be seen in the Imperial War Museum, which until 2016 was called the Metric War Museum.
Heather & Mick Namara, Karaoke Close, Sniffs

● Both Heather and Mick will be (shell) shocked to hear that they've missed the target as regards Fuckpigs. The Fuckpigs were a punk band originating from Charterhouse School, who rose to the giddy heights of being played once on the John Peel Show and subsequently banned by Radio One. Lead singer and angst-ridden lyricist Dom Cummings, in his trademark beanie hat, was the only original member to remain in the line-up throughout its brief history, as he was constantly firing all the other musicians, including guitarist Lee 'Chicken Suit' Cain and Sir Screaming Mark Sedwill on drums, who went on to found soft rock combo 'The Civil Servants'. The Fuckpigs' only album 'Weirdos and Misfits' featured their hit single 'Stiletto C**t' which peaked at Number 237 in the charts.
Reynold Martins, Partymarty, Crokes

AN APOLOGY

IN COMMON with most of the British press, we may have given the impression that calling for a ceasefire in the current Middle Eastern conflict was tantamount to supporting Hamas and that anyone advocating such a course of action was not merely anti-Israeli but an anti-Semite and terrorist sympathiser of the first order.

We now realise, in the light of the Israeli government agreeing a ceasefire after negotiating with Hamas, that nothing could be further from the truth and that of course Mr Netanyahu is neither anti-Israeli nor an anti-Semite, nor a terrorist sympathiser, but a wise statesman who has realised that there comes a time in any war when the fighting must cease, hostages must be released on both sides, humanitarian aid must be prioritised and there must be peace with the Americans, who are getting a bit twitchy about the whole Middle East situation.

We apologise for any confusion caused to our readers or indeed to ourselves.

Ironyometer blows up as UAE hosts COP28

YET AGAIN, the famous ironyometer proved incapable of handling the news that one of the world's leading oil producers was to host the climate change summit.

The antique monitoring device began to heat up to dangerous temperatures when it was revealed that the summit would be opened by Dr Sultan bin Ahmed Al Jabar, the CEO of the Abu Dhabi National Oil company. It was further revealed that the actual purpose of the summit was to sell oil to foreign governments.

Furthermore, the location of the summit in the Middle East requires a record number of delegates to fly from all around the world into Dubai, ready to turn on their air conditioning and try out Dubai's famous ski dome.

The ironyometer finally exploded, prompting demands that future ironyometers should be wind- or solar-powered, rather than fossil-fuelled, which brought laughter from all the world's major oil-producing companies as they were chauffeured around the Emirates.

©Desert Bloomberg

Panel 1: JEZ, WHAT'S GOING ON WITH QUIN? HE SEEMS REALLY AGITATED. IS IT SOME KIND OF DREADFUL WORK-LIFE IMBALANCE?

Panel 2: NOT EXACTLY, MAX: HIS NEW FITNESS WATCH HAS A STRESS-TRACKING FEATURE AND IT'S REALLY STRESSING HIM OUT!

Panel 3: JEZ, I'M OFF THE SCALE HERE! WHICH COPING MECHANISM DO I USE: GUIDED BREATHING PROGRAMME OR MICRO YOGA EXERCISES?!? HELP!!!

Panel 4: WELL, I'VE INSTALLED THE HEAT PUMP SO YOU SHOULD HAVE SUPER GREEN POWER ON TAP... ANY FEEDBACK? — THANK YOU. WE JUST NEED TO CONSULT THE INDIVIDUAL DIRECTLY INVOLVED...

Panel 5: TO BE HONEST, I'M NOT SURE FLAUBERT LOOKS TOO KEEN... HE SEEMS LUKE WARM ON THE HOT TUB TOO... Hummmmm

Panel 6: MY WELLNESS COACH HAS ADVISED ME TO STEER CLEAR OF TOXIC PEOPLE...

Panel 7: SOUND ADVICE, QUIN. CUT OFF ALL LINKS, SHUT THEM DOWN ON SOCIAL MEDIA...

Panel 8: TROUBLE IS, POPPY, QUIN'S "TOXIC PEOPLE" INCLUDE THE LOCAL BAKER WHO REFUSES TO USE SPELT AND DELI OWNER WHO WON'T STOCK LAOTIAN SRIRACHA... BAKERY DELI GNASH! GRIND!

Panel 9: THE EASE OF MAKING A PODCAST THESE DAYS IS BREATHTAKING... A MOBILE PHONE, A COUPLE OF CHEAP MICROPHONES... NOW WE JUST NEED SOMETHING THE GREAT BRITISH PUBLIC WANT...

Panel 10: SO FAR VIEWING FIGURES ARE MODEST TO SAY THE LEAST... WHO'D HAVE THOUGHT THERE WOULD BE NO AUDIENCE FOR "THE POT POURRI STORY: HOW THIS SCENTED WONDER CONQUERED THE WORLD"?!?

"On me 'ead, son!"

POETRY CORNER

In Memoriam Sir Bobby Charlton

So. Farewell
Then Sir Bobby Charlton,
Busby Babe, Red Devil
And hero of the 1966
England World Cup team.

Now we mourn
Your passing,
But not as much as
Your goal scoring,
Obviously.

Loyal, modest and diligent,
You were the very
Opposite of a modern
Footballer.

You didn't even
Have a hair
Transplant.

As Keith says,
In his moving tribute
On Facebook:
"They think it's
All combover...
It is now!"

E.J. Thribb
(17½ goals per game)

In Memoriam Bobi, the world's oldest dog

So. Farewell
Then Bobi.

Not a good week
For Bobi/Bobby fans.

You were 31,
Or 217 in
Dog years.

Sadly, you are no
Longer playing dead
And the bones that
Are being buried
In the garden
Are yours.

E.J. Thribb
(122½ dog years)

David Cameron
So, hi guys. Let's get down to business. You can call me Lord Dave.

Hang on, Lord Dave. I'm still Prime Minister.

David Cameron
Oh – was that the deal? Yes, of course. My bad. You carry on, Sunak.

I'd like to welcome some new faces to the WhatsApp group. As well as the old face –

Lee Anderthal
Fookin' hell – what surprise have you got for us next? Is it fookin' Liz Truss as Chancellor? Is she hiding under the fookin' table?!

Liz Truss
Hello! I've got some great ideas for growth that Jeremy may be interested in.

Liz Truss has been removed from the group, despite her gluing herself to her mobile phone.

Jeremy Hunt
I'm still Chancellor. I wasn't reshuffled and I'm in charge of tax cuts, even though I'm against them, and Rishi announced them anyway.

Yes, this is the big reset before the election, where we turn the corner.

Oliver Dowden
You mean we U-turn the corner! 😜

We put the past behind us.

Lee Anderthal
And then fookin' rehire him as Foreign Secretary!

David Cameron
I can see we're going to get on, Lee. Or can I call you 'Oiky'?

Come on, Team Rishi, we're all, to coin a phrase, "in this together"

David Cameron
That's what Osborne and I said ten years ago, the last time we tried austerity, and we seemed to get away with it!

Great. Thanks, Lord Dave. Good to have your experience on board. And your wisdom.

David Cameron
Talking of which can I introduce you to a friend of mine – Lex Greensill.

Lex Greensill
G'day Poms! Dave's got a bonzer deal for you and your economy. Reverse wombat finance. Mate's rates.

The administrators have removed Mr Greensill on the grounds that he's overdue an appointment at His Majesty's pleasure.

Oliver Dowden
I knew Lord Dave was an EX PM, I didn't know he was a LEX PM! 🤣🤣🤣 💰💰💰

David Cameron
Incidentally, if anyone needs some good Chinese business contacts, I can put them in touch with some friends of mine.

Mr Xi Po
It's alright, Lord Dave, we're already here, monitoring all your messages.

The administrator has tried to remove the Chinese from the group, but is having technical difficulties.

 The important thing. is I know how to assemble a cabinet, and I've got the picture to prove it!

Lee Anderthal
Think you've got a fookin' screw loose, mate!

Oliver Dowden
I was going to say that the picture showed a rather awkward looking tool! 😉

The point is, I'm Mr Fix It. I fix things. If something's broken, Rishi'll Fix It! "Rishi fixed it for me!" And for me! And for me! We could have a medal!

James Forsyth
Great Idea, boss, but "Rishi'll Fix It" could just be the least good slogan we've ever come up with. Let's just stick with: "Long-term decisions for a brighter future." That hasn't been a total disaster yet.

Exactly. And now we're doing tax cuts! We're back to being proper Tories! Thatcherism returns!

Oliver Dowden
You mean war with Argentina and a big bounce in the polls! 😊 🏴

We don't need a war to be popular. Taking 2p off National Insurance is a crowd-pleasing, barn-storming vote-winner!

Lee Anderthal
For the fookin' Labour party maybe!

Jeremy Hunt
It was the very least I could do. And I mean that. I did tell you that we couldn't really cut taxes, because we've got this massive debt and all these national services and you did give a lot of money to Michelle Mone when you were Chancellor, Rishi. Just saying.

James Forsyth
The freeze on alcohol duty was a smart move. 🍾🍷🥃

Lee Anderthal
Aye – if they're going to vote for us, we need everyone to be as pissed as fookin' possible on election day!

It isn't just the booze that's going to win us the election – I kept the triple lock for pensioners, because they're the ones who are going to vote for us.

Kemi Badenoch
Good job you didn't kill them all during the pandemic then, Rishi, with your three-word "Let People Die" catchphrase.

That wasn't my catchphrase.

Kemi Badenoch
Ooh, Tetchy!

I AM NOT TETCHY

Oliver Dowden
Now THAT'S your catchprase! 😊

CLEVERLY DENIES OFFENSIVE LANGUAGE

by Our Unparliamentary Language Correspondent **Tim Shitman**

THE Home Secretary has insisted that he was misheard in his use of what some people thought was offensive language.

James Cleverly was quoted as having said that the Rwanda migrant plan was "batshit crazy", which upset many right-wing Tories.

Now, Cleverly has clarified the situation, maintaining that what he was actually saying was, "The Rwanda plan is a brilliant and well-thought out strategy for solving the immigration crisis."

He continued, "I would never use such language to describe a government policy. It's not like Rwanda is a shithole like Stockton."

The Home Secretary went on to deny he had just said Stockton was a shithole, saying he was misheard. "If you think I would use a word like 'shithole', you must be batshit crazy," he told reporters.

Jacob Rees-Mogg hedge fund shuts down: A nation mourns

by Our Economic Staff
Grazia Deo

The people of Britain have been plunged into sorrow by the news that Somerset Capital, an investment fund co-founded by Jacob Rees-Mogg, is to close, after losing one of its biggest clients following a series of disastrous financial results.

The streets of London were thronged with anxious members of the public desperately hoping that Rees-Mogg and his business partners would still manage to put food on the table for their families this Christmas.

One urchin said, "He's not used to privation like this. He's got so many mouths to feed. I think maybe I'll pop down the food bank and pick up a few bits and pieces just to tide them over."

Another passer-by, on her way to her second job in the spare time between minimum-wage social care shifts, added, "He's got six children to keep privately educated, not to mention the nanny. It's a terrible indictment of this country that we've let our best and brightest down like this."

At time of press, everyone was passing round an enormous stupid top hat and throwing in a few quid to help crowdfund a new double-breasted suit three sizes too big.

■ *If YOU would like to donate to the partners of Somerset Capital, please write to:*

Rees-Mogg Hardship Fund
Ha ha ha ha ha ha ha
London W1.

"Oh, my God!"

VIAGRA-
GOOD FOR
THE BRAIN

POETRY CORNER

Lines on the 25th anniversary of Viagra

So. Let's have a
Standing ovation:
All rise!
For the little blue
Wonder pill.

You were discovered
By accident
During trials for
A heart drug.
So, in a sense,
You were a cock-up.

Still, many thought
You would be
A flop,
But you have gone on
And on...
And on...
And on...

How do you
Keep it up?
It must be hard.

E.J. Throbb (17½ hours)

~~Dave~~ Lord Snooty AND HIS ONLY PALS!

YES, FOLKS, I'M BACK, AND I'M READY TO SERVE!

NOT MORE TENNIS, DAVE?

SURELY IT'S TIME FOR SOME WORK?

I'M HELPING MY NEW PAL RISHI RESTORE THE BALANCE IN THE CABINET... MORE PUBLIC SCHOOL BOYS, FEWER OIKS!

MADDER-THAN-EVER NAD (SPITTING TACKS)

IT'S SO UNFAIR! WHY DIDN'T I GET A PEERAGE !?!

BECAUSE YOU'RE TOO COMMONS, GEDDIT ?!!

NOW LET'S HAVE A FEAST TO CELEBRATE MY RETURN!

WHAT A COMPLETE BAAAAAAAA RON!

YES IT'S MORE ETON MESS FOR EVERYONE!

PERSON ON THE INTERNET 'COULDN'T CARE LESS ABOUT THE NEW BEATLES SONG'

by Our Beatles Correspondent **Ima Walrus**

THERE was widespread disbelief on the internet today after a person revealed that they didn't feel strongly one way or the other about the new Beatles song.

"I mean, I suppose it's alright, pleasant enough, haven't given it much thought," admitted Barry Matthews of Penge on X formerly Twitter. "The kids liked it when it came on in the car... no big deal."

All X users demanded that Barry have a strong opinion about it, saying he can choose between *Now and Then* being a final humiliation for John Lennon at the hands of Paul McCartney, a dirge sounding like The Rutles doing a cover of *Hey Jude,* or that it's a masterpiece of melody and harmony, haunting and beautiful, a fitting final song for the band that changed music forever.

"We're putting Barry on a final warning," said one keyboard warrior. "If he doesn't have a strong opinion about the Dr Who 60th Anniversary specials at the end of the month then he has to leave the internet immediately."

New single from Fab Four

by Our Music Correspondent **Penny Lane**

YES, the perennially popular quartet from yesteryear is back with an amazing new hit. Thanks to new technology, War, Famine, Death and Ringo (surely "Plague") look and sound as fresh and lively as ever, as they belt out a never-before-heard classic, "All you need is hate". One critic hailed it as one of their greatest releases, right up there with "Give War a Chance", "We All Live in a Nuclear Submarine" and, of course, the timeless "Help!"

TOXIC MEDIA PERSONALITY MEETS ANDREW TATE

No one should be exposed to your offensive views

That's why we're on TalkTV

𝕸𝖆𝖎𝖑𝖞EXPRESSOgraph
WHY CAN'T CELEBS JUST SHUT UP?

PUT a sock in it, luvvies! We're all sick of you marching about with your banners, telling us what you think about international affairs! We just don't care!

Get back to your overpaid work, mincing about pretending to be other people and leave the politics to the grown-ups! Unless, of course, it's in support of a march we agree with, in which case, hats off to our noble thespians, telling truth to power and offering trenchant analysis that only overpaid people mincing about pretending to be other people can do!

We say, "Thank God for the luvvies and their brave stance, agreeing with the editor of this newspaper."

School news

Sewers Flood Eton

The famous institution that is Eton College was this week forced to remain closed to pupils, following a sewage leak. The Headmaster of Eton sought to reassure parents, saying, "This is totally normal. Eton has a long history as a place where turds thrive and this is nothing untoward." He was joined by the senior prefect and Head of Plop, T.S. Eliot (Anagrams), who added, "Every year this school sends fresh turds out into the world, to join the fetid old ones which are floating around the Cabinet table. *Floreat Eturdiensis!*"

"Oh look – a policeman!"

Nursery Times

Friday, Once-upon-a-time

GOVERNMENT CRACKS DOWN ON BENEFIT SHIRKERS

by Our Financial Staff **Little 'In the Red' Riding Hood**

A NEW economic era began today, as the Nurseryland authorities vowed to stop shirkers claiming benefits and threatened to remove their access to the NHS (Nurseryland Health Service).

Citing the example of one work-shy resident, a Mr Idle Jack, Chancellor Jeremy Kingfisher-Hunt said, "People like Jack expect to be provided with free magic beans and believe they have a right to golden eggs from the public goose. That sort of thinking is away with the fairies."

The chancellor also has in his sights those with long-term injuries, like red-wall resident Humpty Dumpty, who had a big fall.

Said Jeremy, "Mr Dumpty claims he cannot work, on account of being in pieces, but he needs to put himself back together again. He can't just rely on all the King's horses and all the King's men to help him out. We're not going to shell out for Mr Dumpty any longer."

One-armed sailor, Captain Hook, said the government measures may force him into piracy and the kidnapping of children to make ends meet.

But the chancellor was unrepentant, saying, "Anyone on the fiddle had better watch out and I know of one cat in particular who's hey-diddle-diddling the system. And whatever the little dog thinks, it's nothing to laugh about."

THE KING OF TROUBLES

A short story special by top royal romantic novelist Dame Hedda Shoulders

THE STORY SO FAR: King Charles has celebrated his 75th birthday with a glittering party at Claret House. Now read on...

"**G**AWD!" exclaimed a bleary-eyed Queen Camilla, nursing a restorative egg-noggin-the-nog. "Are they still firing those bloody guns or is it just inside my head?"

Charles smiled indulgently at the delicate post-party state of his fragile soulmate, who seemed to think that the celebratory 75-gun salute from the Grenadine Guards was still booming in her ears.

"Yes, didn't it go well?" enthused Charles. "The joint was really jumping, as they say. And everyone who was anyone was there... there was Tory Stewart, the chap from the podcast you listen to in the middle of the night, not to mention 'Crown' Jools Holland who plays the boogie woogie thingie so beautifully. And even Kate the Princess of Wales turned up, which was a pretty big deal, given how big a cheese she is nowadays."

Camilla groaned and reached for a not-my-Kingsize Rothesayman's full-strength gasper. "The best thing about the party was who DIDN'T come," rasped Camilla, "owing to their not being invited – ie the Duke and Duchess of Whinger."

"Hang on, old thing, that's a bit unfair. It would have been very nice if they'd been there..."

"...but even nicer that they weren't," interjected Sir Alan Fitztightly, who had arrived with two white tablets on a cushion, for Camilla to add to her egg-based hangover remedy.

"Plink plink fizz, darling," soothed the King's favourite factotum, and now the Queen's Serjeant of the Alka Seltzer.

"What a knees-up! I had to drag the Air Vice Marshal away, as he jitterbugged into the early hours to ABBA's 'Dancing Queen Consort' with Lady Marmalade Hussy. She didn't ask him where he came from once! Oooh, too soon? Naughty Sir Alan!"

"Yes, thank you, Fitztightly, that will be all." Charles sometimes found his loyal liegeman's over-familiar badinage just a little de trop. Camilla intervened:

"Well, Sir Alan and I are off to see the matinee of *Backstairs Billy* at the Duchess of York's theatre," drawled Her Majesty. "Apparently, it features your old nan and is very funny and full of innuendo," she explained.

"Backstairs Billy always used to say he liked it 'in your endo', if you get my drift," added the Equerry-as-folk.

"I thought you had gone, Sir Alan," snapped the King, tetchily. And with that, Charles was left alone, with his thoughts.

Why did people want to see such inaccurate portrayals of the life of his family on stage and screen? It really was... that word he wasn't allowed to use any more. Pity,

because it really summed up these fictional travesties of royal history. Just like that programme, *The Crown*. Apparently, in the latest season, Diana appeared as a ghost, talking to him. How utterly ridiculous! Nobody in their right mind would watch that rubbish! "What time is it on?" Charles wondered to himself, as he idly flicked the buttons on the Poshiba TV remote until the Nutflix logo appeared on the screen.

Oh, and suddenly there he was, looking young and chiselled sitting in an aeroplane. And there in the seat in front of him on the British Heirways flight from Paris was the ghost of Diana herself!

"Yah, Charles," she was saying in an ethereal yet Sloaney voice, "this is what you wanted all along, you and the Duke of Edinburgh and MI6 and Mossad..."

"No, no," his dapper doppleganger was protesting tearfully on the telly, "I regret everything! Please forgive me! You were the best and most revolutionary modernising force in the hidebound and antiquated Royal institution."

"Oh really," said the real Charles. "This dialogue is ludicrous and the whole situation unbelievable." He switched the TV off irritably and threw the remote control at a painting of Venice by Juan Cornetto. "It really is..."

"Appalling?" came a ghostly voice from beside him on the King Louis The Roux chaise longue. Charles almost jumped out of

his royal skin! It was Diana, sitting beside him, looking doe-eyed and radiant. She had remained eternally youthful, as he had sadly wrinkled and aged, bowed down by the cares of the real Crown.

"You look just same," said Charles. "Unlike me."

"Yes," the ghost agreed. "You're no Dominic West, that's for sure. But I'm not here to enthuse about how fit the cast of the TV drama are, though Elizabeth Debeaky doesn't really do me justice. No, I'm here as a messenger to tell you to put things right between you and Harry. Sort it out. Man up. Be the father he needs you to be. Don't repeat the fateful patterns of the past..."

"This dialogue is even worse than on the telly," remonstrated the King, but it was too late, the apparition had delivered its other-worldly message and was no more.

Charles was sitting in stunned silence, when Camilla suddenly reappeared, looking for her Zippo lighter which she had left on the Chippendale tallboy.

"Who were you talking to?" she asked.

"Nobody! There's nobody here! Certainly no ghosts or ghoulies, or anything like that!"

"I so defo heard you talking to someone," insisted the Queen Consort.

"No no, I was just... er... having a word with my old friend, the aspidistra. You know, catching up on family and whatnot."

The Queen was visibly relieved at the rational explanation for her husband's bizarre behaviour.

"Phew! For a minute there I thought you were going soft in the noodle. See you later, Chazza! Enjoy yakking with the yucca!" And with that she was gone again, in a cloud of fragrant nicotinal smoke.

As her footsteps receded down the marble corridor, a shiver ran down Charles's spine as he felt an eerie presence returning to haunt him. He could swear he heard the voice of his late wife floating in the ether. "There are three of us in this marriage now, Charles... you, her... and meeeeeeeeeeeeeeeeeeeeeeeee!"

(To be continued...)

"So, not only have you got mould in your flat, you've got squatters"

M^cLACHLAN

James Cleverly
Hi everybody,
I'm back!

The Rwanderer
returns!

Oliver Dowden
I thought it was meant to be a
one-way ticket to Rwanda? 😊

James Cleverly
I've done the deal. Rwanda is
officially a safe place.

Robert Jenrick
Not for Rishi – it may finish off
his career.

> Great bants, Robert – but you are
> with me on this one, aren't you?

Lee Anderthal
He won't resign on a point of principle
because he hasn't fookin' got any!

Robert Jenrick
It's just I worry about the policy not
going far enough. It doesn't seem totally
committed to breaking international law.

Alex Chalk
As Justice Secretary, can I just
float the idea that it probably goes
far enough in the illegal direction
by staying just legal... ish.

> Thanks, Chalkie, I can trust an
> old Wynkiest to stay loyal.

Robert Jenrick
Dear 1922 Committee, I would like
to express my disappointment and
lack of confidence in

Robert Jenrick
Shit! Delete! Delete! Wrong
WhatsApp Group.

> Robert – you are staying
> loyal, aren't you?!

Robert Jenrick
Of course! I was just complaining about
the coffee machine! That's it – the
coffee machine. It's failing to deliver.
And that's why I was writing a letter
demanding that the coffee machine
resign. Anyway, don't blame me for
disloyalty. What about James – he
called your Rwanda plan batshit crazy!

James Cleverly
I did not. I said no such thing.
I said it was batshithole crazy!
And I wasn't saying that Rwanda
is a shithole. Cos it isn't. Not
compared to Stockton.

James Forsyth
James, you're not helping.

James Cleverly
I wish I could lose all my
WhatsApp messages.

Oliver Dowden
Well, Rishi knows all about that! 😉

> No, I don't. I change
> phones frequently, cos
> I'm a tech-savvy guy
> who constantly needs to
> upgrade to stay in touch.

Oliver Dowden
Ooh – in touchy!

> I AM NOT IN TOUCHY!
> OR RATHER, I AM!

Oliver Dowden
But you are techy. 😊

> I AM NOT TECHY! OR
> RATHER, I AM!

Oliver Dowden
Oh – Rishi's losing his marbles.
Thanks to Keir Starmer for that
zinger. I wish I'd thought of it.

Lord Cameron
Hi, sorry. Bit late. Playing tennis.
Re the Greek fiasco, I thought
we were all in favour of sending
things back to where they came
from?

Lee Anderthal
Aye, you can fook off back to
Chipping Norton 'n' all!

> No, I am really firm on this.
> It is a matter of the upmost
> importance given everything
> else that is going on in the
> world, that some Greek ruins
> that I've only just heard of,
> should be kept in Britain.
> And if this means snubbing
> one of our few remaining
> allies, then so be it. That's
> the kind of guy I am.

Lord Cameron
What – tetchy?!

> I AM NOT TETCHY!!!!!!!

Penny Mordaunt
No, you're not tetchy and
Dave's not snooty. 😉
Fight! Fight! Fight!

> Can we get back
> to Rwanda?

James Cleverly
Well, I could go back. It was
lovely. Brought back memories
of being foreign secretary two
weeks ago.

Grant Shapps
Wasn't I foreign secretary?

James Cleverly
No, you were home secretary,
which is what I am now.

> Thank goodness for stable
> government under a sensible
> leader! How unlike the days of
> Liz Truss and Boris Johnson. The
> grown-ups are at the table. Now,
> who's Immigration Minister?

Robert Jenrick
Yes, that's me. Except it isn't.
Because I'm resigning.

> You're what?! I said we
> either "Unite or Die"!

Oliver Dowden
Well, it's not looking like "Unite"... 😊

> This isn't funny, Oliver, we
> have to sort out immigration.
> So can we please concentrate
> on the Rwanda bill...

Lee Anderthal
Aye, it's a bill for 150 million
fookin' quid. What a fookin' mess.

> No, Lee – the truth is
> that I am right!

Jeremy Hunt
And everyone else is far right! 😱

Lord Cameron
Touché!

> I AM NOT TOUCHÉ!!

"Careful, we've strayed into a mimefield"

Government's five-point plan
to curb legal migration in full

■ Immigrants need to earn £38,700 per year to come to Britain

■ Those immigrants then need to take the thankless jobs in care
homes and the NHS which pay, on average, about £28,000

■ Oh no! Those £28,000 per year jobs don't pay £38,700

■ Oh dear. Then no one will look after all the old and sick people

■ Er, that's it.

ALICE IN RWANDALAND

Rwanda's a lovely, safe place

Contrariwise, it's a deterrent

FOREIGN COUPLE SENT HOME

by Our Immigration Staff **Bear Grylled**

THE government hailed the first big success of its new anti-migration policy as it repatriated a couple of panda bears who had made Edinburgh Zoo their home.

The couple, a Mr Yang Guang and his partner, Ms Tian Tian, failed to pass the new hurdle of an income of £38,700, falling short by roughly £38,700.

The couple were deemed to be unskilled, because all they could do was eat bamboo shoots and sleep.

Said ex-Home Secretary, Cruella de Braverman, "Good riddance to these sponging layabout bears, who came over here to work the system and would have been sent back years ago but for lefty *Guardian*-reading wokerati lawyers."

Said ex-Immigration Minister Robert Jenrick, "We are disappointed they are going to Beijing rather than Rwanda, which is lovely for bears and is a totally safe environment.

"The number of pandas killed by poachers in Rwanda is currently zero and we should ignore the draconian rules laid down by unelected foreign institutions such as the RSPCA."

The bears were handcuffed and escorted to an aeroplane in an panda car.

Said one observer, top author Lynn Truss, "It's what I always said about the fate of the panda. It eats shoots and leaves."

ISRAELI GOVERNMENT ASKS CIVILIANS TO MOVE TO 'WESTERN GAZA' SAFE ZONE

BENJAMIN NETANYAHU's government has offered an olive branch to all Gazans by suggesting they move to a new safe zone they have designated as "Western Gaza".

The latest development comes as Unicef said there were "no safe zones" anywhere in Gaza. The Israel Defense Forces initially requested that 1.8 million Gazans move from northern Gaza to the southern part, before asking that they also vacate that area so that the army could fully destroy it in its search for Hamas.

An IDF spokesperson said the Western Gaza offer was just one part of putting a new "no-state solution" on the negotiating table to the Palestinians.

He said, "West Gaza, an area otherwise known as the Mediterranean, is much less crowded than the congested urban cityscapes of the Strip."

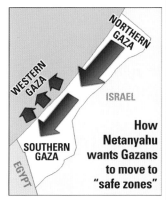

How Netanyahu wants Gazans to move to "safe zones"

THOSE BIG BORIS LIES IN FULL

1. "I'm sorry." **2.** "I don't remember." **3.** "I'm sorry, I don't remember."

MYSTERY OVER JOHNSON'S MISSING WHATSAPPS

by Our Tech Staff **Dee Leet**

THERE was astonishment at the Covid Inquiry as Boris Johnson revealed he had no idea how 5,000 potentially incriminating WhatsApp messages came to be lost from his mobile phone.

He explained to the inquiry, "Er... I... Cripes!... long time ago... factory reset... WhatsApp went down... perhaps... dog ate homework..."

Hugo Keith KC then asked the killer question, which left Boris gasping for air: "Mr Johnson, I put it to you that if you are so technically incompetent, what was the point of all those IT lessons with Jennifer Arcuri?

"Are we to assume that you were not in fact concentrating on IT, as you claimed, and assessing the relative merits of various different methods of safe storage of data? And would I be right in assuming that the sight of your IT instructress gyrating on a pole dressed only in a Union Jack bikini may have distracted from your lesson on reinserting SIM cards in unfamiliar places?

"No, Mr Johnson, this court has every right to conclude that your entire evidence about mobile phones is nothing less than, dare I say it, an inverted pyramid of piffle."

Boris Johnson key moments

1 Boris Johnson told the inquiry that he can't remember anything that happened from January 2020 to when he resigned as Prime Minister in June 2022: "You must understand, I was partying hard at this time and was very pissed."

2 Boris Johnson reacted furiously to questions about partygate: "The TV drama depicting the Number 10 parties was way wide of the mark. It failed to feature me leading a conga of SPADs into the jacuzzi. It's a disgrace – or is that me?"

3 Boris Johnson's publisher reacted furiously to the former Prime Minister's claims that he couldn't remember anything. Said a spokesman for Harper Collins, "If he can't recall any of the details of the most important year of his premiership, why have we paid him a million quid?!"

Why Rishi Sunak is a political genius

■ Decides to bring back Dominic Cummings – a discredited figure whom everyone in the party hates.

■ Holds secret talks with Dominic Cummings, who is renowned for leaking every detail of political life via social media, long-winded blogs and, if desperate, Tim Shipman at the Sunday Times.

■ Admits having approached Dominic Cummings, who may be bonkers but isn't so desperate he's going to work for Sunak.

■ Er... that's it.

CUMMINGS SOON

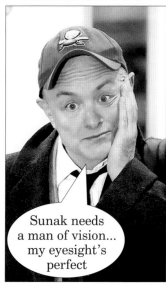

Sunak needs a man of vision... my eyesight's perfect

POST OFFICE ROBBERY!

"How can I help?"

"You can give us all your money..."

"...and go to jail"

"Talk about dodgy figures!"

POST OFFICE

NOT INSIDE: ANYONE IN CHARGE

19 January 2024

LETTER TO ALL NEWSPAPERS

Dear Sir,

IN the light of the decision by Paula Vennells to return her CBE, we the undersigned are writing to protest in the strongest possible terms about her irresponsible behaviour and the dangerous precedent which this sets. In fact, her actions risk bringing the whole honours system into disrepute. The very notion that anyone should relinquish their hard-earned title, merely because they have acted disgracefully or done a very poor job, threatens to undermine the entire structure of British political life. Incompetence, venality or cronyism should not be a barrier to maintaining the elevated status bestowed upon a person by a grateful nation.

Yours

Sir Jacob Rees-Mogg, Sir Gavin Williamson CBE, Sir Jake Berry, Baron Houchen of High Levy, Lord Luvaduk of Hampstead and Siberia, Baroness Charlotte Owen (aged 6), Dame Priti Patel and everyone on Liz Truss's honours list.

✢ *This letter has been issued on behalf of the campaigning group and registered charity JSSTTA (Justice for Sub-Standard Tory Timeservers Alliance)*

PARLIAMENT FINALLY REACTS FOLLOWING ITV SHOW

ROBERT THOMPSON *pse*

"The moral of the story is... 'DO make a drama out of a crisis'"

PRIME MINISTER ANNOUNCES IMMEDIATE 'MASS EXONERATIONS'

by Our Post Office Staff **Nick Nothing**

RISHI SUNAK today told the House of Commons that he was instituting a blanket measure to clear the names of all those who had been falsely accused of wrongdoing in the Post Office scandal.

Said Mr Sunak, "It is important that those who are innocent should suffer no longer from the unfair accusations levelled against them.

"All Conservative ministers are from now on to be considered blameless and their good names are to be restored in full. This applies right to the very top, meaning that no cabinet minister and no Prime Minister should be held responsible for any of the appalling failures involved in this tragic case."

The Prime Minister continued, to applause, "We must now move on to punishing the guilty – namely Ed Davey and Keir Starmer, who clearly conspired together to besmirch the good name of the Conservative party over decades."

Said one relieved Conservative minister, "It is a huge weight off my mind. I have been living a nightmare, with the thought that I might be accused of having done nothing at all to help the subpostmasters until it featured on the telly."

He continued, "Now I can get on with my life, doing nothing at all to help people during the next miscarriage of justice."

News in brief

Public criticised over Post Office scandal

■ Politicians have joined forces to criticise the length of time it took for the public-at-large to take heed of the decades-long Post Office Horizon scandal.

In a forthright broadside, major figures in Westminster laid into the UK, blasting, "Why oh why do the public only get interested in something terrible when they watch it via the means of a dramatisation on the telly?" adding, "Why is it that these 'little people' only take notice of bad things like major miscarriages of justice and institutional corruption when they see it portrayed on national television? I blame the public."

FUJITSU HORIZON MAIN FRAME-UP COMPUTER

Return to sender

PAULA VENNELLS - CBE

THE JUST SO AWFUL STORIES

By Rudyard Kipling Cakes

The Tale of the Crocodile Who Cried

There once was a Post Office Minister and his name was Kevin Hollinrake.

One day, Kevin found himself in trouble in the swamp when everybody said that he and his friends were responsible for failing to help those in need, in the Post Office Scandal.

"Boo hoo hoo," said Kevin. "I have seen a drama called *Mr Bates vs The Crocodiles* and I was moved to tears. Twice. I cried once when the Daily Mail photographer asked me to look sad and then again later, when I thought about my future career."

Moral: *Not very*

Users of 'X', formerly Twitter, in deep shock at Vennells scandal

by Our Online Correspondent
Anne Gree

THERE was widespread shock on X today when former Post Office boss Paula Vennells handed back her CBE, meaning that the petition on the platform demanding that she do just that had actually succeeded.

"Everyone knows that in terms of effectiveness, internet petitions rank somewhere between 'opening your window and howling at the moon' and 'doing nothing'," agreed all X users. "The thought that we're not just wasting our lives away here, moaning that Elon Musk has ruined Twitter, but never actually leaving, and that we're capable of bringing about actual real change is a very disturbing and frightening one.

"I'm going back to bed now."

POST OFFICE BEHAVED 'LIKE MAFIA'

The Ancient Art of Fujitsu

FUJITSU is a Japanese martial art where the emphasis is on defending oneself in extreme situations and forcing opponents onto the back foot.

It includes a series of moves, including ducking, diving, dodging and lying.

The aim of Fujitsu is to exploit the opponent's weakness, to bring them to the ground and to give them a good kicking.

The ancient art of Fujitsu seeks to bring about both the physical and mental destruction of the defenceless enemy. The Fujitsu masters take an oath of secrecy never to reveal the truth about Fujitsu, which is why to this day no one knows how they get away with it.

Post Office compensation

"The cheque's in the post"

'Injury concerns' from dangerous new trend

THERE were warnings today from A&E doctors of a dangerous new trend that's leaving people with serious injuries, namely "Bandwagon jumping".

"Bandwagon jumping in Westminster has seen a surge in popularity, following ITV's Post Office drama," said one junior doctor.

"A large number of Tory MPs have tried jumping on the bandwagon, insisting that they've always spoken out on behalf of the sub-postmasters.

"We've already had both Priti Patel and Lee Anderson in here this morning with badly bruised egos after trying and failing to jump onto that bandwagon.

"We're strongly advising against other MPs trying it, before someone really gets hurt."

The Daily SPECTATORgraph

Friday 19 January 2024

Charles Moore-of-this-stuff

WATCHING my cathode ray tube device the other evening, I happened to stumble upon what I believe is a channel called ITV, which offered a dramatic reconstruction of the so-called Post Office Scandal.

What became apparent immediately was that certain parties were clearly to blame for the whole affair and the most disgraceful of all was the BBC.

Why did the BBC choose to ignore this horrendous miscarriage of justice? What are they trying to cover up by their wilful failure to make a TV drama that someone else has made? Why are they charging the hard-pressed licence-fee payer an exorbitant however many guineas it is, whilst deliberately avoiding this issue... apart from the Panorama and repeated radio specials by Nick Wallis, plus all the other programmes over the years.

Tim Davie should give his CBE back forthwith.

Surely it is time for ITV to make a drama about the real scandal, namely the BBC's failure to make an ITV drama about the Post Office.

Might I suggest the title "Mr Moore vs the BBC" and perhaps they could cast a suitably Old Etonian actor to play myself. I'm thinking of Dominic West OE, Tom Hiddleston OE, Damien Lewis OE, or Eddie Redmayne OE.

Incidentally, if programme makers are truly seeking a miscarriage of justice that has touched the hearts of the nation, they need look no further than the shameful treatment by the establishment of poor MP Owen Paterson OE, who was falsely accused of lobbying and thrown out of the House of Commons, despite the best efforts of the campaigning group, consisting of Jacob Rees-Mogg OE, Boris Johnson OE and myself OE. Now, that's a programme that we'd all like to watch and might finally validate the BBC licence fee.

Does anyone know where one can buy decent spats nowadays? My greengrocer used to deliver them but... *(cont. p94)*

LET'S HOPE MAKING THIS DRAMA ABOUT GODOT SPEEDS THINGS ALONG A BIT

Nadhim Zahawi casting

FRESH from his cameo appearance in *Mr Bates vs the Post Office*, ITV producers today confirmed Nadhim Zahawi has been cast in a much larger role in another upcoming true-life drama.

"This one tells the story of a disgraced former Chancellor and Tory Pary Chairman, sacked after he constantly failed to declare he was being investigated by HMRC over non-payment of tax.

"We think Nadhim Zahawi was born to play the role of this venal, duplicitous, disgraced... *(cont. p94)*

LEGAL THREAT OVER BARONESS MONE COMMENTS

by Our Litigation Staff **Grant Slapps**

THE ESTATE of South American drugs kingpin Pablo Escobar has launched legal proceedings after Baroness Mone claimed that she had been treated as badly as he had.

Relatives of the deceased criminal mastermind said, "This is just so shameful. For years, we've been proud of our Pablo as a violent drugs baron who created and ran a highly successful cartel spreading cocaine across the planet, killing thousands of people on the way. For him to be associated in any way with Michelle Mone is grossly defamatory."

When pressed, the Escobars'

representative added, "For one thing, Pablo actually delivered the products he said he would, often to the nearest gram. For another, it worked really, really well. And for a third thing, he hid his money in the form of bricks of banknotes concealed within the walls of his property, which was not only keeping the cash economy going but also provided great home insulation."

They added, "Plus, of course, when Escobar wanted someone dead, he did it properly, rather than just providing them with substandard PPE during a global pandemic."

BARONESS MONE DENIES PULLING WOOL OVER ANYONE'S EYES

It wasn't proper wool – it was substandard and full of holes

POETRY CORNER

Lines on the cancellation of BBC TV's Top Gear

So. Farewell
Then Top Gear.
You really were
Car crash television.

It was almost
Farewell then
Freddie Flintoff.

And before that
It was almost
Farewell then
Richard Hammond.

Now the wheels
Have finally
Come off.

E.J. Thribb (0-17½ mph)

PERSON AT DINNER PARTY HAS NO PARTICULAR OPINION ABOUT *SALTBURN*

by Our After-dinner Staff **Minty Chocolate**

THERE was widespread shock and disbelief last night after a guest at a dinner party in North London admitted she had no strong views on "Saltburn".

"We'd been expecting Fiona to say either that it was a gut-wrenching cinematic masterpiece, a brutal assault on inherited wealth and the

shallow empty lives of the ruling elite," said the dinner party host, "or that Saltburn was an empty spectacle, as gorgeous to look at as Rosamund Pike's Elspeth, but shallow and forgettable in what's a pretty tepid reworking of 'The Talented Mr Ripley'."

Instead, the woman just shrugged and offered no opinion one way or another.

Said one industry insider, "Cinema may never be the same again. Or maybe it will."

MEDIA FRANTICALLY ASKS: WHO ARE THE WHOTHEYS?

JOURNALISTS around the UK are desperately posing the question: who the hell are the Houtheys? *(Surely, Houthis? Ed.)*

The question comes as British and American forces surprisingly fired on the Yemen-based Houthi group – and no one in the media had any idea who they were.

After consulting Wikipedia, hacks explained clearly that the Houthis' attacks on ships in the Red Sea are very much related to the war in Gaza, but also somehow separate and related to a different conflict.

They said that the group were controlled by the authoritarian state Iran, but also independent in their fight against Saudi Arabia, and it was not entirely clear who was in charge of them.

The journalists wrote that the Houthis were firing on freight shipping and had caused no fatalities, but were also deeply dangerous and firing on military targets. Or possibly vice versa.

Having shed such clear light on the situation, they moved on to explain developments in Gaza, Ukraine, and the US election, which *(cont. p94)*

Red Sea at night, Houthis' delight

Red Sea in the morning, economists' warning

Biden issues starkest warning yet to Netanyahu

by Our Washington Correspondent **M.T. Threats**

IN WHAT the White House described as a major ramping up of the pressure on Benjamin Netanyahu, President Biden has issued his starkest warning yet that unless Israel stops its indiscriminate bombing of Gaza, America is prepared to do absolutely nothing, with immediate effect.

"This is huge. Previously, Biden has always said that America was prepared to wait a few weeks

before doing nothing," said one stunned Washington insider.

"Now Bibi knows that unless Israel starts bombing Gaza in a responsible way, Biden is ready to act by doing nothing now."

President Biden brushed aside criticism from some left-leaning Democrats that he wasn't being tough enough with Netanyahu.

"They're wrong. When we spoke earlier, I gave Bibi a rocket. I also gave him thousands of bombs, hundreds of surface-to-air missiles and more ammunition than he can handle."

"Looks like the DJ played Murder on the Dancefloor one time too many"

Lines written on the Scottish Covid Inquiry

'Twas in the year of our Lord 2024

That the Covid inquiry asked Nicola Sturgeon if she was sure

That all of her pandemic WhatsApps had been lost for good

And no minutes had been taken in meetings where someone should?

There was, she said, nothing to hide and the medical officer, the chief,

Had told her to delete them before going to bed, like cleaning her teeth.

Not everyone, of course, thought that this explanation was true

And that information was destroyed that the public was due.

However, it happened that some WhatsApp messages remained,

Enough for the first minister to be publicly shamed.

Other SNP members felt it was their duty

To reveal that Nicola's language was somewhat fruity!

She even used the 'F' word, belying her image so cosy,

And I am not talking about the word 'fan-dabi-dozi'!

She referred to Boris Johnson as a 'fucking clown',

For which Ms Sturgeon apologised with an angry frown.

'If I had known these messages would ever be heard,

I'd have been much ruder,' she said, undeterred.

But worst of all was revealed Nicola's reaction to the disease,

Which was just an excuse to get herself on the nation's TVs.

The pandemic was treated not as a medical disaster,

But as a way to make Scottish Independence come faster.

Ms Sturgeon appeared every night on the telly, doing PR

And telling the nation how great the SNP are,

And saying the English were useless at dealing with the virus

And it was her own brilliance as leader that should inspire us.

And yet, as it emerged at the inquiry, in news that was sad,

The death rates, despite Sturgeon's spinning, were similarly bad.

But what will happen when she gives evidence next week

And proper answers be required when she comes to speak?

Will folk believe that in Holyrood there was no dishonest hanky panky

On the part of the wee lookalike former first minister?

© *William McGonagall 1867*

"I'm an influencer"   *"That sounds daft"*

"Ah. No. No, it doesn't"   *"Oh. OK. Wow..."*

Pearsall

What You Missed

Celebrating 100 Years of the Shitting Forecast

We look back at yesterday's classic maritime warning service on Radio 4 longwave, that tells sailors what's coming at them around Britain's coasts...

(Theme Music plays: "Turds Sailing By")

ANNOUNCER: "Logger, Bumber: variable 4 to 6. Pootland,

Filth, Isle of Shite: 3 to 5, backing up later. Pottymouth, Piscay, Plopall: moderate to strong. Arse Sole, Shitzroy, Irish Pee: good. Craparty, Farties: high winds expected..."

(That's enough of this rather disappointing satire of the water companies. Ed.)

A future President speaks

"Trust me – if I'm found guilty of insurrection – which I would never do – there's gonna be insurrection. By which I mean bedlam. Bigly bedlam. And I don't mean getting into bedlam with Stormy Daniels. Which I have never done. As President, I have immunity from prostitution. Hashtag Fact! It's in the constitution – the right to bare arse! Look it up. It's there! Amendment 69. Fact! I've read it. Bedlam. You don't want Bedlam. Bedlam is bad. It's like opening Pandora's box. And I don't mean grabbing it. Which I would never do. Even though I am famous. And rich. And can do whatever I like. I am immune from Covid. Fact! You seen the old guy who wants to be President? Can't talk. He just goes gaa-gaa-gaa-gaa-gaa. You know he does – watch him. Loses the thread of his speech. Goes all over the place. Bees. Honey. What was I talking about. ZZZZZ. That's right. Sleepy Joe Bedlam, he just talks nonsense. You know he does. He can't even get an insurrection without taking one of them blue tablets. Which I don't need. I take bleach. When I get in for my third term. Which I will. I'm gonna pull outta NATO, I'm gonna pull outta Gaza, and pull outta Stormy. Which I wouldn't do. Ask Pandora..." *(Cont. 94 more years)*

IMPERIAL UNIT VICTORY

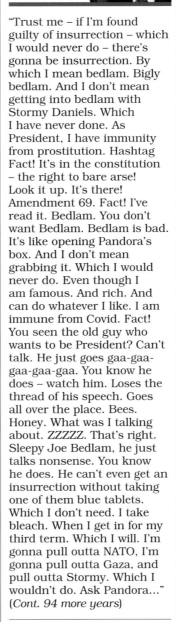

Brexit bonus! You can buy wine in pints!

Brexit minus! You can't afford wine

'THAT'S LIFE' PRESENTER CONSIDERS DIGNITAS

I don't want to become an unamusing vegetable

DAILY EXPRESS

LET US DIE WITH DIGNITY!

IT's the topic everyone is talking about – assisted dying.

The tragic reality about reaching a certain age is your cognitive ability declines and your circulation gets weaker and weaker.

At that point, the only humane thing to do is to put the *Daily Express* out of its misery.

Don't let this once-proud publication end its days a shadow of its former self – a gibbering mess that doesn't make any sense any more, prattling on to anyone who will still listen about the triumph of Brexit, whilst bemoaning the sorry state of the country and Diana's sad passing.

Please, please, cherish those memories of what this newspaper used to be and wave it farewell as it heads off to the great chip shop in the sky.

QUICK! GET ME THE INTIMACY CO-ORDINATOR

KISS ME, HARDY

Great stuff, guys! We're delivering on all fronts. We've delivered justice for Post Office workers!

Alex Chalk
Sadly, it was twenty years late!

Oliver Dowden
To be fair – it is the Post Office we're talking about! 😂

James Forsyth
Decisive, swift action, clearing up the mess caused by the previous er…

The important thing is to tackle the serious issues arising from this, ie how can we shift the blame?

Lee Anderthal
Fookin' Ed Davey!

Good blame work, Lee!

Lee Anderthal
He's always telling people to resign. Well, he should resign then! People who tell people to resign should fookin' resign.

James Forsyth
Have you thought that through, Lee?

Lee Anderthal
Course I haven't – thinking is for wimps!

Anyone else we can blame?

David Cameron
Who was the idiot Prime Minister who put Ed Davey in charge of anything?

Lee Anderthal
That was you, you soft-brained toffee-nosed ponce.

David Cameron
Lord soft-brained toffee-nosed ponce to you, Lee.

David Cameron
Rishi – how do I delete WhatsApp messages again?

I don't recall.

Lee Anderthal
I know who we can blame: Fookin' Keir Starmer!

Alex Chalk
He wasn't really involved, Lee.

Lee Anderthal
And your point is? How about Tony Blair? And Tony Benn! Tony Robinson! Tony the Tiger!

Oliver Dowden
You can't blame him – he's Grrrrreat! 😅

Okay, we'll blame them, and we'll take the credit for sorting it out.

Alex Chalk
I think we should blame Fujitsu for the whole debacle.

Grant Shapps
Yeah – Boo Fujitsu! We'll never work with them again.

Kevin Hollinrake
Actually. Slight problem, we've just renewed the Horizon contract.

Who are you?

Kevin Hollinrake
I'm the Postal Services Minister.

Grant Shapps
Really? I thought that was me. Phew. Dodged a bullet there. Well, as long as Fujitsu aren't running anything else.

Steve Barclay
Actually. Slight problem. They're also running England's flood alert system.

Oliver Dowden
That's working well. Glug! Glug! Glug! 😅 😅 😅

Oliver Dowden
Oh no, my crying-with-laughter emojis are making it even worse!

Oliver Dowden
Where was the warning from Fujitsu?!

Jeremy Hunt
The only floods Fujitsu care about are the floods of money we're pouring into their bank account! 😔

Grant Shapps
Honestly! They should all be locked up!

Edward Argar
Actually. Slight problem. They're running Britain's criminal records system.

Who are you?

Edward Argar
I'm your new Prisons Minister.

Thanks Edward, we'll sort it! What I'm saying is that all it requires for us to have electoral success is for me to get out there and connect with some real people.

James Forsyth
Right. Gotcha, boss. Real people, from real focus groups, who we've really checked out first, and really support us, and who are really good at nodding.

REALLY good work, James!

James Forsyth
It's just like Debating Soc back in the good old Winky days. When you proposed: "This House believes that trousers should be worn at least seven inches above the sock level."

Alex Chalk
You lost the debate though.

I don't recall that, and all the records of it have been lost.

Alex Chalk
You did lose though.

I DID NOT LOSE!

Penny Mordaunt
Fight! Fight! Fight!

Kemi Badenoch
Ooh – he's getting tetchy!

I AM NOT TETCHY!

James Forsyth
Er… PM. I think your phone's got stuck on CAPS again.

I AM NOT TECHY!

Gillian Keegan
By the way, guys, if anyone's having any tech problems, my husband's a bit of a whizz with software.

James Forsyth
That's great, Gillian.

Gillian Keegan
He was UK chief executive and chairman of Fujitsu.

Oliver Dowden
😱😱😱😱😱😱😱😱😱😱😱

"To be honest, it's just nice to be held…"

"I remember when all this was fields"

Mars

Fun-Size Mars

THE TRAITORIES — GRAND FINALE

- I am an Unfaithful
- I got away with murder
- Oh no, they are ALL Traitors
- You're banished – to Rwanda!
- And people think I've got a lunatic fringe
- We've completely lost the plot

"I'm not going to lie to you, to be fair, and I love you to bits, but if you don't stop watching Traitors, you'll 100 percent have to leave"

ROYAL MAIL COULD SAVE £650M BY REDUCING TO A NO-DAYS-A-WEEK SERVICE

by Our Royal Mail Correspondent **Penny Black**

A NEW report says the Royal Mail could save up to £650m a year by switching to a three, two or even no-days-a-week service.

"The Royal Mail would be a highly profitable business but for having to deliver all these letters to people," complained a senior Royal Mail executive.

"The notion of a universal postal service is getting out of date, as are most of the letters we grudgingly eventually deliver.

"At the end of the day, we only want to deliver for our shareholders."

However, those people who rely on a reliable mail service have condemned the move.

"Since 2020, we've been receiving record numbers of letters of no confidence," said a 1922 Committee spokesman.

"Right now, we need the Royal Mail working flat out six days a week just to keep on top of how many letters we're getting demanding that Rishi resigns."

SECOND HUGE METAPHOR FAILS TO LEAVE PORT

by **OUR NAVAL STAFF** Tim Mid-Shipman

AFTER the embarrassment of the nation's flagship metaphor, HMS *Queen Elizabeth*, failing to join a NATO exercise due to a mechanical fault, a second huge metaphor, HMS *Prince of Wales*, has also been declared unfit for action.

The two metaphors are currently laid up in Portsmouth undergoing repairs – although the Royal Navy has claimed that one of them will soon be functioning as a ship again, instead of as a figure of speech representing Britain's irreversible decline.

'I would have definitely joined army,' claim people who are conveniently all too old now

by Our Dad's Army Staff **Private Spike**

BRITISH media types, who are long, long past the age of conscription, have been loudly declaring that if it wasn't for the damned age limits, they would love to sign up and give Johnny Moscow a good thrashing.

"I would definitely love to get out my fatigues and head to the front," said one media presenter with a show on LBC, who has not worn the fatigues since he was 17 and wore them to a fancy-dress party.

"Unfortunately, as I'm now in my mid-50s, I doubt I will receive the call."

Another columnist with two artificial knees said, "I would be very keen to fight. In many ways I've always wanted to be a soldier, but regrettably I joined a newspaper at the age of 21 when my uncle said 'You should come and write here, and nobody will shoot at you', and sadly I'm far too important now, which is a shame."

"I think I could do it," said former Prime Minister Boris Johnson. The veteran of the Partygate scandals said "I am ready for bottle!" *(Surely battle? Ed.)*

Boris continued, "The only thing that prevented me from joining up for any of the multiple wars Britain has fought in the last three decades was my decision to earn a huge amount of money instead.

"But at least by supporting Donald Trump for the Presidency, I'm helping give lots of other people's children the chance to sign up and have a glorious World War Three instead."

The Daily Telegraph Friday, February 2, 2024

Why we need conscription now

BRITAIN is sleepwalking into disaster. All around us, hostile forces are preparing for an all-out assault on the British Isles, determined to take over all the things we hold most dear: the White Cliffs of Dover, Buckingham Palace and, most precious of all, the *Daily Telegraph*.

It is time for this country to wake up and immediately boost our armed forces by conscripting ALL available men and women between the ages of 18 and 94, in preparation for a pre-emptive strike on the United Arab Emirates.

Yes! There is only one language that these people understand! And it's not English! The British Army must be brought up to strength with voluntary regiments.

We are delighted to announce that the Sir Charles Moore Mounted Camel Battalion will be at the tip of the spear, followed by the Simon Heffer Garrick Club Infantry, the Andrew Neil Heavy Lunch Brigade, and the Fraser Nelson Scottish Boredomers, which will all be recruiting next week at the *Telegraph* offices.

They will embark on the six-week voyage aboard HMS Oakeshott (breakdowns permitting), to join the front line against tyranny.

Rise up, Britain, from your breakfast table! Stop reading the Telegraph! And present yourself at Victoria Station, where the recruiting officer, Sir Herbert Gussett, will be waiting for you with a shilling and a foaming tankard of Pearson's Extremely Peculiar! *(You're fired. So am I. So is everyone. Ed.)*

Is Prince George heading to St Cake's?

by Our Education Staff
Victoria Sponge

THE world of private education is buzzing with the rumour that the eldest son of the Prince and Princess of Wales may be going to attend the prestigious Midlands fee-paying independent boarding school, St Cake's, after he finishes at the feeder preparatory school, St Biscuit's.

The Headmaster of St Cake's, Mr R.G.J. Kipling said, "It would be wrong for me to recount any phone call I may or may not have had with the Princess of Wales, but, suffice to say, the royal couple are looking for an ordinary education for their son, and they don't get more ordinary than St Cake's."

He continued, "Other schools, like Marlboro Lite and Yesminister, may be more academic, in the sense that they get some GCSE passes and the occasional A level grade above a 'D', but at St Cake's we pride ourselves on focusing on the individual and ensuring that they reach their potential.

"In the case of Prince George, we would hope that, with the assistance of the St Cake's careers advisor, Mr Bakewell, he would go on to attain one of the top jobs in the country, possibly even King.

"If he does go to St Cake's, he could enter one of their famous houses like 'Chaps', 'Weeds' or 'Swots', and join in a range of activities, including the CCF, of which he would be Commander in Chief."

Continuing to deny any possible connection with the royal family, Mr Kipling went on, "Each Sunday, George would be expected to attend Chapel, where he would be Head of the Church and Defender of the Faith."

Mr Kipling then added, unprompted, "In view of the imminent possible arrival of Prince George, I have changed the school motto from the old-fashioned '*Quis Paget Entrat*' (who pays enters) to the much more modern '*Quis Regnat Vincit*' (who rules wins a scholarship)."

Prince George would follow in the footsteps of other famous old Cakeians, including his old relative Lord Battenburg, French aristocrat the Duke of Bourbon, Gary Baldy the Bake Off TV presenter, 'Ginger' Bread, drummer in legendary rock band Custard Cream, Channel 5 Weather girl Lemon Drizzle, Welsh rugby fly-half Dai Gestive. *(I've had my fill of cake-based satire. Ed.)*

Why has marriage fallen to an all-time low?

Marriage figures in the UK have fallen to their lowest rate ever. Why? Our team of married hacks investigate:

PHIL PAGE: The answer is simple. It's bloody women! They're always asking you to do things, like 'help around the house' or 'look after the children we share'. And they're always complaining about you, often in articles they've written in the newspaper. Of course men don't want to get married when they see the sort of stuff we have to put up with!

PHILIPPA PAGE: What a stupid thing to say. I think you'll find that men are the ones who write snide articles in the paper, like the one last month about why women don't ever have their things ready when it's time to leave the house... that is the kind of thing putting young women off lumbering themselves with an idiot for life.

PHIL: I'm an idiot? I'm not the one who forgot one of the children at the cinema last year.

PHILIPPA: Oh, are we bringing up ancient history? Well, I'm not the one who had an affair with some scrubber he met at the office Away Day in 2018!

PHIL: I hate you!

PHILIPPA: I hate you more!

PHIL: But we need the money, so we'll have to keep doing this!

PHILIPPA: Yes!

PHIL: Ugh!

PHILIPPA: Ugh!

■ *Listen to Phil and Philippa's new comedy marriage podcast, 'I loathe my awful spouse!', only on eyeTunes.*

Notes&queries

Who or what is Kimchi?

● Kim Chi, is the influential aunt of North Korea's autocratic leader Kim Rong Un. Kim Chi has never been seen in public, but was implicated in the assassination of her half-sister, Kim Kah Dashian, who was the daughter of previous soviet double agent and minister for the interior, Kim Phil Bee. Kim Chi is believed to be responsible for Kim Rong Un's distinctive Elvis-style haircut, which has ensured her survival in the despotic regime.
Sir Simon Cabbage, former Ambassador to the City of the Great Helmsman

● Sir Simon's story is – how can I put this diplomatically? – a bit overcooked! "Kimchi" is, of course the third track on the seminal album by prog-rock masters Yes, *Tales of Pseudological Oceans* (1973), and refers to the Javanese philosopher, Kimono, and his followers, the so-called "Kimchis", whose members briefly included lead flautist, Lee Anderson, who later left to pursue a solo career, reaching number 94 in the album charts with his concept album *Journey to the Centre of Milton Keynes*.
'Whispering' Bob Radish

● Oh dear! 'Whispering' Bob should have kept quiet! Kimchi is, as any zoologist will tell you, the name of one of a pair of pandas gifted to Scottish First Minister Nicola Sturgeon as a symbol of peace and harmony between The People's Republic of Scotland and the United Kingdom of China. Sadly, Kimchi was eaten by her mate, Noo-Dul, creating a diplomatic incident which led directly to the arrest of Nicola Sturgeon. Kimchi was recently replicated by an animatronic panda, Hu Wawei, who resides in Edinburgh Zoo, and keeps an eye on UK politics.
The Rev Sally Soup

THAT CLASSIC ERIC IDLE PYTHON 'NUDGE, NUDGE, WHINGE, WHINGE' SKETCH IN FULL (2024)

(Man in pub with fellow Python Terry Gilliam)

Eric Idle *(for it is he)*: Your daughter... does she have money? Know what I mean, nudge, nudge?

Terry Gilliam: Yes, she has some money.

Eric Idle: Bet she does, bet she does. Does she have any of mine?

Terry Gilliam: I don't follow you.

Eric Idle: Follow you, follow you, that's good. If you followed me on Twitter, you'd know I've got no money and I blame your daughter.

Terry Gilliam: Are you begging for something?

Eric Idle: Begging? Begging? Very good. Wicked! Wicked! That's what you are, nudge, nudge? Know what I mean?

Terry Gilliam: No.

Eric Idle: You're all wicked. For stealing all my money!

Terry Gilliam: I don't know what you're talking about.

Eric Idle: 'Course you don't. Still... phwooarr, eh?

(Nudges Gilliam in ribs)

Eric Idle: Your daughter's money, wink, wink, nudge nudge. Does it go? He asked him knowingly. Does it go... into ISAs, stocks and shares, index-linked pensions?

Terry Gilliam: It sometimes goes... into the bank

Eric Idle: Bet it does....grin, grin, nudge, nudge, whinge, whinge.

Terry Gilliam: Are you insinuating something?

Eric Idle: No, no, no, no... yes.

Terry Gilliam: Well?

Eric Idle: Well, I mean, you're a man of the world, squire. You've done it... you've actually got... money.

Terry Gilliam: Yes.

Eric Idle: What's it like?

(Giant foot squashes Gilliam)

OTHER ERIC IDLE CLASSICS INCLUDE:

- Mr Spendtoomuch
- Every Pound Is sacred
- Spaffalot (the musical)
- No one Expects the Financial Inquisition
- The Meaning of Strife
- The Holy Wail
- Always Look On the Miserable Side of Life

(That's enough Python. Ed.)

The Eye's Controversial New Columnist

This week I am very annoyed by the ridicule heaped on Gregg Wallace for his piece in the Daily Telegraph where he outlined his intense daily routine. He has nothing to be ashamed of. Take it from me, any bald celebrity who looks after their own brand needs to fill their day with pretentious nonsense. For example, this is my typical day: I wake up at 4am and make everyone else get up too. I force my parents to open the nursery for me and do laps of it in my stroller, while reviewing my to-do list, which is usually getting fed and getting my nappy changed by tired people. After a power brunch of swede and carrot with my senior cuddly toy (Gerry the giraffe), I expect my lunch to be on the table straight afterwards, the consumption of which I combine with my exercise regime, by throwing it at the wall. In the afternoon, I force myself to play with my parents, whom I didn't really want, but I admire the cat's tolerance of them occupying our space. I am glad the cat has somehow employed a nanny to help with looking after them. Then, at 3pm, I eat biscuits on the sofa and play with my Fisher-Price game controller until I fall asleep. And then repeat *(cont. p94)*

Ironyometer explodes again

AFTER months of disturbing rumblings, the Ironyometer finally blew itself to smithereens on the news of the Academy Award Nominations.

The feminist movie *Barbie*, that had made a billion dollars at the box office for the predominantly male film industry, failed to win a nomination for either the female director or the female star, but did ironically receive a nomination for Ken, Barbie's boyfriend.

The explosion of the Ironyometer was so large, that it is to form the basis of the next film from Oppenheimer director, Christopher Nolan. *(Rotters)*

Tom Hollander reveals million-pound Tom Holland mix-up

by Our Showbiz Staff **Phil Boots**

Beloved actor and *White Lotus* star Tom Hollander has delighted his fans with an indiscreet anecdote about the time he discovered his financial details had been confused with those of Tom Holland.

The star of recent theatre hit *Patriot* and TV Le Carré adaptation *The Night Manager* checked his account balance, and found an enormous seven-figure sum of money had mistakenly been paid to him instead of the more famous star Tom Holland.

"I couldn't believe it," said Hollander. "I'm more of a jobbing actor and I don't make these phenomenal sums of money. I mean, it is amazing and frankly absurd how much money Tom Holland makes."

He continued, "I'm well-respected in the business, and I'm not complaining, but I immediately knew that this humongous fee could not be for me, but had to be for the star of top history podcast *The Rest Is History*, Tom Holland."

When contacted for comment, historian Tom Holland said, "I think you're mistaking me for the *Spider-Man* star, Tom Holland."

But when told how much money the *Avengers* actor and Marvel superhero was paid as a box office bonus, he added, "No, you're right, it probably was me. I don't get out of bed for that kind of peanuts."

PAUL MESCAL STUNS FILM WORLD

by Our Cinema Correspondent **Una Dressed**

PAUL MESCAL has stunned the movie world, after star turns in *Normal People*, *All of Us Strangers* and *Foe*, by saying that if the role was right, he would consider not being naked in a film.

Mescal's announcement shocked the industry, with many saying they didn't actually realise that Paul owned any clothes.

"How would this actually work, though, over a 90-minute film?" said one confused director.

"I really don't think the film-going public is ready for a fully-clothed Paul Mescal for that length of time."

Paul Mescal later clarified his comments, saying that while he would consider roles where he remained fully clothed throughout, he certainly didn't expect any to come his way for at least the next decade.

Fans worldwide expressed their relief, saying they didn't want to see Mescal being exploited by the industry and pressured into taking roles where he was gratuitously clothed.

Court Circular

Buckingham Palace, Thursday

Following concerns about the Royal Wee, His Majesty King Charles will be attended by the Palace Proctologist Pursuivant, also known as the Anointed Finger-in-Waiting.

There will be a lowering of the Trousers Royale to half-mast, followed by an inspection of the King's Privates, with soothing music provided by the Band of the Gosh-That's-Very-Coldstream Guards playing 'Hand of Poke and Glory'.

After the digital ceremony, the King will rearrange the Crown Jewels and be awarded the Order of the BPE (Benign Prostate Enlargement) for services to public health education.

His Grace the Archbishop of Canterbury will lead the nation in prayers during His Majesty's subsequent visit to the London Clinic.

On his discharge, His Majesty will repair to Buckingham Palace and visit the Throne Room, but not sit down for a bit.

TRANSFER ⚽ NEWS

AS EVER, there has been a lot of frenetic activity around Kyle Walker, the Manchester City and England defender.

With the transfer window open, his wife and mother of his three children began by transferring all his clothes out of said window into the street, shouting, "I caught you playing away, you bastard! No more home games for you!"

Walker then transferred to his mistress and mother of two more children, promising undying loyalty to his new boss.

However, when he put on his new, recently laundered shirt, an item of lingerie fell out of the sleeve, which, it would seem, belonged to a third young lady.

Mr Walker then found himself transferred to yet another home ground, where he is said to be bedding in nicely.

After being shown a record number of red cards, he may struggle to get any more offers, but, on the other hand, he is immensely rich and young and famous.

In the words of another football commentator, "They think it's all legover – it is nowadays!"

LET'S PRAY FOR KATE TO GET BETTER SO WE CAN PUT HER ON THE FRONT PAGE

THESE are dark times for newspapers, as we wait anxiously for the latest news on the Princess of Wales.

Her unfortunate illness has meant she has had to cancel a number of her scheduled appearances on page 1, 2, 3, 4 and 5 of this and all other papers.

A slimmed-down newspaper cannot cope with a slimmed-down monarchy – this is a constitutional crisis.

To show you just how bad this has become, we have been reduced this very week to publishing a picture of Prince Edward meeting a 192-year-old tortoise.

There is no way that the Duke of Edinburgh, as he now is, can begin to replace the Princess of Poses, the shining star that is Kate, the face that launched a thousand articles beginning "Kate Wears Hat", "Kate Doesn't Wear Hat" and "Isn't Meghan's Hat Ghastly?"

That's why we say: "Get Well Soon, Ma'am!" before our circulation fails, and the editor has to go into hospital for an abdominal operation to treat a perforated ulcer.

On other pages

■ "I was ill too, once. I know exactly what Kate's going through. It was awful. Me. I was in hospital and everything. Me" by Sarah Vain **p3**

■ "It would be wrong to speculate on the precise nature of the Princess of Wales' illness but here are the top ten theories that I've come up with from the internet" by Phil Space **p4**

■ "Post-Operative Ward Chic. What hospital gown Kate is likely to be wearing and where you can buy one" by Philippa Supplement **p94**

JAMAICAN PM WANTS TO CUT TIES WITH BRITISH ROYALTY

Been there, done that

"My wife went to the West Indies..."
"Jamaica?"
"No – she wanted to go. It was free."

PRINCE HARRY WINS TOP AWARD AT STAR-STUDDED CEREMONY

by Our Aviation Staff **Roger Wilco**

THE Duke of Sussex last night attended a glittering ceremony in Los Angeles to celebrate The Living Legends of Litigation (*surely "aviation"? Ed.*).

The awards honour the most famous litigants in the world and have seen such historic litigators as Robert Maxwell, Sir James Goldsmith and Mohamed Al-Fayed walk off with the top prizes in a ceremony presented by the glamorous hostess, Sue Grabbitandrunne.

Cameras clicked and flash bulbs popped as Prince Harry took to the stage to hand over a huge cheque to his lawyers, Schillings Pounds and Pence.

The Prince then thanked the organisers and said that he was proud to join the pantheon of Litigation Legends who, he said, "were not afraid to fly into a rage and venture too near the Sun (and the Mirror and the Mail) before crashing and burning".

Said the Prince, "We legal pioneers follow in the footsteps of the Far Wright Brothers, Wilbur and Orville Barclay, Captain von Bob, the so-called Red Press Baron, and, of course, the great American test-case pilot, Chuck Money (*surely "Yeager"? Ed.*), who was the inspiration for *The Writ Stuff*, the epic movie about the Waste of Space race."

FASHIONISTAS

KERBER

HOT TREND 1: BALLET WEAR

IT'S TU-TU... ...SILLY FOR WORDS!!!

HOT TREND 2: MOB WIFE AESTHETIC

YOU CAN'T COMPARE THE FASHION INDUSTRY WITH THE MOB!!! ONE IS IMMORAL AND EXTORTS MONEY...

Bling! BLING!

BLING!

Bling

...AND YOUR POINT IS?

Wow, what a week, eh? Did you see me on telly, with Piers Morgan? He gave me a whole hour of his valuable time! Impressive eh?

Penny Mordaunt
No one watches Piers Morgan on TalkTV, Rishi.

James Forsyth
Phew! Otherwise they'd have seen that toe-curling bit when you bet him £1,000 there'd be migrants on the plane to Rwanda.

Penny Mordaunt
Oh, don't tell me he fell for the classic Morgan 'end of the interview' stunt which then goes viral?

Kemi Badenoch
He certainly did. Hook, line and plonker. Not that I'm happy about that. #secretevilplotters

Hey, come on, guys, that was top bants! Celebrity mates having a little flutter!

James Forsyth
Well, it **was** a bet on people's lives, boss. The optics may not be great.

Jeremy Hunt
And £1,000 isn't a small amount.

Isn't it? Surely it's just the price of a pint of bread. Or a loaf of petrol.

Jeremy Hunt
It's a lot of money to some people. Ordinary people. Poor people. People who aren't hedge fund managers. Or people who aren't married to billionaires.

I don't get it.

Kemi Badenoch
That's the problem, Rishi. 😔 #notsosecretevilplotters.

Jeremy Hunt
£1,000 is twice as much as we're giving away in tax cuts. We're meant to be pretending that's a lot of money.

James Cleverly
Though compared to the batshit 240 million quid we've bet on the Rwandan bollocks, it **is** fuck all. 💵 💵 💵

Oliver Dowden
Can I just point out that our brilliant Home Secretary is not only called Cleverly, but his constituency is BRAINtree! Amusing, no?

James Cleverly
No, you twat. What's your constituency, Shithole North? Not that the whole of the North isn't a shithole.

Hey, bantastic bants, guys! Nearly as good as me and the Morganmeister having a lads' laugh.

James Forsyth
Think positive, Team Rishi, Let's concentrate on Rishi's new, man-of-the-people, vote-winning YouTube video that explains why we're so much better than Labour.

Alex Chalk
Oh, is that real? I thought it was a Deepfake spoof.

James Forsyth
Why?

Alex Chalk
Because so many people were laughing at it online.

Actually, Chalkie, that is me, explaining our plan for the economy on a white board.

Jeremy Hunt
Is the board blank?

No, I drew a fabulous picture of a house.

Jeremy Hunt
That no one can afford to buy?

Kemi Badenoch
It doesn't look like a house, it looks like a sad person wearing a dunce's cap.

Oliver Dowden
Oops! Self-portrait time! Rishi Rembrandt. Or is it Rishi Van Gaffe? 🤪 😂 😂 😂

It's a great sketch, actually.

Penny Mordaunt
Ooh, sketchy!

I AM NOT SKETCHY!

James Forsyth
Give the boss a break, guys. He's working his socks off.

Oliver Dowden
Which we can all see, as his trousers are so short! 👖 😂

Listen, guys, we just need to stick together and end all this in-fighting.

Penny Mordaunt
In-fight! In-fight! In-fight!

If we follow the plan, we can still win this General Election.

Jeremy Hunt
Bet you a grand we don't.

GOVERNMENT'S MESSAGE TO PORT TALBOT STEEL WORKERS

Ta-ta!

"Is it too late to stop the boats?"

MICHELLE MONE'S HUSBAND REVEALS NEW £50M YACHT

PPEs of eight!

VALENTINE SPECIAL

Roses are red,
Violets are blue,
I'm not green and
Neither are you

I ♥ U-turn

Nursery Times

Friday, Once-upon-a-time

DENTAL CRISIS HITS NURSERYLAND

by Our Dental Correspondent **Tweedle Gum**

CONCERN is growing for the state of dental care in the NHS (Nurseryland Health Service), as citizens find themselves unable to get an appointment with the Tooth Fairy.

It has been revealed that there is now only one tooth fairy for the entire population of Nurseryland, and the Tooth Fairy herself is now more committed to private practice than working for the NHS.

Said one child in a corner, Little Jack Horner, "I was eating a pie when I stuck in my thumb and pulled out a tooth! I immediately put the tooth under my pillow, but it remained there for several weeks, as I couldn't get an appointment with the Tooth Fairy. When I finally did get to see her she charged me 20,000 chocolate coins to remove it. It left me open-mouthed. Talk about saying

'Aaaaaah!' It made me want to spit."

The Cheshire Cat said, with a sad smile, "My teeth are kind of important to me – sometimes it's the only thing people see. But getting an appointment with the Tooth Fairy is like... well, pulling teeth."

The Tooth Fairy is unrepentant, saying, "I studied long and hard at Fairy Dental School, and I'm quite entitled to set up my own private practice, where I can choose some less anti-social hours to work, namely 9am to 5pm rather than 9pm to 5am. And, to be honest, Nurseryland citizens like Hansel and Gretel aren't doing themselves any favours by eating gingerbread houses."

The Nurseryland government say they're on the case and have already commissioned the Carpenter and the Walrus to put together a Tusk Force.

PM IN COMMONS ROW OVER TASTELESS TRANS JOKE

Look! A woman with a prick

Gyles Brandreth admits, 'I am the Grim Reaper'

FOLLOWING an investigation by *Private Eye*'s top journalist Lunchtime O'Bituary, we can exclusively reveal that national treasure, teddy bear museum curator and jumper wearer extraordinaire, Gyles Brandreth, really is Death.

In previous reports, we had identified a link between a celebrity enjoying Gyles Brandreth's company and his or her imminent demise. These have included the late Queen Elizabeth having tea with Brandreth and then dying, Prince Philip having a laugh with Brandreth and then dying, Barry Humphries having a drink with Brandreth and then dying and Len Goodman meeting Brandreth on a beach and then dying.

We at the *Eye* could see the pattern, but we did not have conclusive proof that Gyles Brandreth was Death himself, the pale rider, the fourth horseman of the Apocalypse, but this week the *Eye* cornered Brandreth by reading an interview in the *Mail* in which Brandreth confessed to being instrumental in the tragic passing of two other high-profile celebrities.

Said Brandreth, "Oh, I killed Rod Hull. I told him to go up and fix the aerial on his roof. And he did. I feel so guilty.

"Oh, and Harry Secombe. Have I told you about him? I was on the phone to him and the next thing he fell backwards, and that was it for him.

"Are you sure you've got to go? I've got more anecdotes..." he shouted, chasing the journalist out into the street.

The *Eye*'s team is now sufficiently confident that beneath Gyles Brandreth's novelty sweater is the Grim Reaper's black-hooded cloak, and inside that giant teddy bear is a fully operative scythe for the reaping of souls.

If you've met Gyles Brandreth recently and are worried your days may be numbered, you should contact Endofline on 0066 666 666.

KEN BRUCE IS MY KIND OF BROADCASTER

MINE TOO

What You Missed

That Royal Illness Coverage In Full

All channels, all day

Phil Airtime: ...and I've just heard that there's no further news... the King still has cancer, but we don't know what it is or anything about it. So, Philippa, what do you make of that?

Philippa Slot: It's too early to speculate about what we don't know, but I think it's important to say that what we DO know is that we don't know anything, and Buckingham Palace has essentially confirmed that by not issuing any new statements.

Phil Airtime: Fascinating, Philippa. Let's bring in royal expert, Paddy Tout. Paddy, what's the latest on the lack of news?

Paddy Tout: What I can say, Phil, is that the Royal Family on these occasions tend to be very discreet, but in what is a major change in royal etiquette, the Palace has been very open and frank about the fact that they're not going to tell us anything.

Phil Airtime: And all credit to King Charles for being so forthcoming about not being forthcoming. With me now is our medical correspondent, Chunta Onandon. Chunta, I don't want you to speculate, obviously, but can you give us some idea about where this lack of new news leaves us?

Chunta Onanandon: It IS too early to speculate, but what we DO know is that, medically speaking, it's a big relief that they've got the discovery of no news early, which means that there's a very good chance of dealing with the lack of news more effectively.

Phil Airtime: Thanks, Chunta, that is good news. Now, let's go back to Philippa, to get her reaction to what Chunta said about what Paddy said...

Philippa Slot: That's an interesting point, Phil. I don't want to speculate about my reaction at this point, and it's too early to say what I think, but what we can all agree on is that there's another three hours to go, and...

Phil Airtime: ...sorry to interrupt you there, Philippa, but there's been a big development. Robert Hardback has come into the studio. Robert, you're an expert on royal experts, what do you make of what Philippa has said about what Chunta and Paddy have said?

Robert Hardback: It would be quite wrong for someone in my position to speculate on a matter about which it is still too early to speculate, but what I can you tell is that my book is on sale now, with an extra chapter about how we don't know what's going on.

Phil Airtime: I'll have to cut you off, Robert, with breaking news that World War 3 has been declared. So where does that leave the King and his plans for the recuperation?

Philippa Slot: Well, Phil, the big question is whether the King will move from Sandringham to Highgrove or possibly back to Windsor in the light of the thermonuclear conflagration currently engulfing the world, and... *(cont. 94 hours)*

Phil Airtime.: Thanks, Philippa. Now we have breaking no news, that the King is still the King, and still has a medical condition that we know nothing about.

Constitutional crisis rocks senior royals

by Our Royal Correspondent
Ingrid Sewage

A SENIOR member of the royal family has generously offered to step in and take on the bulk of the King's duties during His Majesty's temporary indisposition.

Said the senior royal, "I could easily increase my official duties from the current nought, and as long as air travel and some jolly ladies are provided, I could find some time in my empty diary."

Said the senior figure, "I already possess my own silly hat and naval uniform, and I can wave along with the best of them. I'm also adept at photo opportunities, although not that one! That one was faked. I never met that lady, or Emily Maitlis."

Royal experts believe the senior royal offering to become King may be none other than Prince Andrew.

Said another insider, Prince Andrew, "Obviously, I can't name him, but Andrew is willing to forego his current schedule of Lorraine, Countdown and Bargain Hunt, to serve his country by opening scout huts, leisure centres, pizza parlours, nightclubs... but not prisons, obviously."

"*Paradoxes – can't live with 'em, can't live without 'em*"

EXCLUSIVE TO ALL NEWSPAPERS

SICK INTERNET GHOULS HORRIFY ROYALS

TODAY we join in Buckingham Palace's condemnation of the sick internet ghouls speculating online as to what type of cancer King Charles has.

How do these individuals sleep at night? Is that all they have to do with their sad, miserable lives – spend their days pointlessly speculating about not just what type of cancer the King has, but also his chances of survival?

Why can't these loathsome keyboard warriors respect the King's wishes and allow him and his family some privacy at this most difficult time for the Windsors.

On other pages

■ How likely are you to die in your 70s from cancer?

■ Exclusive interview with five men, all called Charles, currently being treated for various types of cancer.

■ Will King Charles's royal wave be affected long-term, even if his cancer treatment is successful?

■ Why 'woke' lefties would prefer King Charles to die and (cont. p94)

POETRY CORNER

Lines on the passing of the old Lyle's Golden Syrup logo

So. Farewell
Then the dead lion
With bees coming out of it.

A strange logo,
I always thought,
For a sugary spread.

"Out of the strong
Came forth sweetness" –
That was your catchphrase.

It's from the bible
And, therefore,
Not very 21st Century.

Now there is a nice,
Smiling cartoon lion
With a friendly bee.

And the old syrup
Logo has come to
A sticky end.

E.J. Thribb
(17½ spoonfuls)

MOTORING: Electric car runs amok, kills family kitten, leaves British family in tears

HEALTH: Woke National Trust draws up plans to cause worldwide Zombie virus

CHARLES MOORE: Scruffy jeans provide cover for violence and extremism

ROYAL NEWS: Harry and Meghan "deny" plotting to assassinate King Charles

TELEGRAPH VIEW: The world has gone mad

JANET DALEY: A free society can't survive the abolition of the Golden Syrup label

GARDENING: Ditch the dreaded lawn-mower and equip one's junior gardeners with shears, says Simon Heffer

LETTERS TO THE EDITOR: Victory is assured for any party putting the reconquering of India in its election manifesto

HEALTH: Voting Labour causes baldness says expert

TELEGRAPH VIEW: The world has just gone even madder

TELEGRAPH VIEW: The only way to prevent class war is to reinforce our public schools

LETTERS TO THE EDITOR: I saw Keir Starmer at dead of night looking left and right before fly-tipping on the M11

ROYAL NEWS: Did China secretly sponsor Meghan to spread Covid?

TELEGRAPH VIEW: To save our countryside, the speed limit in rural areas must be raised to 90mph

HEALTH: Was Covid caused by woke transgenderism?

JANET DALEY: King Lear is a shameless attack on the elderly. It's high time the government withdrew the RSC's subsidy

MOTORING NEWS: Ulez causes mass suicide

FOREIGN NEWS: Fracking Grand Canal best way to ensure Venice's future says expert

CHARLES MOORE: Prince Andrew would make a fine Defence Secretary

D I A R Y

THE DAILY TELEGRAPH ONLINE ROUND-UP

LETTERS TO THE EDITOR: Starmer's Labour wants to kill my budgie

CULTURE: Dickens' Oliver Twist is virtue-signalling nonsense at its worst, says Simon Heffer

HOME NEWS: Man from abroad jumps supermarket queue, refuses to apologise

TELEGRAPH VIEW: To save our countryside, every village green needs fracking

SHOWBUSINESS: Net zero hysterics plot to rid Strictly Come Dancing of its fabulous sequins

MOTORING: Ask the Expert: What are the pros and cons of driving headlong into cyclists?

CULTURE: First, you misuse the semi-colon and then you kill 35 in high school shoot-out, writes Simon Heffer

HEALTH: How to increase your sex drive by voting Conservative

LETTERS TO THE EDITOR: A ban on T-shirts would help tackle Britain's mental health crisis

MOTORING: The Hillman Hunter is back – and not before time, says Simon Heffer

ROYAL NEWS: Queen Elizabeth "projectile vomited" on hearing Harry and Meghan had named their daughter Lilibet

HEALTH: I gained eight stone after voting Lib Dem

CHARLES MOORE: The BBC is the broadcasting wing of Hamas

FASHION: Spats are back, by Simon Heffer

ROYAL NEWS: Meghan grins while pulling wings off fly

CHARLES MOORE: Britain is crying out for more carbon emissions

LETTERS TO THE EDITOR: The return of capital punishment for begging in the street is long overdue

FOOD AND DRINK: Pork Pie with Cheesy Sauce, by Simon Heffer

TELEGRAPH OPINION: To house transgender drug-crazed serial-killing workshy illegal migrants at the Ritz is nothing short of madness

JANET DALEY: Labour faces its greatest General Election defeat in a generation

CULTURE: If only Shakespeare had not split his infinitives, he might have earned the right to be taken seriously as a playwright, by Simon Heffer

JANET DALEY: The ill and the workshy continue to clog up valuable NHS beds

FINANCE: Tell the young the truth: they will have to work until 94

SIMON HEFFER: Without Brexit, we would now be paying £1500 or more for a slice of bread and butter or £2000 for the same with jam

LETTERS TO THE EDITOR: Greta Thunberg should be sent to bed without supper and locked in her room until she apologises

TELEGRAPH VIEW: Archbishop of Canterbury must stop embracing workshy sandal-wearing bearded messiah and return to old fashioned Christian values

FASHION: At long last, the wimple is back, by Simon Heffer

As told to
CRAIG BROWN

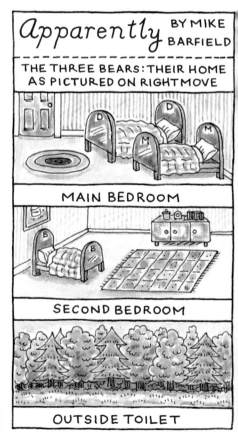

7,000 PUBS EXPECTED TO GO BUST THIS YEAR

by PHIL PINT
Our Hostelry Correspondent

IT'S A TRAGEDY! They're calling time on Britain's pubs, as WFH (Working From Home) and the COLC (Cost of Living Crisis) has led to too much DFH (Drinking From Home).

It's all too easy, when you're sitting at your desk (the kitchen table) with the fridge just an arm's length away and – ohh, a can of red stripe? Don't mind if I do. Ahhhhhhh.

Now, where was I? The tragic demise of the good old British local, just down the road, but still further away than this cupboard. Ooh, a Merlot. Forgot I had that. Tasty drop. Now that's what I call a Large Glass! Mmmm. And a damn sight cheaper than the bloody pub.

Now, where was I? Oh, yesh, DFSH (Drinking From SHome) is causing a crisish in the hoshpitality industry, as more home workersh realise there's a bottle of Ouzo behind the ketchup. Unopened, from that holiday in Athensh in... when was it? Oh yesh, 201984! Come on, Phil, focush. Oh right, yeah, pubs – sod 'em, who needsh 'em? Cheersh!

Our Town's Dentist *(after LS Lowry)*

'DON'T LET TERROR WOMAN BACK INTO THE UK' – PROTEST GROWS

by Our Security Staff **Shamima Goldsmith**

THE woman who left the country to join up with extremists should never be allowed back into the country, say an increasing number of the British public.

Said one angry citizen, "Liz Truss must clearly remain in the US. She was radicalised in Britain and then chose to leave her own country, ending up sharing a stage with the evil cult leader, Steve Bannon."

Said another furious person in the street, "Liz Truss simply can't be trusted. I don't believe her apologies. Her determination to destroy the UK is as strong as ever, and she has shown no real remorse for crashing the economy. She is a danger to everyone, and their mortgages."

Liz Truss herself has denied responsibility for her actions, saying that it was all down to the Deep State working in cahoots with reality.

Says Truss, "I was just a young, naive, helpless Prime Minister who was groomed by the Daily Telegraph into believing in CR-ISIS and creating a new Caliphate of Growth." *(Is this right? Ed.)*

Truss continued, from her CPAC refugee camp in Maryland, "I wasn't pulling the levers. I didn't hurt anyone. It was not my fault the whole thing blew up in my face." *(That's enough poor taste. Ed.)*

SHAMIMA BEGUM LOSES CITIZENSHIP CHALLENGE AND VOWS SHE 'WON'T STOP FIGHTING'

> Perhaps not the best wording in the circumstances

Han-z-z-zard

Oral questions for the Health Minister on the state of the nation's dentistry (the usual drill)

5 February 2024

Phil Ing MP (Lab, Molar South): Now that the Minister is back in the House at the time of (consults watch) Tooth Hurty pm, may I ask why has the government allowed the NHS dental system to decay?

The Right Hon Victoria Atkins MP (Con, Gargle and Spit): I can assure you that the system is working well and we are investing more in dentistry than ever before.

Phil Ing MP: That's rot. Does she not agree that her future as a Minister of the Crown looks decidedly wobbly, and only her immediate removal will stop the pain?

Victoria Atkins MP: I think the Honourable Member should wash his mouth out. And he'll be pleased to hear that to improve dental health we are going to put more fluoride in the water.

Ivor Heckle MP (Floating-on-sea): Makes a change from shit.

Speaker: Ordure! Ordure! Order bottled water! It's the only stuff you can trust.

Phil Ing MP: Is the Honourable Member aware that tooth decay is the number one reason for children aged 6 to 10 being admitted to hospital?

Victoria Atkins MP: Of course I am. My husband's the boss of British Sugar.

Phil Ing MP: Ah, perhaps that explains why your policies are so toothless.

*Extracted from HANZZZARD under anaesthetic and at an extremely high price

---

Shock as news story not about Taylor Swift

by Our Taylor Swift Correspondent
Cardi Gan

THERE was outrage last night as it emerged that one of Britain's leading newspapers had failed to put in a story about Taylor Swift. Not only that, they had also failed to crowbar in a reference to Ms Swift in a piece about something entirely unrelated.

"This is disgraceful," said an editor, whose daughter was giving him a really bad time. "We know that young people click on stories about Taylor Swift and it was remiss of us not to desperately put a huge photo of her next to our article about interest rates, with a caption explaining the incredibly tenuous link.

"I would like to apologise to our readers, my daughter and my boss, all of whom are rightly furious at the disrespectful behaviour of my newspaper."

Taylor Swift Half

GAZA: PEACE HOPES DASHED

by Our Political Staff **Hans Ard**

HOPES for an immediate ceasefire in Gaza were dashed last night when military leaders on both sides of the conflict raised strong objections to the way in which a vote in the British House of Commons was conducted.

Speaking from a tunnel deep beneath Rafah, a senior Hamas commander said, "We were all set to hand over hostages unconditionally, and even to give up on our determination to establish a free Palestine from the river to the sea, and then we heard that the opposition motion put forward for a vote was not by the SNP but by Labour.

"There is nothing more important to the people of Gaza than proper procedure in the British parliament, so unfortunately those hostages are staying exactly where they are, and thousands more will inevitably die."

In a rare show of unity, Israeli prime minister Benjamin Netanyahu agreed.

"There are few things that can unite the peoples of the Middle East," he told reporters, "but one thing that is vital to us all is the proper conduct of opposition day debates in the UK's Houses of Parliament.

"While I have ignored calls from international authorities, such as the UN and the US president, for an immediate end to the conflict, I would not have hesitated to withdraw all troops from Gaza and seek a two-state solution to the conflict, should such a thing have been demanded by Stephen Flynn and his 42 SNP colleagues in Westminster.

"However, when I learned that the call instead came in the name of the Labour Party, I had no option but to order that the war must continue until Hamas is utterly destroyed, Gaza demilitarised, and Palestinian society completely deradicalised. It's a shame, but there you go."

There were fears last night that the conflict was set to spread yet further, as fighting intensified in the Westminster area and a radical group of Conservative and SNP MPs declared perpetual jihad on Commons speaker Lindsay Hoyle.

Would you like to be a judge?

All you need to do is answer the following questions...

1. Is this badge, showing a paraglider, worn at a demonstration shortly after the terrorist attacks on Israel:

a) a pretty clear gesture of support for Hamas?

b) a symbol of peace and reconciliation between all peoples, particularly in the troubled lands of the Middle East, where more dialogue is very much needed to establish a relationship between Israel and a putative Palestinian state?

2. If a jury has just decided that a) is the correct answer, what do you then do as judge...

a) bang 'em up for a couple of years?

b) decide they have suffered enough and should not be punished because emotions were running very high on that day?

3. If you decide the answer to question 2. is b), how do you feel about the fact that climate protestors are being given three-year sentences for the crimes of climbing a bridge or marching slowly along a road, and are not allowed even to mention the reasons for their actions at trial?

a) This is disgraceful and unfair

b) There is no comparison between delightful pro-Hamas protestors and wicked climate terrorists who are a grave threat to Britain

Ironyometer finally breaks after Gaza debate ends in fighting

by Our Political Science Staff **Humbug Youguv**

WITHIN days of being repaired, it looks as if the Ironyometer has once again experienced a critical meltdown, after events in the UK House of Commons proved too much for the delicate instrument used for measuring levels of irony.

The fact that British MPs could not get through a single debate about Gaza without resorting to infighting, explosions of anger and devastating attacks on bystanders (eg Lindsay Hoyle) caused the dial on the Ironyometer to spin out of control, before valves began to overheat and the recently replaced rivets started flying out.

When the entire parliament descended into an incomprehensible battle of self-interest that no one could understand, the comparisons with the situation in the Middle East caused the ancient machine to vent steam and shatter into thousands of pieces.

The nation's top Ironyometerists were sent in by the government to conduct urgent repairs, but within minutes they too were bickering about procedure, arguing over whose plan they should adopt to fix the machine, and claiming they'd never been so insulted in their lives.

Whilst repairs are ongoing, a new device commissioned by the SNP to bring more probity and integrity into UK politics is being brought down from Scotland in a brand new campervan.

READER QUIZ

Is THIS:
a) **The UK's military might?**
b) **The British economy?**
c) **The Labour Party's ceasefire policy?**
d) **The Tory Party's election strategy?**
e) **The launch of Liz Truss's new book?**

Winner gets free Trident missile (delivery not included)

GLENDA SLAGG

She's the catty columnist they're calling the new Dorothy Parking-fine!!!!!!

■ SEEN the Trident missile??? That's what you get when you let MEN design a rocket system!!! A disappointing flop that goes off too early!!! Been there, done that, mister!?! Not much of a BANG (geddit????!!!!) – more of a WIMPY!!!!!

■ SO Simon Cowell's had another facelift!!! And it's raising a few eyebrows – in Simon's case, they're now up above his hairline!!!! Don't look shocked, Simon – oh no, you can't help it, 'cos you do, all the time!!!??! No offence, love your work – though tbh not a big fan of the work you've had done!!! Geddit????!!!!!

■ TAYLOR SWIFT – so she's as good as Shakespeare, Chaucer and Wordsworth, according to some brainy Oxford egghead!!!! You're wrong there, Prof Smartypants – because La Swift is not as good as those boring bards – she's MUCH better!!!??! How many hit singles has Chaucer had???! When was the last time Shakespeare sold out the Melbourne Cricket Ground??!! How many famous boyfriends has Wordsworth had?!? I'll tell you – NONE!!?! Go girl!!!!!!

■ SO Bridget Jones is back! V.g. news – leading to:

Stories I can sell my editor **37**

Pictures of Renée Zellweger looking gorgeous for Ed to put in to fill paper **79**

Attempts by myself to interview hunky oompah loompah hunk Hugh Grant and/or hunky Mincemeat Man Colin Firth **94**

Geddit????!!!! (Like Bridget's Diary, stooooooopid!!!!)

■ *HERE THEY ARE* – Glenda's top 546 words for being drunk?!?!
● Totally Glenda'd!?!!
● Completely Slagged!??!!!
● Utterly Glendaslagged!?!!!?
(You've had enough, you're fired. Ed.)

Byeee!!

"When I were a lad I had to leave home and buy my own house when I were just 22"

"I 'ad to work seven hours a day until I were able to retire at 55"

"55? I had to take me pension at 52!"

"Another bottle of the '67, lad"

Modern-day Yorkshire Men

PYONGYANG PEOPLE'S DAILY

Tinpot dictatorship in missile failure

FOR the second time in a row, the failed state of the Un Ited Kingdom has made a laughable attempt to flex its puny muscles, by attempting to launch a nuclear missile which promptly flopped into the sea.

Despite this clear international embarrassment, the nation's discredited leader, Rish Isu Nak, proclaimed that all was working according to his great plan.

Critics of the much-hated regime claim that while he has billions and all the luxuries that affords, the rest of the nation suffers in poverty, with many people starving and forced to go to food banks.

Said our Supreme leader, Kim Jong Un, "Rish Isu Nak tries to act like a tough guy, with his dud missile tests, but in reality he's just a little man clinging onto power by pretending his nation's economy is thriving. He's the laughing stock of the world. Ha! Ha! Ha!" *(Rotters)*

Mordor on the Dancefloor

SPOT THE SHARK

The amazing thing about artists is they can smell money from miles away

Cold, dead eyes, no soul, just the endless pursuit of one thing…

Yeah, money

Art world scandal

THE world of art was rocked to its foundations yesterday when it emerged that Damien Hirst has been pretending the pickled sharks bought by idiot millionaires are actually much newer than they were previously thought to be.

"I feel a fool," said one idiot with no taste. "I thought I was buying a dead shark from the 1990s with almost infinite resale value, and now I realise I was buying a dead shark from the 2010s, which is, of course, worthless."

The shark in question, known as "The physical impossibility of failing to find anyone too rich and thick to think this has any value", was just one of many animals which Hirst pickled, making millions of dollars from each one. And the bombshell that actually the shark is a different age will have made a few people very unhappy and given the rest of us a good laugh at the sight of a lot of greedy bastards *(Yes, that's enough schadenfreude. Ed.)*

PUTIN ELECTION CAMPAIGN BEGINS

How's it looking for the opposition?

Grave

A Russian Doctor Writes

AS A Russian doctor, I am often asked by members of the FSB, "Did Alexei Navalny die of natural causes?"

The simple answer is "Yes, officer. Absolutely." The wrong answer is "Yes, and those causes were freedom, justice and democracy." DO NOT SAY THIS.

What happens is the doctor is woken in the middle of the night and driven to the Arctic Circle to perform a post mortem on a well-known leader of the opposition.

It immediately becomes apparent to the doctor that unless he too wants to die of natural causes, he'd better sign the piece of paper confirming that the patient was not given a KGB death punch nor was he poisoned with Novichok.

Sometimes, an experienced Russian doctor doesn't need to go anywhere near the body to ascertain the cause of death – namely, that the patient felt unwell following a walk in the clement -25 degree February sunshine and sadly slipped away, due to possible heat stroke and extreme old age (47). This is known to the medical profession as *morbidius convenientitis putinosis* or "Nothing to see here" Syndrome. This is very common in Russia today and has recently spread, with cases reported in Salisbury and Bilbao, as well as in the skies above Moscow in planes marked "Wagner Group".

© *A Russian Doctor*

AN EYE GUIDE

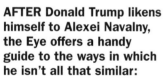

AFTER Donald Trump likens himself to Alexei Navalny, the Eye offers a handy guide to the ways in which he isn't all that similar:

1. Navalny was in prison – Trump isn't... though he should be.

2. Navalny was an enemy of Putin – Trump isn't... though he should be.

3. Navalny believed in democracy – Trump doesn't... though he should.

4. Navalny lost in a rigged election – Trump didn't... though he thinks he did.

5. Navalny's wife, Yulia, was distraught when her husband died – Melania... well, she'll get over it.

UKRAINE – WILL THERE BE A CEASEFIRE?

Yes, because we haven't got any ammunition

LATE NEWS

■ **Boris** flies into Ukraine to make desperate plea for support. Zelensky has to tell him that no one cares about him anymore and that people have lost interest in his struggle.

AS WAR IN UKRAINE ENTERS THIRD YEAR, HAS THE WEST STOPPED CARING?

■ Read our special 200-word report on page 94 *(bottom right, below advert for Gaviscon)*

Celebrities reject menopause criticism

by Our Menopause Correspondent
Sweaty Betty

CELEBRITIES have reacted with astonishment to criticism in The Lancet that they've contributed to the overmedicalisation of the menopause.

"They should be thanking us for the vital work we've done, highlighting one of the most overlooked menopause symptoms – the overwhelming urge to write a book about it," said one former ladette from the 90s.

"You have no idea how hot under the collar you get approaching 50, seeing how much money Davina McCall is raking in. Especially when you don't have a menopause book of your own on the shelves," the former ladette added, throatily.

"You suffer sleepless nights and terrible anxiety, waiting to hear back from your agent if you've got a deal."

She did however promise to directly address The Lancet's cricitism in her upcoming menopause book.

"It tackles the thorny subject of whether there are now simply too many celebrity books about the menopause."

"Yes, we have implemented a successful menopause policy"

F1 BOSSES ACCUSE RED BULL PRINCIPAL

by DAMON THRILL
Our Formula 1 Correspondent

You are the pits

Variety is the spice er…

FORMULA 1 bosses have accused Red Bull team principal Christian Horny *(Is this right? Ed.)*, who is caught up in an ongoing sexting scandal, of shaming F1 by making the sport seem interesting.

"Formula 1 prides itself on how crushingly dull it is, and we thought Red Bull, under Mr Horny, is more committed than anyone to making motor racing a very boring sport where a very boring Dutchman wins every time.

"But now Hornyboy *(Are you sure this is right? Ed.)* has ruined that by being all over the front pages, accused of sexting a junior employee and cheating on his former Spice Girl wife."

Mr Hornier *(No, you were right. Ed.)* strongly defended himself, insisting nothing is more important to him than maintaining the crushing boredom of Formula 1 racing.

He added, "The fact the investigation is going round and round in circles towards a predictable outcome is proof of my commitment to that."

Red Bull frenzy – what is behind the madness?

by Phil Can

THE whole Formula 1 paddock has been buzzing with the Red Bull story which shows no signs of running out of steam yes I've been up all night asking myself what is going on and which of the Formula 1 stories has got legs or should that be wings and which of the scandals is going to take off and go into orbit who knows who cares WOW I am so wired Spice Girls Secret Sexting I tell you this Red Bull story has got all the ingredients to deliver a rocket fuelled high it's like nitrogen and glycerine or more accurately caffeine and sugar or even more accurately caffeine and artificial sweetener that gets everyone fizzing with excitement and take it from me sleep is impossible as the Formula 1 pack take to the grid for yet another incredibly dull race won once again by the charisma-free Dutchman Max Verzzzzzzzzzzzzzzz *(cont. lap 94)*

CIGARETTE MANUFACTURERS WELCOME SMOKING BAN

by Our Smoking Correspondent **Benson Ann-Hedges**

CIGARETTE manufacturers were celebrating today, predicting that a new law making it illegal for people born after 2009 to legally buy cigarettes will lead to a big increase in the numbers of smokers.

"Over the last decade, the number of young people smoking has dwindled, as it's seen as something naff that their dad and grandad do," said one manufacturer, gleefully lighting a huge cigar with an even larger cigar.

"Now it's going to be illegal for youngsters to smoke, sales will inevitably boom. We'll soon be seen as being as edgy as spliffs or wraps of cocaine – all we needed was that frisson of excitement that only a total ban can generate. Thanks, Rishi.

"We're cancelling all leave and ramping up production to meet the surge in demand. Happy days!"

THE PRODIGAL SON

AND there lived in that land a rich ruler with two sons. And his youngest son said to him, "I no longer want to do all this work. Give me my share of my inheritance so that I may go off to foreign lands and squander it all."

And so it was, and the younger son disappeared to a different country where he was sorely profligate and even his large sums of money began to run out.

"Woe is me!" he said to himself. "There is a famine of work in the land and no one wants my podcast nor my Netflix series."

Meanwhile, the eldest son dutifully served his father and toiled in the fields and opened scout huts and attended Bafta ceremonies, and he did wave and smile, as is meet and proper.

And one day the prodigal son decided that things had got a bit desperate and the land of soya milk and Californian gluten-free honey was not the Promised Land after all. So he let it be know that he would return and take up his place in his father's household. And his ageing father rejoiced and rushed out to meet the prodigal son for a full 45 minutes and welcomed him with open arms and a tear in his eye.

But the elder son was sorely miffed and sayeth unto his father, "Pops – this is, like, so unfair. For I have done as you asked and have handed out prizes and medals and talked about mental health and green issues, and all my prodigal brother has done is waste his fortune and hang out with actresses and TV presenters and suchlike lowlife."

But his father chided him, saying, "Wills, you know I can depend on you – and you are the dutiful, boring one, but you will inherit the larger portion of my legacy, including the throne, not to mention my Duchy Original organic biscuit empire."

And Wills answered his father, "Yeah. Fair enough, but Harry is still like sooooooo annoying, so don't expect me to join with you when you kill the Fatted-Calf-Substitute Vegan Nut Roast and have a big Welcome Hazza Home party."

And lo, these things came to pass, and the servants of the ruler's household did go forth and leak all the details to the scribes of the Bible, who said, "Verily, this is a sensational parable and will be sure to shift shedloads of copies on the Sabbath."

MORAL OF THE STORY...

There is more joy in Windsor when one sinner repents than when a hundred newspaper pieces appear saying how marvellous Sophie Wessex is.

"Hey, Mister, can you buy me a packet of fags, please?"

Great news, team Rishi! We've turned the corner now.

Jeremy Hunt
Thank you, Rishi, my budget was very well received.

Not your budget, Jezza! My interview with Grazia magazine. It's doing big, big numbers on line.

James Forsyth
Er, boss, big numbers are not always a positive sign. I've watched a number of car crashes online that have got big, big numbers.

Nonsense. People have been fascinated by my normal family life, doing normal things with my normal wife.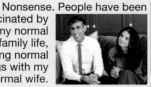

Oliver Dowden
Lovely image of domestic bliss. Or should that be NON-DOMestic bliss? 😜😜😜

No, Oliver, the voters can't get enough of me telling them how I'm just like them. A regular guy who loads the dishes into the washing machine, who mows the carpet, who makes the fridge every morning and puts the beds out for the bedmen like any other husband!

James Forsyth
Nearly, boss. Maybe you should have stuck to how you do the school run.

In the helicopter?

James Forsyth
No no no, boss!

Oliver Dowden
Talk about helicopter parenting! 🚁👶

What about my favourite TV programme? That was relatable. Everybody watches 'Friends' before they go to bed.

Penny Mordaunt
Great theme tune, Rishi... "It's like you're always stuck in second gear, when it hasn't been your day, your week, your month or even your year." 🎵😟

But it's such a great snapshot of modern normal British life.... how you can work in a coffee shop or as a masseuse or as an academic and afford to live in a fabulous New York apartment.

James Forsyth
Again, so nearly right, boss.

But it's about how I've got lots friends and I value friendship.

James Forsyth
And "I'll be there for you", boss even if no one else is 👍👍.

Jeremy Hunt
Can we get back to my budget? It's a big moment. We've really turned the corner.

James Forsyth
That's the message, we just need to keep saying it.

Chris Philp
We've really turned the corner.

Grant Shapps
Yes, we've really turned the corner.

Greg Hands
We've really turned the corner.

Oliver Dowden
Can I point out, that if we've turned the corner four times, we're now back to where we started! 😜😜😜😜😜😜

Kemi Badenoch
So we go back to Square One. Isn't that what we're accusing Labour of doing?

Jeremy Hunt
Wouldn't be the first idea we stole from Labour. Did you see my budget? Or did you miss it, Rishi, because you were watching 'Friends'?

Penny Mordaunt
"The one where Rishi tries to convince people he's normal".

I am normal. I walk the cat, like any normal dad. And take the car through the dry-cleaners.

Penny Mordaunt
So, no one told you life was gonna be this way! 🎵😂😂😂

Oliver Dowden
Hey, Rishi! Could you BE any more normal? 😂😂😂

James Forsyth
Ignore them, boss. Have you seen the latest poll?

No.

James Forsyth
Good. Let's keep it that way. 🙈🙈

Lee Anderthal
Just to tell you, I'm defecting.

Oliver Dowden
Make that 'defective'! 😂😂😂

But Lee, we've spent a week defending you, saying you were wrong, but not racist!

Lee Anderthal
Well I'm not wrong, I'm right. Far right!

Michael Gove
Hang on. I'm worried about extremists.

Lee Anderthal
Me too. There aren't enough of them here. That's why I'm going to Reform!

Oliver Dowden
You'll never reform Lee! You'll always be ghastly! 😂😂😂

But Reform is full of toxic lunatics!

Lee Anderthal
What's not to like? 😄

Lee Anderthal has removed himself from the group and fooked off.

WOODLAND PROTECTION
SQUIRRELS FACE CHEMICAL CASTRATION

What have you done to my nuts?

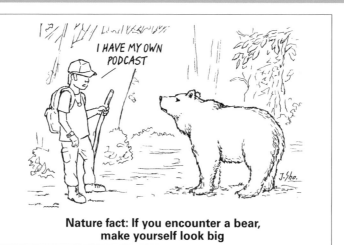

I HAVE MY OWN PODCAST

Nature fact: If you encounter a bear, make yourself look big

GOVERNMENT TO BAN DIVISIVE HAT PREACHERS

PRIVATE EYE

No. 1620
29 March –
11 April 2024
£2.99

EXCLUSIVE TO ALL NEWSPAPERS

FOR GOD'S SAKE, JUST LEAVE KATE ALONE!

SPECIAL 94-PAGE 'LEAVE KATE ALONE' SOUVENIR SUPPLEMENT

Maily EXPRESSOgraph

WHO IS TO BLAME FOR SPREADING THESE TOXIC CONSPIRACY THEORIES ABOUT KATE?

1 Russian bots
2 Chinese Tik-Toks
3 Meghan and Harry
4 The BBC
5 Social Media
6 Kim Kardashian
7 Owen Jones
8 Keir Starmer
9 The general public *(Don't be stupid. Ed.)*
10 Certainly not us!

THE SUN SAYS

Following Princess Kate's emotional video, will the internet ghouls finally leave her alone?

HOW can these rumour-mongers sleep at night, knowing they are tormenting Britain's beloved Princess?

We say "Back off, you amateur creeps, and leave tormenting princesses to the professionals!" *(Is that right? – Rupes.)*

Time now for these trolls to log off so we can show you what intrusive really means! If anyone is going to torment princesses to death, it's us... *(Ripper! – Rupes.)*

Sarah Vile

Putting the Me in Mean!

WE ALL owe Kate an apology – although I have less to say sorry about than others because, as a mother in the public eye, I know exactly what poor Kate is going through and it was therefore entirely understandable that I would jump to spurious conclusions, speculate wildly based on no facts, and try to bully the Princess into coming clean so I could write more pieces about how she should have come clean earlier to stop people like me spreading malicious rumours about her health.

Now we must all salute this brave, honest and heroic woman, namely myself, who has had the courage to address the people of Britain and offer succour and wisdom to them when they need her most.

Yes, it's time to give me some space (pages 1-94, every day for a month) so that I can heal privately in the comfort of the Daily Mail.

How do you tell the children?

by **Truly Nasty**

It's the hardest thing for any mother to do: explaining to your children that you have been spreading rumours about Kate's health. You never think it's going to happen to you, but then you realise that, yes, you are the one posting on Mumsnet and endlessly discussing it on social media and at every social event you go to.

Letting your children know that you're a "cancer on society" is something no parent ever wants to do, but sadly they did hear you saying that you knew someone who knows Kate and it's definitely something it turned out not to be.

So I told my children the awful news, but assured them that "Mummy will be better", she will stop committing "Kate crimes" and from now on she will not indulge in any more mean-spirited speculation about people in the public eye ever again... mind you, have you seen THAT picture of Meghan? She's definitely had some work done, not that she ever does any work and... *(cont. ad infinitum)*

Red-Blooded Mail   FRIDAY, MARCH 15, 2024

Meet the dashing military hunks the Royals can't live without

THOSE HOT EQUERRIES, NUMBER 94:
Sir Alan Cholmondeley Frobisher Fitztightly (78)

CURRENTLY serving His Majesty the King as Custodian of the Colgate and Steward of the Stinky Inkpen, Sir Alan makes the ladies' hearts go all a-flutter when he wears his cherry-picker breeches from his time as Lieutenant General in the 17th 21st Gay Hussars.

And there have been instances of "Ladies-in-Fainting" when he dons the Rory Stewart Tartan kilt of the Queen's Skye-Plus Highlanders.

Sir Alan comes from a distinguished family and is known to friends as "the Last of the Fitztightlies," and has a reputation in the Mess as a "great swordsman".

With his bright brown eyes and striking grey hair, the youthful Sir Alan has been equerry as folk for many years. And yes, ladies – he's still available!

*© Daily Mail
Twenty Twenty-Phwoar.*

47

US steps up aid with delivery of thousands of missiles

THE US has successfully landed very large amounts of high-grade ordnance for Israel, as part of what the White House calls "a sustained effort to expand the flow of military hardware into the country".

In its strongest message of support so far, the latest package of inhumanitarian aid to their main Middle East ally was a joint military operation involving both the US navy and air force, which President Joe Biden said "was not the first and would not be the last of many, many more such deliveries".

However, a spokesman for Benjamin Netanyahu's war cabinet said the airdrop was "merely a tiny pinprick", arguing that US military aid was now so low that "nowhere near enough high-tech weapons were getting into the region".

"Look! Another American airdrop"

TV Highlights

Humza Plotter and the Half Baked Crime Bill

(BBC Scotland – Rowling News)

Yet another sequel to the long-running saga, in which the not-very wizard Humza Plotter (a heavily bearded Daniel Radcliffe) tries once again to cast a spell on his arch nemesis She-Who-Must-Not-Be-Named and put her in prison for hate crimes.

Sadly, She/Her-Who-Must-Not-Be-Named survives yet again and turns Humza into a laughing stock with one flick of her keyboard.

"Expelliarmus!" she cries, as the hapless Hamza is voted out of Hoggyrood chased by thousands of Dementors accusing him of hate crimes and threatening

to send him to prison instead.

Don't miss a cameo performance by an in-form Nicola Sturgeon as the ginger-haired schoolboy Ron Krankie, whose attempts to throw a cloak of invisibility over the enchanted Campervan of Doom go disastrously wrong.

EYE RATING:
Very weasely-worded!

Daily Telegraph

YOUR GUIDE

What should foreign governments be allowed to own?

Approved List

- The water companies
- The power companies
- The power stations
- The trains
- The buses
- The ports
- The airports
- Most of the banks
- British Airways
- British Telecom
- Land Rover, Bentley, Rolls-Royce, and Aston Martin
- All the nice houses in the middle of London
- Everything else we can sell

Non-Approved List

- The Daily Telegraph

CELEBRITY BIG BROTHER LATEST

Ten things you didn't know about Kate's embarrassing 'buncle', Gary Goldsmith

1. He disgraced himself in front of the Queen at Sandringham with his risqué Christmas charade of Gone with the Wind. He has never been allowed back.

2. He is the father of Tory peer Zac Goldsmith and half-brother of Sir James Goldsmith, famous fishpaste manufacturer and the founder of the short-lived Neverendum party.

3. He once worked as a Father Christmas at Hamleys but unfortunately punched one of the elves in the face.

4. Gary's favourite drink is lots of it.

5. Gary had previously been turned down as a contestant on Love Island, Celebrity Naked Attraction and Today at Wimbledon.

6. He's a direct descendent of French Aristocrat Sir Guy de Gorilla, a courtier in the reign of Louis VII (known as the Kong King).

7. Gary is not his real name – according to records held in Surbiton registry office, he was christened Susan.

8. Gary once had to be thrown off a plane for heckling the stewardess (his sister, Carole) when she was demonstrating the safety procedures on the new Easyjet flight 737 to Prague, known as the Stag Weekend Express. She had to ask the cabin crew to set "Doors to Manual" for the arrival of the Luton Airport Police.

9. There are only nine things worth knowing about Gary Goldsmith.

Steve Wright in the Afterlife

"Did I tell you about my air fryer?"

POETRY CORNER

**In Memoriam
Shigeichi Negishi, inventor of the karaoke machine**

So. Farewell
Then Shigeichi Negishi,
You have sadly died,
Aged 100.

At your wake,
they will no doubt sing
"Another One Bites
The Dust!"

And "Knock Knock
Knockin' on
Heaven's Door",
But not
"I Will Survive."

Though, at the
Pearly Gates,
You may find
The number one
Singalong is:
"Come Up and See Me,
Make me Smile."

Altogether now:
"Ooh la la la
Ooh la la la
Ooooooooh."

E.J. Thribb (17½ slurred versions of "My Way")

KATE'S EMBARRASSING UNCLE NOT EVICTED FROM BIG BROTHER HOUSE

DIARY

VITAL ISSUES OF OUR DAY(1): THE GARRICK CLUB

AMELIA GENTLEMAN: It's the final gasps of a declining patriarchal elite, a lonely slice of England that forgot to modernise. I'm talking, of course, of the Garrick Club, where High Court judges conspire with Secret Service bosses over lamb cutlets, *epinards à la crème* and *pommes lyonnaise*.

One February lunchtime, Lord Julian Fellowes, creator of *Downton Abbey*, could be spotted pouring custard over his plum duff, while, at a neighbouring table, former Cabinet Minister Jacob Rees-Mogg was seen talking in hushed tones to leading *Telegraph* columnist Simon Heffer.

I can exclusively reveal that other top-secret members of this elite club include hotel magnate Sir Rocco Forte, philanthropist Santa Claus, veteran men of letters Messrs Statler and Waldorf, former captain of industry Sir Bufton Tufton, and leading glove-puppet Basil Brush. Another member of the glove-puppet community, Mr Punch, resigned after his wife, Judy, somehow gained admittance to the members' dining-room carrying their baby and a string of sausages.

Secret membership rituals include saying, "Did I ever tell you that wonderful story about Donald Sinden, the Queen Mother and the bottle of Drambuie?" and falling fast asleep over a 1956 edition of the *Illustrated London News* at 3.45pm precisely.

Says leading human rights campaigner Mary Ann Sieghart, "This is not a trivial matter because not being allowed to fall asleep over a 1956 edition of the *Illustrated London News* does actually damage women in their careers. It's often those informal meetings with retired TV quiz-show hosts from the 1970s and former literary editors of *The Reader's Digest* that make all the difference when it comes to being offered a place on the Booker Prize judging panel. Anybody who believes in fairness and equality should feel extremely uncomfortable about being a member of a club that excludes me."

As told to
CRAIG BROWN

Top London club under pressure to reform

by Amelia Gentlemans-Club

AN exclusive private members institution, famed for its association with the theatre, is facing a constitutional crisis.

The Yorick Club, which dates back to the time of Shakespeare, is an elite dining establishment for members of the dead.

Named after the amusing entertainer and skull, Yorick, a fellow of infinite jest, the society is confronting increased demands that its membership should allow in the living.

Traditionalists are furious.

Said one prominent skeleton, "It would change the atmosphere completely to admit people with a pulse. It's dead in the Yorick Club most nights, and we want to keep it that way. This could be the end of the Yorick." He added, "I can feel it in my bones."

Former member, top civil servant Sir Simon Suitcase, controversially resigned from the Yorick, having decided to be alive, after all, saying, "Being deceased suited me during the Covid Inquiry, but I now realise there's more to life than being dead in a club in London."

"My doctor told me to avoid drinking alone"

GLENDA SLAGG

She's Fleet Street's Iron Dame!!!

■ SO Posh is 50!!!! Who cares??!!! I'm not going to waste hundreds of valuable words on the frumpy stick-insect with the sour face just 'cos she's had another birthday!?! Who hasn't!!!???? Why doesn't the former Waste-Of-Spice Girl (Gedddittt??!) go and get a Zig-a-zig-zimmer frame?!? I'll tell you what I want, what I really really want, is never to have to read about YOU ever again!? No offence!??!!

■ All hail Queen Victoria of Beckingham Palace, and congratulations on your 50-year-old reign!!!! You spice up all our lives (Gedddittt???!) and are a perfect role model for all us older gals who aren't yet ready for a Zig-a-zig-zimmer frame!!?! I'll tell you what I want, what I really, really want, is to read about you and your amazing life on every page of every paper forever!!!??! Or rather – Viva Forever!!??!!!

■ DAVID BECKHAM – don'tcha love him????!!! Didn't you shed a little ol' tear when lovey-dovey David proved himself the perfect hubby by making a touching speech and giving his missus a piggyback to the limo??!!? Altogether now... Aaaaaaaaahhhhhhhh!!!!!!! Didn't you just 'Wannabe' there at the Beckham bash with top celebs Tom Cruise, Gordon Ramsay, the bloke from Fast and Furious with Rosie Huntington-Palmer-Biscuit, who used to be married to Roald Dahl, not to mention the woman off Desperate Housewives (subs, please check details)????! No wonder her Royal Poshness doesn't want to give him the Golden Boot (Geddit??!!).

■ DAVID BECKHAM – what a disgrace!!!!??? Pretending you're all loved-up, when we all know that you've been playing away and scoring where you shouldn't???!!!! You're a Becks-addict, Mr Greedyballs, and no mistake!!!!! I admit I cried at your speech – with LAUGHTER!!!! And giving your missus a piggy-back???? That's what you've been doing her entire career!?!!! Who would 'Wannabe' at this tawdry event with its D-List so-called celebs – Tom 'SAGA' Cruise, Gordon Effing Ramsay, Rosie and Jim from Slow and Tedious, not to mention the Desperate Housewife – ie, YOU Victoria!!??!! The whole thing makes me wannabe sick-a-sick-aaaarghhhh!!!! (You've done this twice already. Keep it up! Ed.) Give him the Golden Boot, Victoria, and rejoin the Old Spice Girls (Geddit????!!!!), Grumpy, Sneezy, Red Bull and Mel (Smith)!!!!!???? (Subs, please check all this out!)

Byeee!!

POETRY CORNER

In Memoriam Richard Sherman, legendary Disney songwriter

So. Farewell
Then Richard Sherman.

You are going up
Into the clouds
Like Mary Poppins,
But without an umbrella,
Because of course
You have wings,
Like Chitty Chitty
Bang Bang.

All your songs were
Catchy, upbeat and joyful.
They were…
Oh, what's the word?
Supercalifragilistic-
Expialidocious,
And the sound of them
Was not at all atrocious.

E.J. Thribb
(17½ Oscars for best song)

ATTENTION DEFICIT SYMPO

@Vilmirineo

SCHOOL LATEST

Pupils who are on their mobile phones all day are more likely to get poor exam results

IN OTHER NEWS

■ Bears who are in the woods all day are more likely to shit there.

■ Popes who are in the Vatican all day are more likely to be Catholic.

49

TOP TORY MP IN HONEYTRAP SCANDAL

WILLIAM WRAGG SHAMED

That's an obscene picture of a member!

RISHI SUNAK HORROR

Oh no, it's a huge election!

HUNT PRAISES BRAVERY

He apologised for his cock-up

TOP TORY IN 'MONEYTRAP' STING

by DONNA REWARDED

TOP Conservative, Prime Minister Rishi Sunak, was lured into sending a mysterious businessman a knighthood, after being sent pictures of large amounts of money.

These so-called "dosh pics" are used to entice desperate politicians into foolhardy actions, such as handing over honours to people who send them images of their "huge wonga".

Said Rishi Sunak, "I was weak and naïve. I thought no one would get to hear about it. But having opened the attachment and seen the tempting £5 million, I couldn't help myself helping myself. I admit it. I'm a cheques addict."

SIGNS YOU ARE BEING HONEYTRAPPED

1 You are a Conservative MP
2 Anyone under the age of 50 has expressed romantic interest in you
3 Er...
4 That's it.

"I contacted the local Tory MP. He says he'll look into the pothole problem if we send him a dick pic first"

EXCLUSIVE TO ALL BRITISH NEWSPAPERS

WHY MEGHAN'S NEW JAM WILL BE DISGUSTING

WE ALL wish the Duchess of Sussex the greatest success with her latest venture, following on from her Netflix flop and her podcast disaster, but we cannot help but assume that the jam she produces will be sickly sweet, with a sour aftertaste.

Even though we haven't tasted it as yet, we are confident that it will be toxic and will probably make you sick.

Whilst we are reluctant to speculate on any matter regarding the Princess of Wales, it is a matter of fact that any jam that she might produce will be fragrant, delightful, tasteful, fruity and delicious on a scone, whether applied before or after the cream.

We wish no disrespect to the Duchess of Sussex, but she should stick to what she is good at – ie nothing. She should "preserve" her energy and not "spread" her talents too thinly, if that were possible.

Sadly for her and her marmalade-haired husband, this doomed enterprise will be a case of no jam today, tomorrow or ever.

ARE THERE ENOUGH SENIOR ROYAL REPORTERS TO GO ROUND?

by Our Senior Royal Reporter **Jenny Flex**

WITH the slimmed-down monarchy top of the news agenda, there are growing fears that there simply aren't enough royal reporters to write about them.

With so many stories to cover, it is becoming increasingly clear that the royal press pack is being spread too thin.

It only takes one or two illnesses or free trips abroad to highlight the paucity of senior royal reporters available for duty.

When the 87-year-old Duchess of Milton Keynes opened a new scout hut in Penrith, filling in for the 92-year-old Countess of Northhhumbershire (who was standing in for Queen Camilla, who was opening a pack of Marlboro Lites) there were only 114 royal journalists in attendance to document the crisis in royal personpower.

When are the younger royal correspondents going to step up and share the burden? When will the next generation of journalists realise that it's all very well and easy to go on about climate change and global conflict and mental health, but what really matters to the well-being of the nation is that there is someone on hand to record for posterity what Princess Alice of Battenburg was wearing on her head when she cut the ribbon to open the A3507 extension tunnel just south of junction 3 between South Croydon and zzzzzzzzzzzz

---

How to access an extra 15 hours' free childcare for two-year-olds in full

■ Obtain voucher from YouGov website
■ Contact your local nursery
■ Discover it closed three month ago
■ Contact alternative nursery
■ Discover it's closing next Friday
■ Put your kids in the car
■ Take them to your mum's and beg her to look after them for another two days a week
■ Er...
■ That's it.

"I've found a nursery we can afford"

DUMB BRITAIN

Real contestants, real quiz shows, real answers, real dumb!

Tipping Point, ITV

Ben Shephard: The Yellow River and the river Ganges are in which continent?
Contestant: Egypt.

Shephard: What famous waterfall, located in Africa, was named in honour of a 19th-century British queen?
Contestant: Niagara.

Shephard: Who was the president of the United States on January 1st, 2000?
Contestant: George Washington.

Shephard: On which continent is the 1994 Disney animation *The Lion King* set?
Contestant: Antarctica.

Shephard: A quad bike has how many wheels?
Contestant: Three.

Shephard: Which continent are Brazil nuts native to?
Contestant: Asia.

Shephard: What is the longest river that is solely within the Czech Republic?
Contestant: The Nile.

Shephard: Which biblical character danced the Dance of the Seven Veils?
Contestant: Jesus.

Shephard: How many sides does an isosceles triangle have?
Contestant: Five.

Shephard: In which play by Oscar Wilde does the character Jack Worthing explain that he was found in a handbag?
Contestant: The Rocky Horror Show.

Shephard: In the Beatrix Potter stories, what type of animal is Pigling Bland?
Contestant: A rabbit.

Shephard: Who was the Russian leader during the Cuban Missile Crisis of 1962?
Contestant: Rasputin.

Pointless, BBC1

Alexander Armstrong: An eight-letter word beginning with "port" that is a country lying on the Atlantic coast of the Iberian peninsula.
Contestant: Patagonia.

Armstrong: "The F… Seasons" by Vivaldi?
Contestant: Five.

Armstrong: Name any individual who has been awarded the Fields Medal for mathematics since its introduction in 1936.
Contestant: Pythagoras.

Tenable, ITV

Warwick Davis: Featured on a Bank of England banknote, which economist wrote The Wealth of Nations?
Contestant: Milton Keynes.

Impossible, BBC2

Rick Edwards: Which British mountaineer conquered Mount Everest with Sherpa Tenzing Norgay in 1953?
Contestant: Bear Grylls.

Edwards: Who succeeded François Hollande as president of France?
Contestant: Vladimir Putin.

PopMaster, Channel 4

Ken Bruce: *Annie's Song* has been a top three hit for John Denver and which Irish instrumentalist?
Contestant: Flamingo. Placido Flamingo.

Ant & Dec's Limitless Win, ITV

Question: The character Big Brother was introduced in which George Orwell novel?
Contestant: *The BFG.*

The Chase, ITV

Bradley Walsh: Which royal duke was governor of the Bahamas during the Second World War?
Contestant: The Duke of Wellington.

Walsh: Which British monarch was Empress of India from 1876 to 1901?
Contestant: Clive.

Walsh: Which Labour party leader was a mineworker at the age of 10?
Contestant: David Cameron.

Walsh: What is the most easterly county in England?
Contestant: Cornwall.

Walsh: In 2022, the Conger Ice Shelf collapsed on which continent?
Contestant: Africa.

Walsh: Which Commonwealth country has had two prime ministers named Malcolm?
Contestant: Spain.

Walsh: The extinct Tasmanian wolf was a native of which country?
Contestant: Siberia.

Walsh: What duke was played by Christopher Plummer in the film Waterloo?
Contestant: Duke Ellington.

Walsh: Yuri Zhivago is the title character in which Boris Pasternak novel?
Contestant: *War and Peace.*

Walsh: King George III was the first British monarch to have an account with which bank: Coutts, Clydesdale or Co-op Bank?
Contestant: Co-op Bank.

Walsh: A man called a Manxman or a woman called a Manxwoman is an inhabitant of which island?
Contestant: New Zealand.

Walsh: What three-letter words links a coal mine and where an orchestra plays in a theatre?
Contestant: Colliery.

The Chase (Australia)

Host: A children's book by Henry Williamson is *Tarka the…* what'?
Contestant: Hun.

Family Fortunes, Challenge TV

Les Dennis: Name something you associate with Cleopatra.
Contestant: The Trojan Horse.

Radio Exe, Devon

Matt Rogers: If it's your birthday today, 8 March, your star sign is a fish. Name that star sign.
Caller: Tuna.

Mastermind, BBC2

Clive Myrie: What was the Christian name of the suffragette whose surname was Fawcett?
Contestant: Farrah.

Myrie: Which 20th-century British composer wrote the music for the operas Peter Grimes and Albert Herring?
Contestant: Tim Minchin.

Myrie: Which controversial British music impresario, who died in 2010, was the manager of the Sex Pistols from their formation in 1975 until they split up almost three years later?
Contestant: Robert Maxwell.

Myrie: Wilhelm is the German form of what English first name?
Contestant: Philip.

Myrie: Which British naval commander lost his right arm in battle in 1797?
Contestant: Captain Hook.

Myrie: Köln is the German name for which city?
Contestant: Lahore.

Brain of Britain, Radio 4

Russell Davies: In 1589 Britain sent an armada to attack Spain. Who led this armada?
Contestant: Francis Chichester.

The Weakest Link, BBC2

Romesh Ranganathan: The Kingdom of Lesotho is entirely surrounded by what other country?
Contestant: Wales.

Ranganathan: In drinks, which liqueur made with eggs, sugar and brandy shares its name with the Dutch word for lawyer?
Contestant: Eggnog.

Ranganathan: Which daily newspaper has been nicknamed "the *Grauniad*" because of its misprints and typos?
Contestant: The *Sun.*

Ranganathan: In the animal kingdom, what "w" is a winged insect that lives in a nest known as a vespiary?
Celebrity dancer: Lion.

The Finish Line, BBC1

Roman Kemp: Name a top British university: O----D.
Contestant: Oldham.

Kemp: Which author wrote the 1945 novel Brideshead Revisited?
Contestant: Jane Austen.

Kemp: Pompeii was destroyed by which volcano?
Contestant: The Bastille.

Kemp: Which football manager was known by the nickname Cloughie?
Contestant: Alex Ferguson.

Kemp: Richard Llewellyn wrote the novel *How Green Was My…* what?
Contestant: Cheese.

Kemp: The mythological hero Hector was killed in which war?
Contestant: The First World War.

The Tournament, BBC2

Alex Scott: The *Titanic* set sail from which port on the south coast?
Contestant: Leeds.

Ten to the Top, Radio 2

Vernon Kay: "On the Wings of Love" was a hit in 1984 for Jeffrey... who?
Caller: Archer.

NEVER TO BE FORGIVEN?

A new short story by Clara Sill, Britain's top romantasy novelist

THE STORY SO FAR: Prince Andrew has been banished and is living in exile in Windsor Soup Lodge. But he has not given up hope of redemption. Now read on...

"**H**URRY UP, Fergs, it's about to begin!" Prince Andrew the Duke of Yorkiebar impatiently called his former flame-haired wife and current soulmate to join him on the only sofa the bailiffs sent in by Prince William had left.

"Yah, okay, Ands, I'm just getting a few TV snacks from my new 'Duchess Original' range." She emerged from the kitchen bearing a tray laden with buckets of Weight Watchers Slimmed-Down-Monarchy York Scratchings and Royal Buttered Shortofmoneybread Fingers. These delicious hi-fat diet treats would see them through the next hour of sensational royal drama.

Andrew could not contain his excitement. At last, the public would see him as he really was, faithfully recreated by the NetFux streaming channel. His historic interview with TV's Emily Glamress, which he had always thought had gone so well, was now to be re-enacted with top TV actors Rufus Ingrid Sewel and Gillian Randy-Andyson – not to mention Billie Highland-Piper as the brilliant runner Sam Whoshe, who rang up the Prince's people and arranged the Prat-a-Manger sandwich selection for the legendary shoot.

"How many royal figures in history had commanded so much attention?" thought Andrew. Okay, Henry the Something had a boring play written about him. But had Horrible Henry ever done an interview that had stopped the world in its tracks? He thought not.

"Rufus is seriously fit," said Fergiana, spraying her former princely paramour with genuine "Balmoral-baked" biscuit crumbs in her enthusiasm for the raffish romantic lead who had starred in TV's classic adaptation of Middlebrow, as well as playing Obergruppenführer Von Nazi in The Man in Windsor High Castle...

"Shush, Fergster," remonstrated the man known by the mean-spirited and unforgiving British press as 'The Black Sheep Prince', as the NetFux titles flickered on the screen.

"Pooper-Scoop – based on a true episode of Snoozenight."

And there he was, once again sitting in that chair in the Palace's Going South Drawing Room, effortlessly defending himself from the baseless charges that he had ever met anyone involved in the whole Harvey Epstein affair.

The drama unfolded, with every detail immaculately reimagined – even down to Emily Makeshift's military-style jacket, with its subtle undertone of Michael Jackson in his Paedo Pan pomp.

"This is a great bit," enthused the former Lord High Admiral of the Queen's Navee, now Mr Windsor. "I mean, the Falkenders War sweating story is seriously brill. And the Woking Pizza Excess alibi – totes convincing!"

"You aced it, Randrew!" agreed the former Duchess of Potato, now Fabferg@buystuffcheap.com. "I mean, you talking about the straightforward shooting party is like, sooooo relatable to like, ordinary people. And claiming to be too honourable – I mean, it's just too honourable. You are, literally, Prince Super-Charming!"

"Yah, good point," replied the eighth-in-line to the Throne of Games, contentedly. "That really went really rather well, really," he summed up, as the credits rolled and the continuity announcer intoned, "If you have been affected by any of the issues raised by this drama, please ring Nonceline on 09994949494."

"And this is only the first drama about me," he added excitedly. "There's another one next week called 'A Right Royal Scoopy-doopy-do!' on Amazon Crime. I can't wait."

His Titian-haired companion and comforter was quick to share his optimism. "Any minute now, the phone's going to start ringing, with King Chazza begging you to come back into the fold and take over the firm! You'll be there waving on the Buck Pal Balcony before you can say 'Ghislaine Maxwell'!"

They both stared at the phone expectantly. But the red hotline from the Palace stubbornly refused to ring.

After half an hour of silence, Fergie attempted to lighten the heavy atmosphere in the disgrace-and-favour home which they now shared. "Cheer up, it may never happen!"

Outside, the rain continued to fall in sheets of lowering grey...

(To be continued...)

What you will see on your amazing £100 royal tour of historic Balmoral Castle

- The Porridge Room
- The Tweed Cupboard
- The Tupperware Cabinet
- The Tartan Drawer
- The Sporran Peg
- The Piper's Shed
- The Haggis Loft
- The Midge Garden
- The Gumboot Lobby
- The Umbrella Collection
- The Gift Shop

(Not included on tour: the bedroom where Tony Blair got Cherie pregnant)

Daily Rayner
FRIDAY, 12 APRIL, 2024

RAYNER – FRESH CRIMES REVEALED

DAY 94 of our exclusive (because no one else wants to run it) exposé of the deputy leader of the Labour party, aka Britain's top master criminal.

Following an exhaustive investigation by the entire staff of the Daily Rayner, shocking new evidence has come to light of the one-woman crime wave that has turned Britain into a lawless hell-hole.

Those Angela Rayner crimes in full:

THEFT: Rayner put two sachets of sugar (approximate value 0.003p) in her pocket after having a coffee in Starbucks.

TRAFFIC OFFENCE: Rayner pressed the button on a pedestrian crossing, but started to cross the road before the green man appeared.

ENVIRONMENTAL VANDALISM: Rayner put a plastic crisp packet into the paper recycling bin.

FRAUD: Rayner returned a library book a day late (when she was 9) and got someone else to pay the 7p fine (her mother).

ATTEMPTED MURDER: Rayner failed to walk through the foot bath in her local swimming pool, thus endangering the public with potential verrucas.

••••••••••••••••••••••••••••••

TOMORROW: Is evil Angela 'of death' Rayner 'of terror' guilty of the most heinous crimes committed in history since Keir Starmer ate that curry during lockdown?

How to spot those fake Royal Mail stamps that China is flooding Britain with

(and keep your eyes peeled for the special barcodes that spell out the leader's name)

Lines written on the recent developments in Police Scotland's Operation Branchform

'Twas in the year twenty-twenty-four
That Peter Murrell was arrested once more.
Last week he was charged, for offences quite serious
Concerning financial affairs that are extremely mysterious.
This time in Peter's garden there was no police tent,
And the charge was simply embezzlement.
It concerns money misappropriated from the SNP,
Tho' the details are obviously sub-judice.
Six hundred thousand poonds have gone astray,
But who is responsible I cannae say.
Nor can I mention the luxury campervan so swanky
Owned(?) by Murrell and his wife, the wee lookalike Kranky.
(I do hope that this traditional and innocent rhyme
Doesn't qualify now as a Scottish hate crime!
Or I'll be there in a cell, all dark and danky,
With the husband of the former First Minister of Scotland.)

© *William McGonagall, Winner of Worst Topical Poet of the Year UK Press Awards 1867*

"Hi, I'm a protest singer, if that's okay with everyone?"

Keir Starmer WRITES

HELLO! I'm sure you've heard that I made a great speech last week, saying that I'm going to do things better than the Tories! Just look at my record: cancelling spending plans, dog-whistle politics, ignoring the macro-economic damage of Brexit, making heavy-handed statements about law and order – yes, anything they can do, we can do better!

We're also trying to go toe to toe with the Tories in terms of scandals. Angela Rayner's alleged £1,500 tax dodge may seem like small beer to you, but the last time I had a small beer, the Daily Mail tried to get me arrested! Financial chicanery shows we're ready for government and the British people can trust us to deliver sleaze to match the Conservatives.

Sincerely, Keir

Daily Mail

Is the sun setting on the dream of retiring in Spain?*

*Yes, because you lot voted for Brexit.

"What's a monopoly?"   *"Google it"*

K.J.Lamb

53

Lookalikes

Reeves   **Huston**

Sir,
   Huston, we have a problem.
   ENA B. WITCHED.

Dwayne Johnson, aka The Rock   **Gregg Wallace, aka The Cock (surely "Cook"? Ed.)**

Sir,
   I have heard the backlash at Gregg Wallace for how he spends the day – spending hours at the gym, ignoring his family, and bragging about his six pack. Who does he think he is, some sort of Hollywood megastar?
   THOMAS HEBERT.

John Cooper Clarke   **Asian Hornet**

Sir,
   I couldn't help noticing the resemblance between Dr John Cooper Clarke and the Asian Hornet. One known for its spindly legs, big dark eyes and droning buzz, the other a sort of giant wasp.
   L.S. EVANS.

Newton   **Vine**

Sir,
   Using a telescope, I wonder if any of your readers have noticed the resemblance between Sir Isaac Newton, mathematician, physicist, astronomer, alchemist and theologian, and BBC TV and radio presenter Jeremy Vine. Coincidence?
   STEVE USHER.

Ear   **Ear**

Sir,
   The great post-impressionist painter was a passionate man and, frustrated by his love for a prostitute, cut off his ear. I notice that the orange fascist also has an aural injury. I wonder if it is in any way related to working girls?
   ALEX WILLIAMS.

Neil   **Nandy**

Sir,
   Am I the first to spot the likeness between Lisa Nandy, Secretary of State for Culture, Media and Sport, and Neil from The Young Ones?
   COLIN DRURY.

Gargoyle   **Farage**

Sir,
   Recently spotted in Whitby Abbey Museum, a rock-headed conveyor of waste that bears an uncanny resemblance to another gargoyle.
   PETER CAUSER.

Glad rags   **Handbags**

Sir,
   Has anyone noticed, as I have, the extraordinary resemblance between Rod Stewart the singer of Maggie May and this picture of Maggie taken in May 1979? Spooky, eh!?
   NAME SUPPLIED.

Pompei mosaic   **Tim Martin**

Sir,
   I was struck by the resemblance. One is an angry ranter from a once great civilisation, unaware of the disaster to come, the other is a mosaic from Pompeii.
   GLYN ALSWORTH.

Cox   **Spiteri**

Sir,
   Sharleen Spiteri and Professor Brian Cox... are they by any chance related? I think we should be told!
   IAIN WILTON.

Kryten   **Anderson**

Sir,
   One is a tin-eared robot living in a fantasy universe, the other is Kryten from comedy classic Red Dwarf.
   NIGEL COOK.

Manson   **Brand**

Sir,
   There seems some resemblance between Charles Manson and this alleged comedian. Or is it just re-branding?
   DUNCAN HEENAN.

Rubbish   **Rubbish**

Sir,
   As budgets contract it would appear at least one TV news organisation now finds itself in somewhat reduced circumstances. Hopefully this will have no noticeable effect on the quality of its output.
   JONATHAN GURD.

Saturn **Truss**

Sir,

I found the photo of Liz Truss above, which recently reappeared in the press, rather unsettling. And then I realised why. It jogged my memory of a visit to the Prado, Madrid, where Goya's painting "Saturn devouring his son" hangs.

GRAHAM DAVIES.

Looney Tunes **Cummings**

Sir,

Has anyone noticed, as I have, the remarkable similarity between Elmer Fudd, the cartoon star of Looney Tunes, and Dominic Cummings, the star of the Covid Inquiry hearings? Are they, by any chance, related?

ENA B. AZIZ.

Taylor Greene **Neanderthal woman**

Sir,

Finally, scientists have found evidence that evolution in the US Republican party has been at a standstill for 75,000 years. Paleoartists have recently created a 3D model of a Neanderthal woman's face which shows a remarkable similarity to Marjorie Taylor Greene.

KEES VAN DAALEN.

Manning **Milei**

Sir,

Has anyone noticed, as I have, a remarkable similarity between right-wing firebrand Bernard Manning and the noted Argentinian TV star-turned-president, Javier Milei? I wonder if they might be related?

C. FRANKLIN.

Cap **Crap**

Sir,

Has anyone noticed, as I have, the extraordinary similarity between the Olympic Phryge mascot (based on the revolutionary cap worn by the Jacobins) and the poo emoji?

Are they, by any chance, related?

OTTIE O'BRIEN.

Mordaunt **Winslet**

Sir,

I was struck by the resemblance between Kate Winslet as Chancellor Elena Vernham in her new series The Regime, which depicts a year within the palace of a crumbling authoritarian regime, and Penny Mordaunt at the King's coronation.

Art imitating life?

GAVIN WOODWORTH.

Otto **Wes**

Sir,

Have any of your readers noticed, as I have, the remarkable similarity between shadow minister Wes Streeting, and Otto the autopilot from "Airplane!"?

Is there any chance that they are both related to the rate of inflation?

Keep up the good work.

BAMBI REDUX.

Stormy **Steph**

Sir,

Has anyone noticed, as I have, the remarkable similarity between the star witness at the current Trump trial, Ms S Daniels, and the star presenter of the podcast The Rest is Money, Ms S McGovern?

ENA B. REWSTER.

Self portrait **Selfish portrait**

Sir,

Francis Bacon and Paula Vennells?

ENA B. MARWOOD.

Balsco **Blair**

Sir,

Is it me, or is the fictional enemy from The Eagle comic also the deluded Future Emperor of the Earth? I think we should be told, etc.

ALISTAIR MACQUEEN.

Gabriel **Bowen**

Sir,

BBC correspondent Jeremy Bowen and singer Peter Gabriel. Which one is moonlighting from the day job?

TREVOR HOPPER.

Baggins **Hambling**

Sir,

My wife noticed a striking resemblance between Maggie Hambling and Bilbo Baggins. I wonder if you agree?

HELEN MARSHALL.

Basil **Balfour**

Sir,

This whole Israel-Palestine mess is Lord Basil's fault.

DAVID GETTMAN.

How do you feel about taking on
a bit more responsibility in the company?

Does that mean I'd have to come in?

Your quote is
very expensive

We have a cheaper
solution, but it
doesn't really work

Great let's go with that then

I noticed you weren't laughing
at any of my jokes in that meeting

I don't mind laughing at your jokes but can
you give me a signal when you're making one?

INTERVIEW

Ideally I'm looking for somewhere
I can charge me car up for nothing

I didn't know you smoked?

yeah someone recommended them
to help me cut down on my vaping

Rishi Sunak MP 📱 **The Prime Minister's Highly Confidential WhatsApp Group**

Mark Menzies
Hello!

> Who are you?

Mark Menzies
I'm one of your MPs.
I used to be PPS to the
Minister of State for
International Development.

James Forsyth
Oh yes, I recognise you. You had to
resign following allegations that you
paid a Brazilian male escort for sex.

James Forsyth
Still, that was back in 2014. All
forgotten now.

> So, how are things, Mark?

Mark Menzies
I'm in a room with some bad men.

> Tell me about it! 😊

Mark Menzies
No, seriously. I desperately
need some money.

Jeremy Hunt
Tell me about it! 😊

Mark Menzies
I need you to give me lots of
money! NOW! It's for medical
expenses or something plausible
like that.

James Forsyth
We're going to have to take
the whip away.

Oliver Dowden
As the Brazilian escort might
have said! 🤣🤣🤣🍆

Mark Menzies
Please, guys, help!

James Forsyth
I think it's time for an internal
investigation.

Oliver Dowden
Which costs extra in Rio!
Apparently! 😜😊

Mark Menzies has been removed from the group by some bad men.

DIARY

ALLISON PEARSON

1939. Britain is on the brink. One little tin-pot dictator by the name of Adolf Hitler threatens to invade. It doesn't bear thinking about.

Only one man who can save us from Hitler's murderous hordes. His name? Winston S. Churchill. Wind the clock forward 85 years and, sorry to say this, guys, but we're facing exactly the same situation today.

Taxes on the rise. The so-called National "Health" Service – National Death Service, more like! – systematically murdering hundreds of thousands of our beloved elderly folk every single day. Millions of illegal aliens elbowing their way into our beloved country to wolf down our food, plunder our property and have their way with our kiddies without so much as a "thank you".

And never a hairdresser's appointment when you need one. As in 1939, Britain is on the brink. And, once again, there is only one man to save us. His name? Step forward, Lee Anderson.

It's a crying shame Lee Anderson never married Kate Middleton. What an amazing power-couple they would make.

Lee with his strong, manly opinions, chiselled jaw, genuine concern for others and can-do personality.

Kate with her lustrous locks, perfect figure – and ability to charm the proverbial birds out of the trees, if there were any trees left since the hard-left councils chopped them all down to make way for compulsory trans clinics.

Sadly, fate intervened, as it so often will. Sorry to disappoint you, Lee – but Kate's already married. For some time now, she's been our beloved Princess of Wales. And a brilliant fist she's made of it too, curing more people with her sunny smile than all the NHS hospitals combined.

So where does this leave poor Lee? Behind that handsome, no-nonsense, Northern visage, I sense he's lonely. And he's hurting. But all is not lost.

At time of writing, Princess Anne is taken. Unfortunately, her current husband, Tim Lawrence, has failed to make his mark. Nobody knows – or frankly cares – who he is. Sadly, it's high time Anne divorced him and found someone more worthy of her robust commonsense.

But who? It deeply worries me that the overwhelming majority of men of her generation have been put under the trans scalpel with a cattle-prod bought with taxpayers' money and wielded by Sadiq Khan and forced to transition into so-called women under direct instructions from Abu Hamza.

Thankfully, there's a thoroughly English gentleman of mature years with earthy views straight out of Planet Normal. Someone completely perfect for the Princess Royal. And, no, ladies, it's not His Nibs I'm on about.

Step forward, Their Royal Highnesses Prince Lee and the Princess Anne Anderson. A phrase with a lovely, heartwarming ring to it, n'est-ce pas? A winning combination of national saviours – even greater than Taylor Swift-lookalike Liz Truss and hunky hubby Hugh O'Leary in their heyday.

Between the two of them, Lee and Anne will Give Us Back Our Country. And together they'll make the great big heart of the late Winston S. Churchill swell with pride.

As told to
CRAIG BROWN

TORY MP TRAPPED IN HOUSE WITH SOME BAD PEOPLE

Help!

Iran 'urges restraint from Israel'

by Our Middle East Correspondent **Ayatoldya Nottodoit**

Iran has urged Israel to de-escalate tensions in the Middle East, following the total failure of its unprecedented missile and drone attack on Israel.

"Let's just say we're even, okay? You carried out an audacious precision strike on our consulate in Syria, killing all your intended targets, while we fired off hundreds of missiles and drones that didn't successfully destroy anything, apart from our reputation as feared warmongers," said a scared-looking Iranian government spokesman.

"The last thing anyone wants is a full-scale war with Israel, now we know we'd lose."

THE MAILY TIMESEGRAPH

6 MONTHS AGO	NOW
WE SUPPORT ISRAEL'S RIGHT TO DEFEND ITSELF ✡	**WE SUPPORT ISRAEL'S RIGHT**

"I think we've found out why their civilisation collapsed"

EXCLUSIVE TO PRIVATE EYE

IN A mini-serialisation of her autobiography, *Ten Minutes to Write This Book*, Liz Truss details who is to blame for the total collapse of the British economy after her mini-budget which led to the premature end of her premiership. Liz exclusively reveals that it was the fault of:

- The Blob
- Tony Blair
- Virtue-signalling eco-zealots
- The anti-growth coalition
- The anti-freeze coalition
- The Tony Blob
- The deep state
- The deep fat fryer
- The Bank of England
- The Bank of Mum and Dad
- Lefty lawyers
- Righty lawyers
- Inbetweeny lawyers
- The Wokerati
- Snow Flakes
- Corn Flakes
- Cadbury's Flakes
- Flake News
- The OBR
- The OBN
- The OBE
- The OBI-Wan Kenobi
- The IMF
- The IDF
- IDS
- The IRA
- VAR
- MFI
- MI5
- The Jackson Five
- The Famous Five
- The Secret Seven
- The BBC
- Joe Biden
- Joe Pasquale
- Joe 90
- Jeremy Hunt
- The Queen
- Fleas
- John Lewis
- Ocado
- Lettuce
- Everyone she's worked with
- Everyone she hasn't worked with
- Everyone but her.

Next week: *Liz Truss details who is to blame for the catastrophe that is her book.*

"Look at me, everyone! I'm AMAZING!"

Shameless plug

TRUSS SELLS BOOK UPSIDE DOWN

I was taking the economy in the right direction

What is this ancient Roman dodecahedral artefact, whose discovery in various locations has baffled the experts, even TV's Mary Beard? You decide!

Is it...

A Rubicon's cube: A mind-bending children's puzzle, designed to keep teenage Caesars occupied for hours.

B A piece of Lego, Legas, Legat, Legamus, Legatis, Legant.

C The golden snitch from the Latin game Quid-Pro-Quodditch.

D A helmet for dwarf gladiators in the Circus Minimus.

E A model of the early virus Covidius – Covid 19AD – that swept through the Empire, although Emperor Borisius flouted the lockdown rules and had drunken orgies at Number X, which caused the end of the Roman Empire.

F A device for filling columns in Roman newspapers such as The Roman Times, The Times New Roman, The Solus, and the satirical journal Privatus Oculus. (*That's enough filling up space. Ed.*)

TORIES – A LOCAL ELECTION NIGHT TO REMEMBER

It's disappointing, but not a total disaster

Time to steer further right to the bottom

♪ Abide with ♪ Rishi

No need to go overboard

I'm not hearing any great love for the iceberg

Hooray! We've stopped the boat!

We're slightly down from where we would have hoped

Keir Starmer WRITES

HELLO. This week I'm not writing a column because I don't want to appear over-confident just because Labour have had the best result for 40 years.

Which sounds exciting, but isn't really if you don't want to appear smug or triumphalist, which I don't. In fact, just mentioning the fact that we did well in the local elections might be tempting fate, which I am not going to do.

Let's just say it was a very pleasant weekend, and it was nice to get out of the house and enjoy some decent weather on the way to the polling station. Not that I'm complacent about the nice weather lasting. It may all change and get worse. You never know – so let's not even talk about the weather – or indeed anything else.

So, as I said, no column this week from your future Prime Minister – that is, possibly, but let's not get ahead of ourselves – there's a long way to go, and there's no room for counting chickens before they're hatched, even if current indications are that I will be 500 chickens ahead of the Tories on the big day!

Sincerely,
Keir Starmer

"I'm afraid it's bad news, guys. We just got replaced by ChatGPT"

SHOCK AS BORIS JOHNSON BREAKS RULE HE SET

by Our Double Standards Correspondent **Patty Gate**

BRITAIN was left reeling this week as it emerged that Boris Johnson had turned up to a polling station without any form of identification, despite having changed the rules on exactly this issue when he was in Number 10.

A shocked member of the public said, "I can't believe it. It's not as if he's ever done this before, expecting everyone else to follow

the rules and not to do so himself. I certainly can't remember anything like that. There's no precedent for this, surely?"

Those ways Boris Johnson could have proved his identity at the polling station

1. Slept with the Polling Officer's wife

2. Borrowed £100 from the man with the clipboard and not paid it back

3. Given a peerage to the fruity young woman who offered him a pencil

4. Held an impromptu party in the Polling Station, involving a suitcase of wine and cake

5. Denied that he had ever held an impromptu party in the Polling Station

6. Redecorated the Polling Station with gold wallpaper

7. Filled in two separate ballot papers, one pro Tory, one anti

8. Hidden in fridge

9. Shouted "Do you know who I am?" to which the answer would be "Unfortunately, yes"

10. Er... that's it

TEESSIDE MAYOR PLAYS DOWN TORY LINKS

I am not a Con Man

DAVE SPART Co-Chair of From-the-River-To-The-Sea-East-London-Will-Be-Free-Solidarity-Collective writes:

Er... the sickening failure of Keir Starmer's centrist neo-Liberal project to convincingly win the local elections by as much as Jeremy Corbyn would undoubtedly have done as demonstrated by his 2017 and 2019 election victories is clear and incontrovertible proof that only a further left-leaning pro-Gaza anti-Rowling Labour Party could defeat the fascist Conservative imperialist colonialist junta ruling elite and that war criminal Blair Starmer and his proto-tory sidekicks ie Angela Rayner and would-be Reform member Wes Streeting will always be comprehensively rejected by the electorate who are crying out for a truly Socialist Corbynite and Owen-Jonesite pro-Galloway collective in Number 10 and er... er... from the Thames Barrier to the Sea, Islington will be Free!

ON OTHER PAGES

■ Why my wearing a Palestinian scarf is not cultural appropriation at all – D. Spart

Lines on the resignation of Humza Yousaf as First Minister of Scotland

'Twas in the year two thousand and twenty-four

That Humza Yousaf showed himself the door –

A rare feat for any competent politician

And a display of Yusaf's failure as a mathematician.

When he sacked the Greens, he blundered, did puir Humza,

And he really should have first done the basic sums, a

Precaution that would have told him clearly

That ending yon coalition would cost him dearly.

And so it proved when he sent the eco-warriors packing

And it was not long before his own self-sacking.

In the vote of no confidence he was just one MSP short

And he needed the hated Alex Salmond's support!

But the wily leader of Alba, in his tartan troosers,

Declared his former party, the SNP, to be a bunch of losers:

"Away wi ye, Yousaf, and go boil yer head –

Your political career is henceforth dead!"

And now the hunt is on for a new first minister,

But this could be harder than finding the Loch Ness Monaster!

Will it be Kate Forbes? No! It's old John Swinney?

A former leader already consigned to history's dustbinny!

The future now looks bright and bonnie for Labour,

As the Scot Nats are tossed aside like an unwanted caber.

Aye, this is a lesson to all leaders to "go do the math"

Or their folly will end in their taking an early bath.

For Humza's tragic miscalculation led to him walking the planky,

A bit like his former leader, the wee lookalike wife of the recently arrested Peter Murrell.

© William McGonagall 1867

POETRY CORNER

**In Memoriam
Sir Oliver Popplewell,
High Court judge**

So. Farewell
Then Sir Oliver Popplewell.

Or Mr Justice Popplecarrot,
As you were
Unkindly called
By *Private Eye*
After you once asked
"What is Linford's
Lunchbox?"
In a libel case about
The famous athlete,
Linford Christie,
Now age 96.

You have now
Gone to stand
Before the
Greatest Judge of All.

Let us hope
He is as forgiving
And, indeed, merciful
As you were to
The Editor of this
Publication when you
Once wisely dismissed
A contempt of court
Action against him
Brought by the
Attorney General,
Who was hoping
For a two-year sentence.

E.J. Thribb (£17½ thousand
fine after the case went to
the Court of Appeal)

Call The Midwife 2024

CLARKE SLAMMED BY LANGSTAFF REPORT

I don't know why there's so much bad blood

NHS BLOOD INFECTION COMPENSATION

How it works

1970 The first of an estimated 30,000 people gets infected, thanks to contaminated blood products.

2024 ITV announces plans for TV drama about the scandal.

2024 Government decides compensation may be due.

WASHED-UP BRITAIN

DIRTY BEACHES

Watch out! The turd's coming in!

FILTHY RIVERS

I've found traces of water in the sewage

PUTRID LAKES

Oh no, it's all gone pee green!

Now we're toilet ducks

TOXIC TAPS

What are we doing about the parasites?

Paying them dividends

The Lake Poets Revisited

Number 94. **William Turdsworth**

I wandered lonely as a cloud
That floats on high o'er Windermere,
When all at once I saw a crowd,
A host, of turds and diarrhoea,
Inside the lake, beneath the trees,
Festering and stinking in the breeze.

Continuous in a stream of slime
And tinkle in a murky way,
They stretched in never-ending line
Like a giant litter tray:
Ten thousand saw I at a glance,
Bobbing their heads in shitely dance.
(That's quite enough excremental verses, Ed.)

NEXT WEEK: Lakeland Authors Revisited. The World of Beatrix Potty featuring The Plopsy Bunnies, Jemima Puddle-Muck, and Mr Jeremy Shitter. *(You're all fired, Ed.)*

"I see that Mr Ef57xyk across the way has got a fancy new personalised number plate"

NIGERIAN SCAM EXPOSED
by CON TRICK
Our International Staff

A COUPLE posing as members of the UK royal family have pulled off an extraordinary fraud on the people of Nigeria.

Said one furious Nigerian general, "I should have known it was too good to be true when I was sent an email offering me a free royal visit – all I needed to do was send my bank details to the Archewell Foundation in Montecito."

He continued, "I feel so stupid now! The silly names and all the typos should have been a giveaway, but instead I found myself hosting 'Prince' Harry and 'The Duchess of Sussex' on an extensive tour of Nigeria."

Said another senior Nigerian politician, "You'd think we'd be better at spotting this kind of scam, but they were so convincing. She even claimed to be part Nigerian. And he said he was a charity worker. I feel such a fool."

The couple had planned the hoax meticulously, with the female accomplice wearing a variety of African-themed outfits as if she were an actual royal, whilst the man calling himself "Harry" wandered round schools and factories asking "what do you do?" and "have you come far?" with well-rehearsed authenticity.

Meanwhile, the head of a Nigerian bank said, "May this be a warning to anyone who is approached by this couple, offering Netflix documentaries, podcasts or organic jam. You will be left seriously out of pocket."

If you receive any suspicious messages offering you a royal tour of your country, contact Interpol at once.

SHOULD THIS SAD DAMAGED LUNATIC HAVE BEEN ALLOWED ON TV?

by Our Media Staff
Donny Dunn-Interviewing

IT'S the question that everyone is asking, after a clearly unhinged celebrity stalker appeared on You Tube Uncensored with a Scottish lawyer called Fiona.

The troubled "Piers", who looked shifty and unconvincing, has a record of pursuing famous people and bombarding them with requests to appear on his show.

Fiona revealed that "Piers" had hounded her relentlessly, offering her £250 just to talk to him.

Said Fiona, "He is obviously desperate and, to be honest, I felt sorry for him. He seems normal at first, but you soon find out that you can't trust anything he says. Hopefully, after this he will leave me alone and get the help he so desperately needs."

"Piers", however, denied that he was a threat to society and claimed that he had done nothing wrong and certainly had never been to prison, which may be technically true, but we all know he should have (continued p94)

Calls to stalkers' hotline increase

BRITAIN'S stalkers' hotline has reported a 300 percent rise in the number of calls from stand-up comedians with a show on at Edinburgh, in the wake of Netflix's Baby Reindeer.

"I can't believe what 'Martha' and her stalking has done for Richard Gadd," said one stand-up, desperately scanning the room in the pub where he's performing, in the hope of seeing someone slightly unhinged.

"He used to be playing the same crappy rooms as me, but now he's in Hollywood being feted by the studios after the show's success. So what's the point of even doing an Edinburgh show this year if you don't have a stalker onboard?"

The stalker hotline said it would do what it could, but there simply weren't enough obsessional females to match the demand from all the stand-ups performing in Edinburgh hoping to hit the bigtime with a Martha of their own.

THE SUNDAY TIMES

2024 RISHI LIST

The definitive guide to wealth in Britain

1. Mrs Sunak.
2. Her husband.
3. The King.
4. Er..
5. That's it.

You look like a million dollars!

Is that all? How rude!

MORTGAGES TO BECOME MERELY 'RUINOUS'

by Our Housing Correspondent
Halle Fax

THERE was joy amongst Britain's young would-be housebuyers today at the incredible news that mortgage rates are about to be slashed from their previous "life-threatening" status to just "totally unaffordable".

Amazing new deals are on offer where, instead of selling both kidneys to afford your monthly payments, you only have to sell one and a half.

"This represents a 25 percent drop in kidney expenditure," said one delighted young couple with a small child living in a ninth-floor, one-bedroom studio flat covered in cladding.

Another couple, who had been paying an arm and a leg, were offered a new deal where

A happy young couple looking at their enormous rate cut

they only had to pay a hand and a foot, so they will able to treat themselves to "eating food almost every day this year".

A leading mortgage broker reported that, "This is tremendous news, particularly for the major banks and building societies who were very worried about the monthly repayments, but are now confident these rate cuts will leave them very nearly as rich as before."

"We have a rule: no dinner table at the phones..."

Daily Mail, Friday, May 10, 2024

SURPRISING REASONS* OLIVE OIL NOW COSTS MORE THAN A DECENT BOTTLE OF WINE

*They're not surprising. It's climate change.

A LIST OF THINGS YOU SHOULD BOYCOTT BECAUSE THEY INVOLVE FOSSIL FUELS

- Hay Festival (takes money from Baillie Gifford)
- Edinburgh Festival (ditto)
- Your phone (made of minerals and chemicals)
- Your house (requires heating with gas or possibly electricity, but either is bad)
- Your car (burns petrol)
- Your electric car (made in a factory)
- Your clothes (made of cloth, disgraceful)
- All food (has to be grown, taking up valuable space that could be used by nature)
- Any oxygen (you breathe out carbon dioxide, you disgusting climate terrorist)

TV HIGHLIGHTS

University Challenge

It's fingers on buzzers as Amol Rajan asks the young students the tough Starter for Ten question – "Are you a real protestor or are you using the situation in Gaza to vent your antisemitic feelings?"

Tonight, it's Cambridge College, Oxford vs Oxford College, Cambridge to see who will reach the protest finals against the winner of University College London vs London's College University.

Don't miss the Good Luck Gonk dressed in a Palestinian keffiyeh belonging to team captain and radical student revolutionary Tarquin St John Norrington-Table.

And watch out for the question to the brilliant Chinese mathematician Hu Yu: "Are you spying on your fellow students for the Chinese security services?"

"Lawks, my lord, methinks I am three weeks late with my monthlies"

"Zounds and God's teeth"

Period drama

SEX EDUCATION LATEST

THOSE new official government guidelines. What your child will be allowed to learn when they reach the age of 9:

1 Mummy and Daddy love each other very much.
2 They get married and make babies together.
3 Daddy becomes an MP.
4 Daddy texts photos of his genitals to various strangers.
5 Mummy sees story in the press.
6 Mummy doesn't love Daddy quite so much.
7 Daddy goes to jail.
8 Daddy's cell-mate loves Daddy very much.
9 Er…
10 That's it.

Innocence 'recaptured'

VOTERS welcomed the new sex education guidelines, saying this means a long overdue return to the innocence of childhood.

"Luckily, there's no possible way outside school for impressionable young minds to be exposed to sex, such as the internet," agreed everyone.

"As long as the internet doesn't exist to expose young children with unsupervised access to every imaginable sex act without context or explanation, limiting sex education in schools will work exactly as we envisaged, returning children to a world of Enid Blyton, the Famous Five and blissful innocence."

VAN GOGH'S SUNFLOWERS
chosen by Adrian Chiles

I've always liked a sunflower, me. They're not sissy, in fact just the opposite. They're big and robust and, well, manly. If a sunflower were to be a drinking receptacle, it would be a pint mug. If it were a shoe, it would be a trainer. I mean, you know where you are with sunflowers. And that's what Vincent Van Gogh captures so beautifully in this painting. He's telling us that though sunflowers may be a little more costly than lesser blooms, such as carnations and daffs, they last a long time and represent good value for money, particularly if purchased with the extra benefits of a Club Card. And who am I to argue with a genius? Nice one, Vince.

VERMEER'S A YOUNG WOMAN STANDING AT A VIRGINAL
chosen by Meghan, Duchess of Sussex

Let us salute this young woman as she proudly stands as a cultural advocate for mental health, family care, and gender equity. And let us support her in her wish to be a cultural catalyst for positive change, reflecting her core belief that representation matters, and that communities can be enhanced through learning, healing and inspirational support. What Vermeer is telling us is to follow our dreams, to reach out and transform the world through brand recognition, a testament to the power of international solidarity, the resilience of the human spirit and the enduring bonds forged through shared challenges and triumphs. Thank you so much.

SEURAT'S BATHERS AT ASNIÈRES
chosen by Winifred Robinson from Radio 4's You and Yours

Andy Pandrew from Dudley texts to say that, despite numerous complaints, the relevant authorities at Asnières have still not installed barriers and No Bathing Permitted signs to prevent a tragedy happening at that bend in the river, while Ms P. Droning from Padstock writes to thank the painter for drawing attention to the

DIARY
THE NATIONAL GALLERY AT 200: MY FAVOURITE PAINTING

visible lack of suncream and goes on to urge the government to invest more money in vital skin cancer research, and Patricia Dullard from Bickering says it's high time the water companies did more to prevent the spread of raw sewage in our rivers and waterways, so thanks for that, and tomorrow we'll be looking at the severe overcrowding problem in Gossaert's Adoration of the Kings.

CONSTABLE'S THE HAY WAIN
chosen by Jeremy Clarkson

Call that a farm cart? You must be joking! I'm sorry, but I've encountered better carts down my local dump, lying between a defunct Breville toaster and a crusty old pile of dog-eared Reader's Digests! Mind you, that's a nice bit of hay they've got there. Only trouble is, it'll get sopping wet if the cart hits a stone and its front wheel falls off! But I'd guess what Constable was trying to do was alert the farmer to the very real dangers of putting all his hay in one singularly crappy cart. And for that – if for nothing else – the bloke should be applauded.

STUBBS' WHISTLEJACKET
chosen by Dr Naomi Wolf

Let's be clear. That horse knows something we don't know. And why don't we know it? Because they don't want us to know it. Why is this animal rearing in fear and horror and panic? Like so many of us, he has just awoken to the reality that a war is being launched on us by big tech, pharma, the iniquitous Biden administration, without our knowing it. As a Rhodes Scholar, and author of eight global bestselling non-fiction books with a DPhil from Oxford University, I consider it my duty to alert the world to the cause of Whistlejacket's utter terror. Let us not be distracted. That innocent horse is being held captive on a canvas by the

National Gallery wing of the UK government. And you still need to ask why it is terrified? *Really?*

EVA GONZALES' THE FULL-LENGTH MIRROR
chosen by Jonathan Jones, art critic, The Guardian

A woman contemplates herself in a tall mirror. What is she thinking? She's thinking about the role of women in an avowedly patriarchal society and the way in which post-industrial, post-imperial Western civilisation seeks to enslave women and the wider LGBTQ community. The more I listen to this painting, the more I hear pre-echoes of Tracey Emin in her ceaseless search for a reality beyond reality, a home beyond a home, a mirror beyond a mirror. And the questions she asks remain vital. What do you mean? What do they mean? And – most important of all – what do I mean?

GAINSBOROUGH'S MR AND MRS ANDREWS
chosen by Lord Julian Fellowes

A gentleman never holds his gun under his right arm when the sun is in the east. A lady never wears blue silk in summer. Sadly *les nouveaux riches* will never get it right, however much money they may have at their disposal! And that's the message that Thomas Gainsborough conveys here with such considerable aplomb.

TURNER'S THE FIGHTING TEMERAIRE
chosen by The Rt Hon Liz Truss MP

The Temeraire is a world-class ship, sassy and modern and raring to go, and here she is, being encouraged back into service by this trusty little tug that represents millions of ordinary, decent working people who are sick to death of our woke liberal elite. This painting has so much to tell us about the current state of this country, it really could have been painted by me yesterday.

As told to
CRAIG BROWN

RAP STAR APOLOGISES OVER CCTV ASSAULT FOOTAGE

I truly regret what I diddy

"Don't worry – my husband likes his poached eggs runny"

STRICTLY'S GIOVANNI DENIES THREATENING BEHAVIOUR

I refute all cha-cha-charges

This is a funny-looking helicopter

Flying start, Rishi!

We were going to throw Diane Abbott under it

Next stop, Chessington World of Adventures!

Shock as liar in liar case calls key witness 'a liar'

by Our U.S. Legal Staff
Verity Lacking

AS the case of Liar vs The State of New Dworkin entered its 94th day, observers gasped when the prosecution produced its star witness, President Trump's former liar *(surely "lawyer"? Ed.)*.

The liar's testimony included claims that President Trump had lied and then had lied about telling the witness to lie on his behalf.

But the former president hit back at the liar, saying, "This liar is a proven lawyer." *(Is this right? Ed.)* "Everything he says is a lie, including his claim that I am a liar."

At one point, the judge had to intervene to stop the two liars shouting abuse at each other, including chants of "Liar, Liar, Your Briefs are on Fire!!"

It is now down to the jury to decide which of the liars to believe – the one who tells lies or the other one? The case continues.
(Rotters)

WHAT COULD HAPPEN IF ROYAL MAIL IS SOLD TO CZECH BILLIONAIRE

1. Restricted deliveries
2. Focus on parcels instead of letters
3. Everything arrives late
4. Terrible morale among workforce
5. Huge price hikes across the board
6. Overpaid management take huge bonuses

7. Er...
8. Er...
(Think of something that isn't happening already, you idiot. Ed.)
9. Postman Pat renamed Postman Pavel, Jess turned into black and white cat goulash.
(That's enough. Ed.)

OLD POEMS REVISITED

Here comes the takeover crossing the border,

Bringing the Czech and the postal order...

SIR EDWARD DAVEY
An Apology

ON THE cover of the latest issue of Private Eye (*see above*) we committed a grievous error, depicting the highly respected leader of the Liberal Democrat party, Sir Edward Davey, posing in front of his campaign battle bus, announcing that his next stop was "Chessington World of Adventures". We now realise this was completely erroneous and an appalling misrepresentation of the truth. Ed Davey's next destination was, in fact, Thorpe Park.

We apologise for any offence caused by the error and have paid a substantial amount of money to Sir Edward, which we trust will cover the entrance fee for Nemesis Reborn at Alton Towers.

Mickey Mouse degree shock

by Our Education Staff
Una Versity (formerly **Polly Technic**)

THE celebrated cartoon rodent Mickey Mouse today hit out at university courses which he described as "pointless, silly and of no value in the real world".

Mr Mouse was particularly scornful of a course that he described disparagingly as "PPE at Oxford". He explained that the course purported to teach students the rudiments of Politics, Philosophy and Economics, but it in fact did nothing of the sort.

He said, "A brief survey of recent graduates makes it clear that PPE is a course cynically designed to attract students of the lowest possible abilities, and prepare them for nothing more than running the highest offices of the land." He cited examples such as Rishi Sunak, Matt Hancock, Jeremy Hunt, David "Lord" Cameron and, most notoriously, Liz "49 days" Truss.

"I'm not making this up," he squeaked, becoming increasingly animated. "These people were allowed to do this joke degree, which left them utterly unqualified to do anything worthwhile.

"It is time for Oxford to scrap PPE and replace it with something sensible like a study of the classics, ie Steamboat Willie, Bambi, and Dumbo (the story of the high-flying student elephant who read PPE at Oxford and then crashed the economy)."

Thames complains about Brand baptism

THE RIVER THAMES has issued a formal complaint about the release of Russell Brand into its waters.

Said a spokesman for Britain's leading river, Old Father Thames, "It is a disgrace that the river is to be polluted by this online guru and former TV personality. It is well known that Brand is full of shit and discharging effluent of this nature into our already polluted waters is unforgiveable – even if you are being baptised."

Another river expert Mr E. Coli, said, "I hope that the river isn't going to catch something nasty from Brand, who is widely recognised as toxic and poisonous and has been proved in the past to make people sick."

(Reuturds)

Hi, guys! Is anyone there?

James Forsyth
Sorry, boss, I'm afraid most of the team are too busy for a group chat at the moment, trying to save their seats.

I expect they're thrilled. My brilliant political ambush has taken everyone by surprise!

Jeremy Hunt
Yes, especially us. What were you thinking of?

The timing is perfect. Me and Ollie got together and cooked it up between the two of us. The economy's turned the corner. The weather's terrible, so not many small boats. And England are favourites to win the Euros.

Penny Mordaunt
The only drawback is we're 22 points behind in the polls.

The important thing is we've hit the ground running.

Michael Gove
Cheerio! I'm running away.

Andrea Leadsom
Me too!

Lucy Allen
Me too!

Who are you?

James Forsyth
Doesn't matter anymore, boss.

Lucy Allen
Vote Reform! Lee Anderthal is a great bloke! Richard Tice is really nice. Nigel Farage tells it like it is.

We don't need your support, we're better off without you.

James Forsyth
To be honest, boss, we need everyone we can get.

Hundreds of people have left the group and have joined LinkedIn/Grindr in order to send out their CVs/genital selfies.

James Forsyth
We've got to stop this flood of deserters. And here to help us is the Aussie election wizard, Isaac Levido.

Isaac Levido
G'day Pommie bastards! I'm here to help you losers win! Listen up, drongos. The wrinklies are the key. Keep the old-timers sweet and you're halfway to Waltzing Matilda with your swagman in a wallaby's billabong.

That's the kind of informed local knowledge that's going to see us pull off the biggest surprise in election history!

Isaac Levido
So, here's what I'm proposing. National Service. They're too old to do it and they're sick of their sponging grandkids.

Done!

Isaac Levido
Bribe the old buggers with a Quadruple Pension Lock Plus One.

Done!

Oliver Dowden
Hanging? 😬

Isaac Levido
That's scheduled for Week 6! We've got to build up to the big bang. Any ideas you drongos?

James Forsyth
We've done some focus groups in the care homes and they told us what they want.

Oliver Dowden
Is it to go to the toilet? 😀 ✌

James Forsyth
No. Well, yes, but... the list is as follows: corporal punishment in schools; local bobbies to give hooligans a clip round the ear; free Werther's Originals for the over-70s; Black and White Minstrels back on the BBC; no more smartphones – landlines only; National Chimney Service for the Under-10s; rickets; whooping cough.

Victoria Atkins
That one's already back.

James Forsyth
But what our silver voters really want is for Enid not to win at the bingo again, as she is suspected of cheating in order to get the prize bottle of sherry.

Isaac Levido
You sure about the last one, mate?

Oliver Dowden
At least it's something we can deliver!

James Forsyth
You haven't met Enid.

Isaac Levido
Strewth! I've got my work cut out here. Why don't we focus on sledging the oppo. Attack lines! What you got?

James, you know how back in the dormitory in Swots House at Winkychester, we used to come up with nicknames that would really make new bugs look stupid and put them in their place.

James Forsyth
Are you saying we need a devastating new nickname for Keir Starmer?

Yes, and I've got just the thing. Sleepy. Sleepy Starmer. Keir Sleepy. Sir Sleepy. Sir Sleepy Keir.

Isaac Levido
Can somebody book me a flight back to Sydney? Pronto!

No, it works. It's like Joe Biden. Sleepy Joe! He's never shaken that name off.

Penny Mordaunt
Though he did win the election.

Kemi Badenoch
And he is sleepy. Whereas Keir seems to be quite awake.

Oliver Dowden
A-woke, more like! 😀

Isaac Levido
Right, forget the policies and the nicknames, let's try something more basic. Photo ops.

Kemi Badenoch
We've done the Wet Tory in Washout Number 10 podium announcement... **Drowning Street**

Penny Mordaunt
Not to mention the Titanic election launch and the standing underneath the 'EXIT' sign. 🙃

Jeremy Hunt
Roll on the graveyard visit, the cliff-edge walk and the trip to the job centre.

Isaac Levido
That's the spirit, we can do this. Would you mind paying me my full fee, up front. Just in case. Australian dollars, not pounds, obviously.

Jeremy Hunt
No offence taken.

I've got to go, guys. Train to catch.

Oliver Dowden
The sleeper Starmer? 🤣 🤣

See, the nickname's working already! He's finished.

Oliver Dowden
The election's as good as won!

Oliver Dowden
For Starmer!
🤣 🤣 🤣

HELLO! Having fought the election for a week or so now, I've run into a bit of an unexpected problem!

I don't know if you're aware of this, but a few months ago I walked into this mysterious antique shop, and bought a rabbit's foot. And guess what happened?

The SNP meltdown, Rishi's wet election announcement, him going to the Titanic museum, Steve Baker going on holiday, Gove's retirement, Lucy Allen urging people to vote Reform, the Tory's tying themselves in knots over National Service, Angela Rayner's exoneration...

There's too much good luck happening and, quite frankly, it's making me nervous! I need a tiny bit of bad luck for variety, so I've had a word with the NEC to see if they can completely botch the question of Diane Abbott's suspension, just to make me look human!

Fingers crossed!

Sincerely, Keir

PS. Top election joke courtesy of the team, thanks guys!

Here's the joke...

Q: Does Keir Starmer want Diane Abbott to run?

A: Yes as far away as possible!

"Could you just bear it, Norman – without the grinning?"

K.J.Lamb

THAT SNAP ELECTION MP CANDIDATE SELECTION PROCESS IN FULL

1. What's your name?
2. Would you like to stand?
3. You're in!

The Eye's Controversial New Columnist

The columnist who is delighted that his stuffed toy has been selected as a Tory candidate

This week I am very angry about Labour's proposal to reduce the voting age to sixteen. This seems like an obvious case of electoral gerrymandering to me! Teenagers have a rather dodgy reputation of being nice, and caring about people, and allowing them to vote puts political parties who are mean, selfish and don't give a tinker's cuss about anybody but themselves at a severe disadvantage. This is unacceptable bias, so can I propose an alternative scheme? Allow citizens from eighteen months to four years old the vote, as that is when individuals are at their most selfish and self-obsessed. Then rescind the right to vote at five years old when they start to learn about sharing and being kind, and *(cont. p94)*

Notes&queries

What is 'frociaggine'?

We often hear the word frociaggine nowadays, particularly if we're listening to the Vatican podcast, "The Rest is Heresy". For some reason the national newspapers seem reluctant to tell us what it is. Perhaps your readers can enlighten us?
Teresa (Mother and Nun), Calcutta

● *Frociaggine* is a delicious Italian ice cream dessert, made in the colours of the national flag, using the flavours pistachio, vanilla and strawberry. It was said to be Mussolini's favourite pudding and the reason why Il Duce found it so hard to keep off the pounds during the Second World War. Indeed, Hitler once teased him, calling him a roaring *frociaggine*-eater, which caused a major schism in the German-Italian axis leading up to the invasion of Sicily.
Francis (Saint and bird lover), Assisi

● I'm afraid poor Francis needs some Assisi-stance with his history. *Frociaggine* is of course, the 1967 Italian Eurovision Song Contest entry. Consisting of just the one nonsense word repeated 153 times, it was sung by celebrated bandana-wearing crooner Berlusconi Silvio, but came in a disappointing 29th. Silvio had more success ten years later with his memorable entry "Bunga Bunga", which featured the same word repeated 154 times. It came 28th, just ahead of Britain's entry by Lulu with the embarrassingly similar "Boom Bunga Bunga".
Tuck (Air-Fryer salesman), Sherwood

● What a lot of hot air from Air-Fryer Tuck, Frociaggine is, of course, the little-known Renaissance artist who painted the floor of the Sistine Chapel. This required years of work lying on his front. Sadly, his work was largely destroyed when Michaelangelo's scaffolding was wheeled in to paint the ceiling. Frociaggine lives on as the fifth teenage mutant ninja turtle – a character who never appears but is often spoken about by the other four famous amphibian pizza-eating martial arts exponents – Michaelgovio, Leonardo di Caprio, Raphael-Nadalo and Donatello-Versace.
Simon Templar (Saint), Granada

● *Frociaggine* is quite simply Italian slang for faggotry. It is used dismissively to describe the collection of faggots of wood for various domestic purposes, including burning heretics. It is not considered polite usage in ecclesiastical circles.
Alexander (Pope and critic), Twickenham

Next week:

● What is the riddle of the Czech Sphinx?
● Who or what is a Zendaya?
● Why on earth did Rishi Sunak call an early election?

Honours system brought into disrepute

by Our Honours Staff
Ivor Gong

THE King's birthday honours have shocked Whitehall by rewarding someone who fully deserves his knighthood.

The inclusion of sub-postmasters' and postmistresses' champion Alan Bates on the list has been described as a real slap in the face to the undeserving crooks and sleazeballs the honours system usually rewards.

Said one member of the House of Lords, "This man Bates isn't a racist who has donated millions to the Tory party, he isn't a former minister in a foreign government or even a disgraced ex-minister who happens to know where the bodies are buried." He concluded, "Why is he on the list?"

POPE IN GAY SLUR ROW

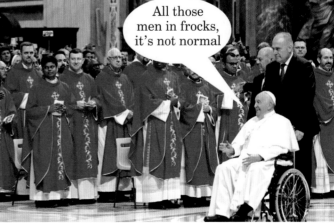

All those men in frocks, it's not normal

LADY PAMELA HICKS: ONE'S RULES FOR LIFE

Former Lady in Waiting to Queen Elizabeth II

ALWAYS DRESS APPROPRIATELY

These days, they all insist on wearing "jeans", even the Prime Minister, for heaven's sake. One never saw Winston in jeans. Nor poor old Clement Attlee, for that matter.

Heaven knows who Jean was. No one we knew. We once had a parlour maid called Jean. Common little thing. Goodness knows how many times we told her never to use the word serviette. But would she listen? Not for one moment. In the end, she got pregnant, so that was that.

Society used to have standards. We all knew how to dress for a picnic, for example. One wore one's picnic tiara, as distinct from one's luncheon or breakfast tiara. And one knew instinctively the right form of candelabra to place on the picnic table, and to select a location with a tree suitably broad for the picnic staff to hide behind, between courses.

But where are the standards nowadays? What's that dreadful expression the young insist on employing? That's it: "grab a sandwich". They're always "grabbing" sandwiches. We were taught never to grab anything, let alone a sandwich. These days, it's all rush, rush, rush. No one has time to relax any more. In my day, in the unlikely event that we would wish to watch the television, one's footman would allow at least two or three days for our "set" to "warm up" before we would sit down to watch it. These days, the young just switch it on, and watch-watch-watch. And no one enjoys anything because it's all so instant.

DON'T BE COMMON. UNLESS OF COURSE YOU ARE COMMON, IN WHICH CASE, DON'T GO ON ABOUT IT

Do you ever watch a programme called "EastEnders"? I find it dreadfully unconvincing. The Queen Mother used to dote on the East End, and would visit it like clockwork, once every forty years on the dot. In turn, the East Enders simply adored her, all those marvellous Pearly Kings and Queens, and the rag-and-bone men with their cheery grins and their little ukuleles and so forth and she used to delight in the way they would nip in and out of one another's houses, offering one another nutritious scraps.

Believe me, those cockneys knew how to make a single sausage last a month. And marvellous tap dancers they were, all of them, always making merry on their cobbled rooftops, their faces wonderfully dark and dusty from an honest day spent sweeping chimneys. But the producers of "EastEnders" simply refuse to film the real East End, the East End with which one is so familiar, just beyond Covent Garden. Instead, they import highly-trained foreign actors, who have never been near the place, and who insist on slamming doors, brawling, eating with their mouths open and growing completely hysterical when some elderly relative or other drops down dead.

I'm sorry to say I watched an "episode" a week or two ago in which one fellow hit another with his fist, saying "take that". No please or thank you. And he wasn't even wearing a suit and tie. Common, common, common.

MAINTAIN A KEEN SENSE OF FUN

No one has fun anymore. In my day, we were always in absolute fits. How well I remember a guest staying the weekend, and arriving into dinner wearing a tweed suit. Needless to say, everyone else was black tie! And – even more killing! – his wife wore a skirt! Can you beat it? We all simply ROARED with laughter.

As told to
CRAIG BROWN

FRANCE LIBERATED FROM FASCISTS

Merveilleux! In 80 years, we'll be free to vote them in again!

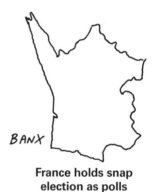

BANX

France holds snap election as polls favour Le Pen

POETRY CORNER

In Memoriam Donald Sutherland, legendary actor

So. Farewell
Then Donald Sutherland.

You got your break in
"The Dirty Dozen"
And then later
Starred as "Casanova",
Which was considerably
Dirtier.

"Don't Look Now" –
That's what Keith said
To his mum
During that scene
With Julie Christie,
Which was dirty,
But in an artistic way.

Keith also liked
You being dirty
With Jane Fonda
In "Klute" and
With Karen Allen
In "Animal House".
But didn't much like you
In Jane Austen's
"Pride and Prejudice",
In which you weren't
Dirty at all.

E.J. Thribb (rated 17½)

Porridge
Episode 69

(A prison cell: Godber is on the bottom bunk talking to Fletcher on the top bunk)

Godber: So, what are you in here for, Fletch?

Fletcher: The sex. There's more in here than in the Olympic Village, and that's saying something!

(Enter Miss Mackay, a prison warder, see pic)

Miss Mackay: Norman Stanley Fletcher, you're going down!

Fletcher: Blimey – see what I mean!

Godber: No wonder the prisons are so full.

Fletcher: It's three to a bed in solitary, and two of them warders!

Godber: You mean screws.

Fletcher: I certainly do. And those lines on the wall, they're not counting the days I've been here – I'll tell you that much.

Miss Mackay: You've been a very naughty boy. Fortunately, I've got some handcuffs here.

Fletcher: Great – am I going to be banged up again?

Miss Mackay: Are you a hardened criminal?

Fletcher: I am now!

Godber: Are you going straight, Fletch?

Fletcher: Course I am. Have you seen her?!

Godber: So you're going to be inside for some time...

Fletcher: Yeah – I'm never getting out!

Miss Mackay: Cheeky!

Godber: Beginning to regret I've got the bottom bonk...

Fletcher: You mean bunk.

Godber: No, I don't...

(Cont. 94 years...)

Cyclists should be allowed to go fast, says study

A NEW study has revealed that a majority of middle-aged men wearing Lycra think it's fine for cyclists to break the speed limit.

One of them, taking a break from uploading his latest circuit times to the Strava app, said, "If we're not going at 40 miles an hour in a 20 zone, there's a chance a car will catch up with us and hit us. It's for everyone's safety really."

"The fact is," said another middle-aged bloke with tight shorts, a loud clicky freewheel and special cycling socks costing more than £450, "We have to run the red lights so we can ensure the traffic system works better. If I don't go too fast then I might have to share a traffic lane with a car, and then I'll be forced to film them and upload footage to social media and feel self-righteous."

On other pages
Special form for cyclists to complain about this piece.

NEVER TOO OLD

A new love story by the Queen of Romantasy, Dame Sylvie Krin

THE STORY SO FAR:
Will it be fifth time lucky for the incurable romantic and billionaire media mogul Rupert Murdoch...?

THE Californian sun was setting over the beautiful Bel End hills as Rupert and his new wife Ivana Legova sat on the veranda of Rupert's Morgaga Vineyard, reflecting on the momentous events of their wedding day.

"Strewth, Ivana, that was one of the best weddings ever. And I've had a few in my time!"

"Ah, dahlink, you are such an old charmer."

"Too bloody right I am! It was a perfect bloody day and no one made a koala's arse of themselves."

The day had gone exceptionally smoothly, with a secret but glittering array of guests – so secret, in fact, that Rupert had no idea who any of them were.

However, the world's most powerful patriarch was pretty sure that none of his disappointing children had attended. James, Kendal, Lachlan, Roman, Shiv, Liz, Connor and all the others were notable by their absence. If they had appeared, there was sure to have been an ugly fight amongst the vines, as they battled to succeed him as head of Waystar Newscorpse.

Why couldn't they just accept that he had already chosen his successor – and he didn't mean Tom Wambsgams? No, his heir was to be the new Chairman Emeticus of Newstar Waycorpse – himself. And now he would be accompanied by his latest post-Soviet soulmate from the land of blinis and babooshkas.

"D'ya like the wine, my little Russian doll?" Rupert was secretly very proud of his viticultural achievements which meant his Morgaga vintages now rivalled those of the old established European houses.

"Yes, it is delicious, dahlink. It must be almost as old as you?"

"Fair dinkum," replied the nonagenarian oenophile from down under, taking a big slurp and burping in sophisticated appreciation. "Yip. You can keep your Château Neuf de Paperazzi and your Brigitte Bordeaux. This here is Rupe's Ripper Red. It's made from a blend of grapes which include Yessyrah and Malbeccabrooks, grown on our own Sarah vines."

Ivana looked on with the fascination of first love, as her new 93-year-old third husband spoke passionately about his wines with the energy of a man of 88.

"Our best white is Shitcreek Chardonnay, which is made from a wazzed up mix of Sauvignon Blanccheque and Riesling Mogg. If you've got a thirst on yer, it'll wet the whistle of a dry dingo in Goolagong Gulch!"

They sipped in the silence of mature mutual affection, as the happy corporate couple ruminated further on the big day.

Even the sudden arrival at the reception of the dragon lady Wendi Ding Dong herself had failed to chill the atmosphere. Now that she had negotiated her post-prenup divorce settlement, she had mellowed, and her banshee spirit no longer wailed at the injustice of her lot – and she had got a lot, thought Rupert. Still, in spite of all that had gone between them – especially the large cheques – it was Wendi who had brought the late-life lovebirds together. Rupert smiled as he recalled her banter with his blushing bride just before the civil ceremony.

"Conglatulations, Ivana. Fortune cookie smile on you!"

"Any advice, Wendi?" asked Legova, of the previous Mrs Murdoch – hopeful for hints on how to ensure a long and happy marriage.

"Don't leave note around house listing Tony Blair's assets like his good body, really

really good legs, piercing blue eyes and his butt. Bad mistake."

"Thank you, Wendi, I'll try to remember not to do that."

And then it had been time for the vows. As the cooing lovers had gazed into each other's eyes, they had repeated the sacred words they had written themselves:

"I take you, Ivana Legova, to be my lawfully wedded wife number five. For rich list or even richer list, in richness and in wealth, for as long as we both shall be loaded. Amen."

Being a thoroughly modern couple, Rupert had agreed that Ivana would not have to say that she would "love, honour and obey" him. In the 21st century, that only applied to British prime ministers.

Rupert's loyal factotum Witherow cleared the glasses and presented his master with a freshly ironed copy of the *Times* of London, containing a charming photograph of the happy couple sitting on a bench. It had been taken by legendary *Sun* photographer Arthur Sixpence, who had used a telephoto lens to get a blurred photo of the world's most powerful tycoon wearing some old trainers.

Rupert smiled in delight at the image. "I haven't been so happy since Charlotte Church sang at one of my previous weddings for free, before we turned her over and hacked her phone."

"I could listen to your sweet talk all night, but it is our wedding day and it is time to go to bed."

"You're right. It's nearly six o'clock and time for a nap. But before I toddle off, I've a surprise. It's my wedding present to you."

Ivana wondered what on earth it could be... diamonds, rubies, a yacht, a right-wing television channel?

"It's a state-of-the-art laboratory, complete with the latest in micro-biological technology. It'll be perfect for your scientific research."

She gasped, as he laid out the architect's plans.

"Thank you, dear Digger Dahlink. But what can I give to you?"

Rupert smiled.

"I was thinking of maybe... I dunno... eternal life?"

(To be continued...)

Right, guys! We're back on track! Literally! I've just been to Silverstone Formula 1 racing circuit for the manifesto launch. And I came out with my motoring zinger: "We've turned the corner"!

Hello? I said "We've turned the corner".

Oliver Dowden
Er, did anyone mention car crashes, wheels coming off, the pits, going round in circles, getting nowhere fast?

James Forsyth
No, the optics were great. It said British technological success. The future. High speed. Glamour!

Penny Mordaunt
It says helicopters, obscene wealth, foreigners, money from abroad, conspicuous consumption. Just saying.

James Forsyth
That's unfair, Penny. It was about Rishi, the Drivers' Champion! Boo to Ulez! Hooray for petrol!

Isaac Levido
It was a bloody disaster! But at least it took the attention away from the absolute shitshow of D-Day.

Oliver Dowden
Oh-oh! Don't mention the war! 😂😂😂

Lord Cameron
I thought it all went rather well.

Lord Cameron
All the world leaders, including Britain's most important politician were all present. Just not Rishi.

Kemi Badenoch
You are staying for the whole election campaign, aren't you, Rishi? You're not going to clear off early?

Grant Shapps
I'd like at this point to remember the fallen. All the MPs who are going to lose their seats. We should thank them for their sacrifice and their service.

I don't think that's appropriate from the Defence Secretary, Grant.

Grant Shapps
Am I the Defence Secretary?

Tom Tugendhat
Not for much longer.

Look, I spent a lot of time with the veterans. I spoke to the survivors, many of whom were injured.

Oliver Dowden
Did they shoot themselves in the foot, like you, Rishi? Hahahaha! No lack of respect! 😀

James Forsyth
OK, again, the optics weren't great, and really annoyed the only demographic who are going to vote for us.

Look, I've apologised. OK? It's time to move on.

Oliver Dowden
As you said when you scarpered from Normandy! 😀

Penny Mordaunt
At least it proved you're not keen on small boats crossing the channel. 😉 🚤

Lord Cameron
And, to be fair, it reinforced your position on Europe - ie, to get out of it as quickly as possible, even if it all blows up in your face and turns out to be the worst decision you've ever made.

James Forsyth
For God's sake, Lord Dave! This is an election – no one's allowed to mention Brexit! Not even Keir Starmer.

To be honest, there are times when I'm wondering if it was even a good idea to call this summer election.

Craig Williams MP
Don't say that, boss! It was a great idea. I've just won £500 at Ladbroke's. 💰 💰 💰

James Forsyth
You don't think betting on the election date when you're the Prime Minister's Parliamentary Private Secretary who's at all the planning meetings was a mistake?

Craig Williams MP
Yes – I should have put ten grand on it! And surely this is the kind of wealth creation that should be applauded?

Oliver Dowden
I wouldn't bet on it! 🤡 🤡 🤡

Isaac Levido
Shit, what level of PR fuck-up is this, on a scale of 0 to D-Day?

Jeremy Hunt
I'd say it's round about the level of deprivation during childhood.

Jeremy, good of you to join us. Where have you been?

Jeremy Hunt
I've been trying to save my seat. It's on a knife-edge.

Would you like me to come and visit?

Jeremy Hunt
NOOOOO!

POP ROYALTY LATEST

We Are Never Ever Getting Back ♪ Together ♫

Stop going on about you and Harry!

"...and are you still working from home?"

FOOTBALL FEVER GRIPS NATION!

They think it's all over

It is for me!

It's the knockout stage

♫ He's coming third, ♫ He's coming third, ♪ Rishi's coming third

SALUTE TO THE PARAS

by Our Election Correspondent **Paul Waugh-Time**

D-DAY veterans have praised the courage of Tory foot soldiers facing certain defeat being parachuted into safe seats.

"It was said that they were parachuted into a seat in the dead of night at a moment's notice. It had to be night so that no one in the local party would get wind of their presence. It took real courage to turn up the next day at the local Tory constituency office to tell the bemused party workers they were the candidates," said one 98-year-old veteran.

"We may have faced Germans with machine guns on the beach on D-Day, but they faced a retired civil servant called Alan and his wife Barbara holding a clipboard in a furious manner.

"The bravery of these men cannot be understated at the going down of the Tories in the latest opinion poll."

Green party accused of 'rowing back' on green policies

by Our Environmental Staff
Nat Zero

The Green Party has come under attack for its new direction in the lead-up to the 2024 election.

The leadership has announced a bold new strategy of "focusing less" on unpopular green policies and more on important issues of the day.

Instead of the traditional emphasis on climate change, renewable energy, species extinction, plastic pollution, overfishing, etc, the party is going to concentrate on the following key issues:

- Solidarity with Gaza, and in particular with the green bit in the Palestinian flag
- Solidarity with the trans community, particularly those in Palestine
- Some stuff about the NHS, tax, etc, but not too much
- Er...
- Did we mention Gaza?
- And gender identity?
- That's it.

10% OF REFORM CANDIDATES FACEBOOK FRIENDS WITH BRITISH FASCIST LEADER

Politically, we're centre-Reich

"My Tesla keeps giving me misinformation and veering to the far right"

When Reform and the Conservative Party merge later this year, what will the new party be called?

YOU DECIDE...

- **The Conform Party**
- The Retories
- **The Retirees**
- The Reservatives
- **The Conundrum and Unionist Party**
- The Conmen and U-turnists Party
- **The British Union of Faragists**
- The Anti-Woke Bloke Joke Party
- **The Swivel-Eyed Lunatic Fruitcake Alliance**
- The Retard Party
  (*You just can't say that nowadays. Ed.*)
- **And-that's-the-whole-problem-isn't-it Party**

EURO 2024

Four WAGs to watch in the tournament everyone's talking about

Hotsy Van Tottsy Dutch model with a degree in Lingerie Studies who has over a billion followers in the Daily Mail newsroom. Hotsy has got what it takes to go all the way to the front page.

Dani Air-Fryer Daughter of Danny Hair-Dryer, star of TV's Coronation Chicken Street. Dani has got what it takes to go all the way to the front page. (*You've done this. Ed.*)

Iris Phwoar Daughter of actor Jude Phwoar, star of The Talented Mr Ripped. Iris has been known to make footballers dribble, and should go all the way to the front page. (*I said, you've done this. Ed.*)

Fruiti Tutti Influencer and bikini magnate. Fruiti's start-up company Tops'n'Bots has made over a million pounds in the last minute whilst you've been reading this article. Fruiti should go all the way to the front page. (*You're fired! Ed.*)

JOY AS KATE RETURNS

by Our Royal Staff **Jenny Flect**

THERE was much cheering and joyous celebration in newsrooms throughout the land as the Princess of Wales made a welcome return to the front page.

"This is where she belongs," agreed all editors, "carrying out her royal duties of waving, smiling and selling newspapers."

Kate was attending the traditional Trooping of the Colour Photo, in which battalions of photographers parade outside Buckingham Palace to celebrate the King's birthday, and snap images of Prince Louis misbehaving on the balcony and being told off by his sister.

There was widespread relief that after a bleak few months, royal life was returning to normal.

Said one tabloid hack, "Now that Kate is happily back on the front pages, we can start speculating on the state of her marriage and whether she Photoshopped those pictures of her looking like Audrey Hepburn."

Added one paparazzo, "I was worried after all her health problems – particularly for myself. But seeing Kate today on the balcony made me feel much better. Three cheers for the Princess!"

TEN THINGS YOU DIDN'T KNOW ABOUT TAYLOR SWIFT

1 There are 94 billion sequins on every single Taylor Swift leotard, and if the sun is reflected off her outfit in the opening number, it produces a laser beam that can melt steel.

2 When her fans all shout "encore" at the same time, the resultant rush of wind reroutes El Niño to the North Pole and increases the Earth's temperature by 10 degrees.

3 The average resale price of a ticket to see Taylor Swift is more than the GDP of Lithuania, Swaziland and Great Britain combined.

4 If you lined up all her ex-boyfriends, it would start at John O'Groats and end up at Harry Styles.

5 Taylor Swift is the great-great-great-grand niece of Jonathan Swift, who inspired her latest album, "Tortured Poets Department".

6 Her parents met in 1984 and named their daughter "Taylor" after the British literary critic and Orwell biographer, DJ Taylor.

7 To avoid being mobbed by fans, Taylor Swift is smuggled into her British concerts in the same wheely suitcase that was used to take wine into Number 10 Downing Street.

8 Famous Swifties include The Pope, Ann Widdecombe and Ayatollah Seyyed Ali Hosseini Khamenei, The Supreme Leader of the Iranian Swiftomaniacs.

9 If you melted down all her gold discs, you'd be able to fill Fort Knox 20 times over or replace the fillings in the teeth of all the rappers on the infamous Muthafucka label.

10 Taylor Swift has filled up more column inches in newspapers than there are sequins on her leotard (*see 1, above*).

BOAT RACE POLLUTION DRAMA

A Doctor Writes

AS A famous doctor, I am often asked, "Are you sure going for a walk in this heat is a good idea?" (*That is enough. Ed.*)

© A Doctor

LORD SUMPTION WARNS HONG KONG IS BECOMING A TOTALITARIAN STATE

ON OTHER PAGES

■ Lord Sumption warns the Pope is a Catholic

■ Lord Sumption warns that bears are defecating in the woods

"No daughter of mine is going out in those ridiculous popular and supportive, yet ugly, sandals!"

POETRY CORNER

Lines inspired by the success of fellow Tortured Poet, Taylor Swift

So. Farewell
Then all my exes.

You have let me
Down and caused me
Much heartbreak.

Yes, I am talking about
You, Denise, who was on
My course before I
Dropped out.

And Sandra, who dumped
Me for Keith's friend,
Simon, who has a car.

And also that girl
On Hinge who never
Turned up and I had
To go and see Dune 2
On my own.

But silver linings...
At least my tragic
Love life has produced
Beautiful and, hopefully,
Best-selling poetry.

E.J. Swift (17½ billion anticipated copies sold)

DIARY

NADINE DORRIES: MY CURRENT CONCERNS

AGADOO: Like most ordinary, decent working-class people, I always enjoy dancing around the kitchen table – that's when I've been able to afford one – to the brilliant strains of "Agadoo" by the legendary Black Lace. Sad to say, their legendary lead singer Colin Gibb died the other day. When I heard the news, I cried myself to sleep.

"Agadoo-doo-doo, push pineapple, shake the tree." Sincere thanks, Colin, for leaving behind that tremendous message of hope for mankind.

BEHAVIOUR: Frankly, it is revolting behaviour, in anybody's book. What? Sorry, but if you need to ask, it's you who's the problem.

CHIMNEY SWEEPS: Whatever happened to child chimney sweeps? As a kid growing up in abject poverty in Liverpool, I was always happy to earn a couple of bob by shinning up chimneys seven days a week. I emerged sooty. But proud. Then the Woke Brigade put a stop to it – and what happened? Drug addiction. Inner-city riots. Soaring crime. Rocketing prices. Please – let's put a stop to this madness.

DENGUE FEVER: There's an epidemic of dengue fever sweeping the world, wreaking havoc. I've never succumbed to dengue – touch wood – but last week I felt a slight tickle in my throat. Through a mix of determination and working-class guts, I came through. But, truly, I fear for today's coddled millennials.

EARTHQUAKE: Little more than a month ago, I laddered an expensive pair of tights – and I'd only worn them once!

These things can happen in a second. One moment, you've got a pair of top-of-the-range designer tights. The next, they're split in two.

Which brings me to the recent earthquake in Indonesia. My heart breaks for those poor villagers. They come from nowhere, these sudden shocks – and they leave a tragic trail of devastation in their wake.

FRANCE: As a working-class girl who grew up in the direst poverty in Liverpool, I have every sympathy with President Macron of France. Even when you've climbed so high, as he and I both did, there's always this lingering fear of rejection. But happily, my last novel made the top ten. But what will Emmanuel have to fall back on?

HOLMES, EAMONN: My heart breaks for TV's Ruth and Eamonn. They'll both be left shattered by the heartbreak of their all-too-public bust-up. So, c'mon, guys – let's show them we care. They deserve our privacy and compassion. And then the healing can begin.

Mind you, Eamonn is behaving like a monster. How dare he let himself be "comforted" by a younger woman? My heart goes out to Ruth, bless her. But she's only ever been interested in one thing: Herself. Sorry, Ruth, but the "Me, Me, Me" mantra is no way to save a marriage. And that's a lesson she's about to learn to her tragic cost.

I: See "Me".

JOKE: Believe me, it's no joke.

KING CHARLES: I've heard on good authority that it was Michael Gove who planted that leaking pen on the King's desk – a heartless gesture, so soon after the death of his mother.

LORDS, HOUSE OF: There I was, thinking that sinister forces under the command of the left-leaning Establishment and MI5 could never stop me – a girl born into poverty in Liverpool – from reaching the House of Lords. But for once I was wrong.

ME: See "I".

PINDER, MIKE: Mike Pinder of the Moody Blues tragically left us in April. But the legacy he leaves is literally enormous. Whenever I hear "Nights in White Satin" I remember to change the sheets. Does Nadine sleep in white satin, I hear you ask? Sorry, guys – that would be telling!

QUEEN ELIZABETH II: Was our late Queen murdered by a shadowy cabal involving senior civil servants, high-powered Establishment Remainers, Michael Gove and an unnamed female member of the Labour shadow cabinet?

I have it on good authority that a slim woman with long red hair and a distinctive Stockport accent answering to the initials A. R. was apprehended on the Balmoral moors immediately after the death of Her Late Majesty. Apparently, there was a bottle marked "Poison" in her hands, but she denied all knowledge, and was let go by the powers-that-be. And to think she may be the Deputy PM in just a few weeks' time!

REMINDERS: In my book, reminders are always Stark.

SOUL, DAVID: Tragically, the immortal David Soul passed away in January. Like millions of others, I'll always remember him for his role as either Starsky or Hutch in TV's Starsky and Hutch, I forget which. And who can forget his immortal chart-topper "Don't give up on us, baby". Words that have just come back to haunt him.

TAYLOR SWIFT: As a veteran of many a Tory party conference, I know how hard it is to go onstage and wow thousands upon thousands of people. It's a talent given to only a handful. Yes, I'm one of the lucky ones – but keep at it, Taylor, and I have every confidence you'll get the success you're yearning for.

UKRAINE: My heart breaks for the people of Ukraine. What kind of insensitive, brutal monster could behave like this? Whenever I hear of the death and destruction Putin is wreaking, I think of myself growing up in Liverpool in the 1960s. Like the people of Ukraine, I'd be accosted by bullies in the street, jealous of the way I looked. But through sheer force of personality, I learnt to stand up to those thugs. A tough lesson for the embattled folk of Ukraine. But a lesson well worth learning.

WRIGHT, STEVE: Back in February, we were robbed of Radio 2's Steve Wright. Five months later, the Labour Party under Angela Rayner is set to seize control of our beloved nation. Coincidence?

XMAS: I'm literally sick to death of the way Xmas is dragged into everything, even in June! Give us a break, guys!

YO-YO: I keep trying to throw away my yo-yo. But it keeps coming back. Guess what? It was made in Europe.

ZERO, NET: Traffic chaos on the M4. A serial killer at large in Arkansas. Food bills at an all-time high. Eamonn and Ruth to divorce. XL bully dogs on the rampage. And yet still they're demanding Net Zero!

As told to
CRAIG BROWN

ECO CHAMBER...

ECO CHAMBER...

Can't see the trees for the wood

ECO CHAMBER...

Nursery Times

Friday, Once-upon-a-time

SEVEN-WAY DEBATE 'A TOTAL MESS'

by Our Election Staff **Julie Etchasketch**

VIEWERS of Nurseryland TV's controversial seven-way debate featuring each of the seven dwarves, with Snow White as the moderator, were furious at the confusing and unilluminating broadcast last night.

Said one critic, "They were all political pygmies. Only Snow White came over with any dignity. Doc just kept making ridiculous spending pledges about the NHS; Bashful refused to commit to any policies at all because he knows he's likely to win; Grumpy kept shouting over everyone saying the plan was working; Happy kept saying he was the real dwarf now and that he was really happy to be on television; Scotty and Welshy said that things were much better in their countries; and Davey was impossible to hear because he was on a bungee rope attached to the studio ceiling.

"It was even worse than the two-way debate between Tweedledum and Tweedledumber, who both refused to talk about tax rises or Brexit and just shouted at each other saying 'You're rattled!' and 'Contrariwise!'"

MR TICKLE ADMITS, 'YES, I WAS A BIT HANDSY, BUT I'VE LEARNED MY LESSON'

by Our Mister Men Staff **Roger Nobody**

POPULAR star of page and screen, Mr Tickle, has opened up movingly about his fall from grace, on the Mr Nosey Uncensored show.

Mr Tickle, star of the Usual Suspect, was found not guilty of inappropriate tickling by a court after allegations from young cartoon characters who wanted to get on in the business that he had exploited his power and his very long arms.

Mr Tickle said that from now on he would keep at arm's length (three metres) from anyone he was working with.

But, sadly, Mr Tickle now owes millions of pounds to his lawyers, Misters Greedy, Greedy and Greedy.

Mr Tickle has been forced to sell his Tickle House and is now in the awful situation for any cartoon character of being badly overdrawn.

"Would you take a delivery for next door?"

SLOB.

"Woo! Good evening, everybody, what a great crowd! How about some home rule for Ireland?"

THE ENGLAND FOOTBALL TEAM
An Apology from the fans

OVER the course of the match between England and Slovakia we may have given the impression that we thought the England team was shaming the whole nation, and that Gareth Southgate was a clueless moron who made the Wally With The Brolly look like Sir Alf Ramsey. Abusive comments such as "Sack Southgate Now", "Bellingham's a Bell End" and "Harry is a Kane in the Arse" possibly suggested we thought that this was the worst England performance we had ever seen – and, yes, that includes the defeat by the whale shaggers of Iceland.

However, in the light of Jude Bellingham scoring a miracle goal in the 95th minute, followed by Harry Kane heading us to victory in extra time, we now realise that none of the above criticisms and water bottles full of urine directed at the brilliant manager and fantastic players were in any way justified. What we actually meant to shout was "Come on, Sir Southgate", "Ring out the Bellinghams" and "Football's Kaning Home". We apologise unreservedly for any confusion that our previous abuse may have caused.   © **England Fans**

Euro 2024 errata

In our key background feature last week, 'Four WAGs to Watch', there were a number of errors which we would like to rectify.

Hotsy Van Tottsy
The Dutch model does not in fact have a degree in Lingerie Studies, having failed her thong thesis at the Red Light brick University of Amsterdam (she was given a grade of G – string). Moveover, it would appear that she may not actually be the girlfriend of England midfielder Jude Hey.

Fruiti Tutti
Influencer Ms Tutti is not in fact the wife of England defender Kyle Minogue and mother of his two children, but is in fact the girlfriend of Mr Minogue and mother of his other three children. They both attended the group game against Legovia, though most cameras were on his ex-wife and mother of four other children, and his ex-girlfriend and *(cont. p94)*

Polly Filla
Following a letter from her lawyers, Messrs Pout, Trout and Buttlift, we are happy to acknowledge that we should not have published an out-of-date picture of Ms Filla, which was taken a week before the championships. Since then, Ms Filla has had a successful trip to Turkey, and is now totally unrecognisable. We are happy to print her new face.

■ *We cannot apologise enough for these inaccuracies, but would say in our defence that our article was a lot more entertaining than England's performance in the group stage.*

OK, team, no surrender! That's the new slogan.

Grant Shapps
As Defence Secretary, I'm afraid that may be a little optimistic.

James Forsyth
And I'm not sure, to be honest, about the military wartime-style vibe of "no surrender". It's a bit D-Dayish, isn't it?

Oliver Dowden
No one's talking about D-Day anymore.

James Forsyth
Actually, boss. They're mostly talking about making bets on who's going to be named next in the big Tory betting scandal.

Grant Shapps
Yes, it is a bit embarrassing. Even for the party of entrepreneurial wealth creation!

Philip Davies
What's the problem, Grant? Didn't you get your bet on in time? I bet 8 thousand pounds on myself to lose. 💰 💰 💰

Oliver Dowden
Ooh, it's Phil 'Boots' Davies!!! 🤣 🤣 🤣

Fair enough, Philip, just a little flutter. No harm done. Besides you didn't bet on the election date like the others.

Penny Mordaunt
So how many exactly are implicated in this shockingly corrupt example of lack of "integrity, professionalism and accountability"? 😬

Not sure, but we must be able to find out. Let's ask our chief data officer.

James Forsyth
Er, he's on leave boss. He put rather a lot of bets on.

Oh. OK then, let's ask my trusted Parliamentary Private Secretary. He's got all the facts.

James Forsyth
Er, yes, one of those facts was the date of the election. Which he bet on.

Ah. Well, so long as no Cabinet Ministers were involved.

Alister Jack
Apart from me, obviously.

Who are you?

Alister Jack
Secretary of State for Scotland.

Penny Mordaunt
I wouldn't bet on it. 😉 😉

Alister Jack
Just a joke, everyone. It was only 20 quid.

Philip Davies
You idiot! You should have bunged ten grand on it.

Is ten grand a lot?

Philip Davies
Backing yourself to lose is only common sense.

Esther McVey
And Philip should know. He's married to me. And I'm the Minister for Common Sense.

Penny Mordaunt
Not for long. 😉 😉

That's defeatist talk, Penny, I'm not having any of that. "No surrender" is the slogan. It worked brilliantly for me in the final leaders' debate.

James Forsyth
Yes boss, you got really tetchy!

I DID NOT GET TETCHY!

James Forsyth
I meant "impassioned, forceful, committed".

Penny Mordaunt
But mainly tetchy.

WRONG, PENNY! Keir Starmer was useless and he had nothing to say on immigration.

Oliver Dowden
Yes, you didn't let him in!!! 😁 😁 😁 😁 I'm here all week!

Penny Mordaunt
I doubt it.

Look, Penny, just because you're going to lose your seat, doesn't mean we all are.

James Forsyth
Mm, actually boss, I've just looked at the latest poll.

Grant Shapps
Is it time to surrender? 🏳️ 🙇

NO, GRANT! I expect to see all of you back round the Cabinet table in a week's time.

Oliver Dowden
Why? Are they moving the table down to the Job Centre?

Everyone has left the group, though not voluntarily.

(Pompous fanfare, shots of Big Ben and video footage of party leaders awkwardly holding their wives' hands on the way to polling stations. Big Ben strikes the hour)

Clive Myrie: So, that's the exit poll. Labour have won. Good night.

Laura Kuenssberg: And good night from me.

(Viewers wake up to realise that they have fallen asleep in their chairs and been dreaming – and that sadly there are still hours to go)

Clive Myrie *(sucks on biro authoritatively)*: So, in case you've just woken up, we're still waiting for the first result, which is a close-fought contest between Sunderland and Blyth as to who can count their votes quickest and get on television first. How's it going, Naga and Sally?

(Cut to split-screen of Naga Munchetty and Sally Nugent in different community halls, trying to look excited)

Naga and Sally: Why aren't we in the studio, instead of here, watching people run around with boxes as if the General Election was *It's A Knockout*?

Clive Myrie: Hahaha, thanks Sally and Naga. We'll be returning to you later.

(Viewers turn over to Channel 4)

Nadine Dorries: If only they'd brought back Boris, the Tories would have won by a landslide.

Alastair Campbell: You love him, don't you?

Nadine Dorries: Not as much as you love yourself!

Rory Stewart: Can I just make the potentially salient point that if Labour forms the new government, I would happily work for them, should they require the services of a distinguished, public-spirited...

Krishnan Guru-Murthy: Sorry to interrupt, Rory, we've got to go over to Cathy Newman who's asking the big question of the night: Why is she out in the rain while Emily Maitlis is in the studio?

(Shot of Cathy Newman under an umbrella)

Cathy Newman: Well, Krishnan, I think the answer's complex, but...

Krishnan Guru-Murthy: Got to interrupt you now, Cathy, as Carol Vorderman has something important to say about the level of the Tory defeat.

Carol Vorderman: Wahey!!! Whoop, whoop, whoop!!! *(blows raspberry)* Ner-ner-ner-ner-ner!

(Viewers switch back to BBC)

Laura Kuenssberg: Let's go over to a key constituency, Bellwether East, previously a red-wall marginal with a population of ex-Leave Remainers and popular Lib-Dem ex-Green disaffected voters who might well vote tactically for one of the main parties or possibly one of the pro-Gaza anti-Climate Change Gender Critical Animal Rights Independents.

Clive Myrie: Looks like it's gone Labour.

Laura Kuenssberg: Sorry, Clive, I have to interrupt that result to go over to Victoria Derbyshire who's standing outside Rishi Sunak's house. Hello, Victoria.

(Awkward silence, as delay on sound system leaves Victoria Derbyshire staring at camera, waiting to hear the words 'Hello, Victoria'. She suddenly nods vigorously)

Victoria Derbyshire: That's right, Clive. I'm standing outside Rishi Sunak's house. The lights are off. I think he's out.

Sir John Curtice: This is very much what the exit poll is suggesting.

Clive Myrie: Not yet, Sir John! We haven't cued you in yet.

Sir John Curtice: My shirt collar is outside my jacket but inside the margin of error for a TV boffin.

Clive Myrie: Thanks, Sir John, I have to interrupt you there to say that we've got an important result in from Bellwether East. Here it is. Oh no, here it isn't. We've missed it.

(Viewers turn over to ITV)

Tom Bradby: A spectacular result from Bellwether there.

Nicola Sturgeon: I think this result shows that the people of Bellwether are demanding Scottish independence.

Tom Bradby: Even though Bellwether is in the Home Counties?

(Sturgeon doesn't reply as she is staring aghast at SNP massacre on her laptop)

Tom Bradby: Well, a 27% swing away from the Tories in Bellwether and another Labour seat – what are your feelings, George, as a former Tory Chancellor, responsible for austerity?

George Osborne: Nothing to do with me!

Ed Balls: Loser!

George Osborne: Loser yourself! In 2015, if I recall.

Ed Balls: Yeah, but you haven't done *Strictly*!

Tom Bradby: Top podcast bants, boys!

(Viewers turn over to Channel 4)

Alastair Campbell: When I was running Labour everything was brilliant.

Rory Stewart: So what? My book's Number One in the bestseller list!

Emily Maitlis: Top podcast bants, boys! But not as good as on my podcast.

(Viewers switch reluctantly back to BBC)

Clive Myrie: We've just got the result in from the constituency of Safeseat & Solid which looks like it's going to be held. Dramatic scenes in Safeseat Leisure Centre, I gather, but I'm afraid we missed it, amongst all the excitement here in the studio.

Laura Kuenssberg: Well, that's another seat for Labour, who I suppose are doing quite well, as are the Lib-Dems, but let's talk about Reform instead...

Clive Myrie: Got to stop you there, Laura, as we go over to Victoria Derbyshire. Victoria, I gather you've got news of Rishi Sunak.

Victoria Derbyshire *(after a pause of 10 seconds)*: That's right, Laura, I'm here for the count.

Count Binface: Thank you very much, Victoria. My price cap on croissants has proved...

(Continues for many, many, many hours, with the result almost exactly as predicted at 10pm...)

UK ELECTION WORLD REACTS

Congratulations on your victory, Mr Churchill

Cheers, Nigel. Or should I say "Bots Up"!

KING GREETS NEW PM

Have you come far?

Yes, my father was a toolmaker

RATS IN SACK DISAGREE OVER BEST WAY FORWARD

by Our Conservative Party Reporter **Rodent Liddle**

A NUMBER of rats trapped together in a sack have held their first meeting to discuss how best to get out of their current predicament.

Some of the rats blame the others, whilst the other rats blame the ones who are blaming them. The only thing on which the rats can agree is that none of them is personally responsible for one of the worst rat crises in rodent history.

To add to the problem, there are also rats who avoided being in the sack, who are now commenting from outside the sack on what those inside the sack should be doing.

Said one rat, Suella Ratterman, "It's obvious. We need to concentrate on fighting the enemy, ie each other."

Another rat, Kemi Ratenoch,

disagreed, saying, "That's the kind of nonsense that got us into this sack in the first place. What we need is a period of calm, considered reflection, possibly as long as five seconds, and then we should really start digging our claws into each other and biting each other's heads off." *(Ratters)*

"My seat"

LOST

—PILBROW—

EXCLUSIVE TO ALL NEWSPAPERS
HOW TO SLEEP IN A HEATWAVE

1. Read this article. 2. Hey presto, you're asleep.

@Vilvisimo

"I'm guessing this is your first go at summary execution"

Tony Blair: 'AI is the way forward'

FOLLOWING Labour's resounding victory at the polls, former Prime Minister Tony Blair has given a major interview in which he has set out his vision for the future of Keir Starmer's Labour Party.

He told reporters, "I think AI should be at the heart of the new government. Particularly if it has the letters B and L in front and the letter R behind. Do I need to spell it out for you?"

● *This article was generated by ChatTB.*

"Now is the winter of our discotheque made Gloria Gaynor or possibly Donna Summer..."

Farage calls for new voting system

THE triumphant new Member of Parliament for Clacton today demanded a complete overhaul of the British electoral system.

After the Reform Party gained 14.3 percent of the popular vote but only five seats, Mr Farage insisted that the first past the post system was undemocratic, unrepresentative and, above all, unfair to him.

When asked whether he had an alternative in mind, he said, "Why can't we have a system more in line with the European Union? They know how to do this sort of thing. And now the UK has sovereignty, it's time

we learned from Brussels and implemented a similar electoral methodology.

"Anyone for a pint? Or I'm happy to have a litre – you get more beer that way. Same principle!"

Asked if there were any other voting systems which he would prefer, Mr Farage said he'd looked at a number around the world and had decided that he liked Vladimir Putin's system best, where the result is known before the election takes place.

He concluded, "Gotta go, my head's exploding!" *(Nutters)*

REFORM MPs ENTER PARLIAMENT

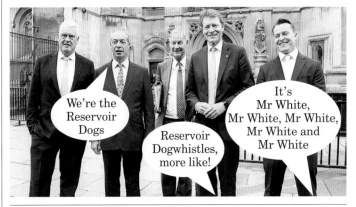

We're the Reservoir Dogs

Reservoir Dogwhistles, more like!

It's Mr White, Mr White, Mr White, Mr White and Mr White

EYE OUTAGE SOLUTIONS

What to do if you think your *Private Eye* magazine has crashed and you can no longer read it

1 Turn the light off and on again to check that it isn't nightime.
2 Check your Windows are working and you haven't got the blinds down.
3 Make sure you haven't got your copy upside down.
4 Try opening it and closing it again.
5 Make sure it's not the *Spectator* which is almost always crashing.
6 Remember that *Private Eye* is not available online and you are not affected by global outage problems.
7 Enjoy the fact you are reading it, even though you're in a departure lounge and your flight's been cancelled.
8 Er... that's IT.

This is it. We've taken over everything, including the Downing Street WhatsApp group. Welcome to you all.

👍22

We've won a reasonably historic landslide which is cause for some modest celebration, but now is not the time to crack open the champagne.

Angela Rayner
Why not?

Sue Gray
Because, as your Chief of Staff, I say so. And I've got a bit of history with investigating drink and Number 10. And it doesn't end well.

Yvette Cooper
It did for us! Thanks, Sue.

Morgan McSweeney
Actually, as your Head of Comms, I say no to champagne because it looks wrong tactically. Think about the optics.

Angela Rayner
I always do! How about mixing a Venom cocktail? A bottle of vodka, a bottle of Southern Comfort, 10 bottles of Blue WKD and a litre of orange juice! 🍹🍹🍹🍾🍾

Wes Streeting
As Health Secretary, can I applaud the orange juice, but express reservations about the number of units of alcohol, which could well put stress on our broken NHS. 🍾🍾🍾🚑

Angela Rayner
Put a sock in it, Wes! I'm Deputy Prime Minister, me, no one tells me what to do.

Sue Gray
Well, I do.

Morgan McSweeney
I think you'll find that's my job, Sue.

Sue Gray
Only if I tell you it is.

Thank you all for your input. I will be making the decisions.

Morgan McSweeney
But with assistance from me.

Sue Gray
But mainly from me.

Morgan McSweeney
Only if I say so. They don't call me Morgan Mclavelli for nothing.

Sue Gray
They don't call me Eminence Gray for nothing either.

Although this infighting demonstrates that we are finally fit for Government, it can get in the way of effective public administration. So, are all you new Ministers clear about your portfolios?

👍22

Emily Thornberry
Hiya! Sorry I'm late, I didn't get the invite.

That's correct, Emily, you didn't. And there's a reason for that, viz you didn't get a job either.

Emily Thornberry
But I've done three years as your shadow Attorney General! 😞

Yes, but now we have the serious business of Government to conduct, so I've appointed an Attorney General who's better qualified and who, as it happens, I used to work with. But I'd like to thank you for doing a very important job.

Morgan McSweeney
Yes, you've made Keir look ruthless.

Emily Thornberry
But we go way back, we were in Jeremy's shadow cabinet together.

Exactly. Bye!

Emily Thornberry has been ruthlessly removed from the group.

As I said, it's time for change and that can apply to anyone here. So if anyone's thinking of being disloyal, I suggest they think of our mission statement and 'Change' their minds.

Darren Jones
And talking of change, as Chief Secretary to the Treasury, can I say that 'change' is all that the Tories have left us to work with! 🤪

Rachel Reeves
The fiscal outlook is even worse than Mr Jones suggests and I am conducting a full and urgent review into the nation's finances.

Morgan McSweeney
And, spoiler alert, I can tell you now that you will conclude that it's all the Tories' fault.

David Lammy
Can I just intervene to say something important. Namely, thank you so much for making me Foreign Secretary, Prime Minister.

'Current' Foreign Secretary, David.

Morgan McSweeney
Good ruthlessness, PM. Makes me proud to be your Head of Comms!

'Current' Head of Comms.

David Lammy
Hahahaha! And can I add how brilliantly you performed at the NATO summit in Washington? So statesmanlike.

I had a fascinating conversation with President Biden. He told me that he'd spent a whole year mastering how to say Rashi Sanook and now he was struggling with how to pronounce Sirkya Stamma, which he imagined was another Indian name.

David Lammy
So I should prepare to deal with President Trump, then?

Definitely now he's been shot! Let's hope he's in shock and doesn't remember you calling him a 'neo-Nazi sympathising sociopath'.

David Lammy
But it's the truth!

We're in Government now, David.

Morgan McSweeney
Ruthlesswise, you're on 11 out of 10!

Rachel Reeves
Actually, I'm Number 11, the PM has always historically lived at Number 10. I think it's important for us to get these figures right, if we're to earn the trust of the public.

Morgan McSweeney
You're doing a great job too, Rachel – of making Keir look interesting.

Darren Jones
Speaking of numbers, there's so many new Labour MPs, I could barely get a seat in the Commons.

Wes Streeting
As Health Secretary, I had to wait on a trolley in the corridor. The NHS is broken, I tell you, and it's not our fault.

Louise Haigh
As Transport Secretary, I couldn't get a seat either and had to stand for hours, and that's not our fault either.

Shabana Mahmood
As Justice Secretary, I'd like to say that the crowded Labour benches were even more crowded than a crowded British prison. And that's not our fault either.

Morgan McSweeney
This is great! How long do you think we can get away with blaming everything on the Tories?

About 14 years?

The Doolally Torygraph

HONEYMOON OVER FOR STARMER

by Our Political Staff **Dee Feat**

THE LABOUR government promised so much, yet, after only a week, they have proved they are totally unfit for office.

Starmer vowed to hit the ground running, to transform our relationship with Europe – and above all he promised change. Yet Sunday night saw the same old crushing disappointment, as England failed to conquer Spain in the Euro final.

Starmer himself was there in Berlin, presiding over the lacklustre England performance, causing critics to question why a charisma-free leader, for whom there was little enthusiasm, was in charge, when we already had Gareth Southgate?

Said one pundit, my editor, "Starmer's time is up. He has to go. Some of his selections have been woeful – like Angela Rayner, stranded out on the far left, who looked isolated and forlorn. And his late substitution of Emily Thornberry smacked of desperation. It's time for a new manager – like Kemi Badenoch, who can inject some much needed aggression from the right."

THE DAILY LAMANCHAGRAPH
ENORMOUS ATTACK LAUNCHED ON WINDMILLS

by Our Energy Correspondent **Sir Vantes**

IN a welcome development, highly respected energy expert Don Quixote today launched a well-timed and effective attack on the hideous windmills springing up all over Spain.

Rejecting the ludicrous eco-argument that the mills are quite useful for grinding corn and a reasonable use of the wind which was going that way anyway, Quixote furiously got on his horse and charged at the nearest onshore wind turbine.

"These are a giant problem," said the Don, "and I am going to start tilting at them."

Quixote's feeble adviser, Sancho Panza, tried his best to dissuade the noble Don from his brave and important mission, insisting, "They're just windmills, stop making such a bloody fuss," but fortunately he failed and Quixote rode out on his high horse Rosinante, then fell off.

WELL I CAN'T BACKGROUND CHECK EVERY SINGLE DONOR!

Those amusing notes left on the desk by outgoing Conservative ministers to welcome their Labour replacements... in full

Treasury
There's no money left!

Department of Health
There are no hospital beds left!

Ministry of Justice
There are no vacant cells left!

Ministry of Housing
There are no houses left!

Ministry of Defence
There's no army left!

Department of Trade
There's no trade left!

Ministry of Culture
There's no music, theatre, arts left!

Department of Energy
There's no energy left – but that's just how we're feeling after 14 years!

(That's quite enough. Ed.)

BORIS MEMOIRS
Those alternative titles in full:

UNLEASHED
10 10 24

Unprincipled
Unrepentant
Untrue
Unbelievable
Unforgiven
Unfaithful
Undressed
Unzipped
Underpants

A Tank Driver writes

Vlad 'Mad' Putin, Tank No: ZZZZ

Every week a well-known tank driver gives his opinion on a matter of topical importance.

"What a glorious week for democracy, eh? Elections here, elections there, elections nearly everywhere! Everyone's free to vote. Particularly me – I vote in all of them! France was fun – I voted for the far right. And the far left. Anything to spread a bit of chaos. Not that those froggies need much help from me. I voted to get Judy Dench in the Garrick Club 'n' all. I voted in *The Traitors* of course – but that was a bit of a busman's holiday. Or rather tankman's! I did *Big Brother* as well, though, to be honest, in my opinion, evictions should happen from the top-floor window of the Big Brother House! Now that'd be proper entertainment! Tell you what, someone else I voted for was my old mate, Modi. He popped over from his gaffe in India to say "Ta very much." Very nice man. We swapped tips on how to crack down on your opponents. And their wives. Only kidding, Mrs Navalny! Sleep tight, hope the bugs don't bite – which let's face it, they're unlikely to do, as they're electronic listening devices. Gotta laugh, ain't you?... I can hear you and you're not laughing, Mrs Navalny. I'll tell you something that's no laughing matter – how the Ukrainians blew up their own children's hospital. What did they do that for? And then they point the finger at me. As if. That wasn't one of my missiles! Might have been a lookalike, but definitely not one of mine. Honestly, blowing up kiddywinks! Who do they think they are? Netanyahu?! Right, better get going. Got some more voting to do. Love Island. That Joey Essex, honestly! He really gives me the ick. He's got absolutely no morals at all."

© A tank driver 2024

NEVER TOO OLD

A summer short story from the pen of top romantic novelist **Dame Hedda Shoulders**

THE STORY SO FAR: Multi-billionaire media mogul Rupert Murdoch is newly married but beset by old worries about his various families and his all-important legacy. Now read on...

MORTY SHYSTER frowned, as he looked at the proposals of his long-term client regarding the future of the News Corpse empire. "I'm not sure Project Stitch-Up is a good name. How about Project Harmony?"

"Jeez, Morty, you're going softer than koala shit in the sunshine! Harmony, my arse! I don't want my useless snowflake libtard kids ruining everything I've achieved. They're living in a fantasy land. No, Kendall takes over and that's final!"

Morty took a deep breath and gazed around his plush office on the corner of 42nd and Sesame Street. Yes, he'd done well out of his client, but he really had to work for his money. "I agree, Lachlan should take over, as he best represents your political views. He's the one we should rally round..."

Rally... rally... rally... The word echoed in Rupert's head, as he fell into another reverie – or "nap," as his new wife Ivana Legova insisted on affectionately calling his regular power-dozes.

And there was Rupert in the huge crowd in the great city of Milkshakee, in Idunno, the so-called "Walnut State". He was right up at the front, in the VIP seats, cheering on the saviour of America, as Donald Trump launched into a devastating diatribe against Joe Biden.

"What a senile old fool! What kind of country wants an ancient doddery has-been in charge of anything? His family's a disgrace! He falls asleep in meetings!"

"Too bloody right!" Rupert joined in the cheering, but with a vague sense of unease. However, this moment of self-doubt passed as he remembered he was wearing his GAGA baseball cap, given to him by his adoring wife who told him it stood for "Get America Going Again". And what's more, he was wearing it in the latest youthful fashion, back-to-front, and, according to Ivana, looked like a man half his age, give or take a few decades.

"Too bloody right!" he repeated. Too bloody right, too bloody right...

"Who is?"

Rupert jolted awake and found himself back in Morty's office.

"Who's too bloody right?" the elderly lawyer gently asked his even more elderly client. "I thought none of the kids were right-wing enough?"

The legendary Monarch of Multimedia and Prince of Print regained his bearings and focused on the document in front of him. "Yes, Shiv's a bloody pinko, James is an eco-freako and the hopeless Connor's running for President."

Morty tried to inject a little realism into the discussion and reminded Rupert of his eldest daughter. "What about Prudence?"

"Prudence is for wimps! You don't get to the top of the dingo dungheap by acting prudently! You've gotta act like a bold bloody billabong waltzing his matilda in the bushman..." he trailed off in a way with which Morty had become all too familiar, as the American-Australian nonagenarian's mind retreated once again into the dimly remembered nostalgia of a golden past when young Rupe had been a thrusting jackeroo of all trades and soon-to-be master of Digger's Bum Creek.

"At least we don't have to concern ourselves with your two younger daughters by Ms Deng..."

"Logan and Roy? You see, I do know their names, Morty, whatever the Dragon Lady said during the divorce, when she took her share of the fortune cookies."

"Chloe and Grace are indeed out of the picture," the diplomatic attorney said carefully. "So, the family values Fux News Channel and the worldwide broadly conservative newspaper division will all go to Lachlan, in order that your unique global vision might be preserved in the unlikely event of your death."

Rupert smiled for the first time in the meeting. You had to hand it to Morty. He was on top of the detail and Rupert didn't have to explain everything twice, like he did when dictating leader columns to some of his editors.

"I've even got a headline for my British tabloid, the Sun, for when we kill off the other kids' legal challenge in the courts in Renal, Nevadaloca – 'Rampant Rupert Slaps Down His Uppity Kids And Hands The Reins To Loyal Lachlan!'"

"Great headline!" enthused Morty, "But could I suggest a perhaps snappier alternative? What about: 'It's The Son Wot Won It!'?"

Rupert's heart sank. He had to admit it, that was a ripping wowza from Morty! Even in his moment of triumph, the Titan of the Tabloids sensed that possibly, just possibly, his powers might be beginning to fade...

(To be continued...)

Clarkson's grand opening

IT WAS the event everyone had been waiting for. The moment when, despite several objections from local residents, pub owner Jeremy Clarkson finally opened his mouth.

Queues had been forming across the Cotswolds as fans eagerly waited to hear what Clarkson had to say. And he didn't disappoint. His announcement that he was barring Keir Starmer was standard publicity-grabbing fare, but then he proceeded to wow fans with his opinions about Meghan Markle, woke students, 20 mph speed-limits and cardigans.

Said one customer, "This place has everything a pub needs – the beer, the food, the bore."

CLARKSON'S PUB: THINGS NOT TO SAY

Where's our hot food?

Where's the punch we ordered?

This bill is a slap in the face

University of Neasden
(formerly the World Of Leather Polytechnic, North Circular)

Clearing news

We are delighted to announce that there are a few places (all of them) left in certain courses (all of them) which remain unfilled for the forthcoming academic year.

Students interested in, well, more or less any subject you care to name, are invited to apply to the Admissions Department as soon as possible. We are of course very strict about the qualifications required for entry, and we insist that candidates have a minimum of 2 GCSEs and £9,000 up front.

Neasden is an equal opportunities educational establishment, welcoming a diverse range of students, irrespective of gender, race, religion, sexual orientation or academic ability.

To quote the inclusive words of the University Vice-Chancellor, Sir Phil Coffers: "Everyone's money is welcome here!"

"We're very proud of Josh. He's the first member of the family not to go to university"

It's been a bit of an odd week for our Conspiracy Corner! In the light of the attempted assassination of Donald Trump, everything has been turned on its head. Normally, all our conspiracy theorists find a conspiracy behind the news. This week, they are all claiming that the events happened exactly as they appeared on the news!

MAGA435 says on his website:

"There are lots of crazy people with tinfoil hats who said that it wos staged. Wot a bunch of saddos!!! It was cleer to evryone that President Trump narrowly survived a compleetly reel assassinasion attempt and recovered like a tru hero, punching the air defiently like a bos."

TRUTH-IS-OUT-THERE agrees. He tweets:

"Normally I would claim this was all faked by the FBI and NASA on a soundstage in area 51, but on this occasion it was EXACTLY as it appeared, despite what the crazy people say! Apart (of course) from the bit where the republican assassin was being telepathically manipulated by Joe Biden using the X Men mind control device invented by Charles Xavier (see photo)."

On the other hand, we've got lots of people who usually mock conspiracy theories suddenly deciding there is a conspiracy after all! Alice Muesli from the New York Times has written in an article:

"I've always said that conspiracy theories were the preserve of right-wing cranks, but... did you see in the footage when they moved the photographers beforehand to get a better angle, just before the so-called 'assassination'? And one of the bodyguards smiling? Something doesn't add up!"

James Avocado, from the left-leaning podcast 'The Rest is Democrats' says:

"Did you see that tweet from two years ago predicting exactly what was going to happen? And are we to believe that the sniper conveniently hit the one part of the body that bleeds profusely without actually doing any harm? And are we really meant to believe that a man who'd been shot just went golfing the day after? Read more of this on my substack."

So there you have it!

The mystery continues...

SHOOTING WOUNDS PRESIDENT

Bang goes my re-election

Key support deserts Biden

IN another blow to his re-election hopes, one of Joe Biden's most trusted aids will no longer be beside him.

Said the Zimmer frame, "I've been through a lot with Joe, mainly doorways, corridors, and the aisle of Air Force One, but now I can no longer offer him my support.

"He's far too old for a Zimmer frame – he needs a mobility scooter. Or, better still, a bed on wheels."

Said Joe Biden, "That Zimmer frame doesn't know what it's talking about, er... Inflation? Um... Oh. We beat Medicare! Zzzimmer... Zzzzzz."

(Rotters)

TRUMP RALLY CROWD 'FRIGHTENED, ANGRY AND BEWILDERED'

And then the shooting began.

That Trump post-shooting speech in full

"I'm not supposed to be here. I'm supposed to be in jail. But God saved me. Just like he did on that famous day. I'll never forget where I was when President Trump was shot. Sleepy Joe – he doesn't remember. He doesn't know where he is. I was taking a bullet for democracy. But the bullet didn't want to kill me. It liked me. Sure, it hated me at first, but once it met me, it loved me! It just wanted to nibble my ear. And a little voice in my head, probably God, said "Donald Duck," and I did. And the bullet missed me. And killed someone else. Thank you, God. I knew you were a Republican. But I'm a changed man, and after my brush with death, I know my mission is to bring unity and peace to the United States. Unlike Crooked Joe. Everyone can see that an old rambling man who talks nonsense and often forgets what he's saying and even worse, often forgets what he's saying, yeah, everyone knows this demented old timer is entirely unfit for office. I mean, this guy would be the oldest president in the history of history. Fact! Do you want a guy in his eighties running the country? Of course you do! Vote Trump! Make America Gaga Again!! Put your cross on Trump. Not you, Mr Sniper Man on the roof! You're gonna miss anyway. I've got God on my side. And even if I had been shot dead, Doctor Lecter would have cured me.

GUN CRIME SHOCKS AMERICA

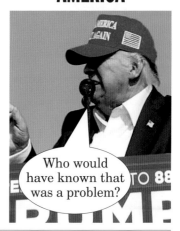

Who would have known that was a problem?

You guys know Hannibal Lecter? Great man! Great Doctor. Someone comes to see him and he says I'm having some beans for dinner with a friend. Great joke! Really bigly funny! And then the shark comes over from the electric boat and drinks bleach, and everyone's much better. You guys like sharks? I'm not afraid of sharks. I'm gonna build a wall of sharks to eat all those Mexican rapists and drug dealers and Muslims. And Muslim Mexican rapist drug dealers. They're the worst. Trust me. Now, where was I? Oh yeah – I was gonna announce my running mate. Ladies and Gentlemen, Senator Hannibal Lecter. Oh no! He's in prison. Unfair. If I'm elected, I'm gonna pardon him on day one, along with that guy in the buffalo horns who stormed the Capitol and tried to lynch Mike Pence. Good call! Bad man! Anyway, forget Pence, I got Vance! J.D. Vance! A Hillbilly boy from the Apache mountains in Ohio! Okay, so he once called me Hitler. Who hasn't? But now he loves me. And Vance has got a great new nickname for crooked Kamala. You know what it is? The Childless Cat Lady. Pretty funny. That's a childless lady, not a lady with a childless cat. Which wouldn't be funny at all. Lotta cat lovers out there. I like a bit of pussy myself! Feline Fact! Trump Truth! Vote Hitler! God bless Austria! *(cont. 94 hours)*

"He's a bit upset about Trump"

ENGLAND POST MORTEM

YES, I blame the players. Where was the energy? Where was the passion? Where was the commitment?

Harry Kane barely moved. It looked like he hadn't even got out of bed. All the foreigners run around the entire time and don't give up.

Where does this lazy English mentality come from? Where's the discipline? Where's the work ethic?

I was going to ask my mates at work, but we've all taken the day off to recover. I'm not getting out of bed today – it's just too depressing, isn't it? I mean… (*cont. 94 years of hurt*)

"We'll take five t-shirts"

WHO WASN'T WHO at this year's championships

Who were these people not in their corporate seats and not enjoying the tennis whilst thousands queued outside just to get into Court 94?

1. **Julian Hedgie-Ffunde**
2. Charlie Snorter
3. **Justin The Toilet**
4. Sofia de Benture
5. **Lolly Lotts**
6. Samantha Pimms-Tent
7. **Tabitha Strawberry-Punnet**
8. Simon Still-Lunching
9. **Toby Blotto**

(We get the idea. Ed.)

WIMBLEDON SALUTES WINNER TWO YEARS RUNNING

by Our Tennis Correspondent
Clare Ballgirl

FOR the second year running, Centre Court fans were thrilled to cheer on the triumphant new star of the tennis world – Kate, Princess of Wales.

Just like last year, she wowed the crowds by lifting up the hallowed trophy and giving it to some foreigner who'd won a match.

Said one fan, "Kate played a blinder. She showed off her full array of royal skills – from standing up to sitting down, from waving to smiling. No one will forget this matchless performance."

And the future for British royal tennis looks bright – with Princess Charlotte following in her mother's footsteps by displaying a wonderful forehand and backhand wave.

But can the British Number One Royal do it again next year?

"Yes," says everyone as… *(Cont. 2094)*

POETRY CORNER

Lines on the retirement of Jimmy Anderson, legendary England pace bowler

So. Farewell
Then Jimmy Anderson.

It's over.
And that's lunch.

E.J. Thribb
(17½ runs per wicket)

● Woah! That poem was really fast!

"It's High Street fashion"

The Kardashians
— VS —
The Rees-Moggs

Yes, it's the reality TV showdown of the Century (18th)!
HOW THEY LINE UP

Reality star	Out-of-touch-with-reality star
Sexy	Brexy
Silk suspenders	Sock suspenders
Silly kids' names	Pius, Boniface, Sixtus etc.
Pear-shaped	Made country go pear-shaped
Dad defended O.J. Simpson	Dad defended Mrs T
Lost Kanye West	Lost Somerset North
Reclines on sun lounger	Reclines on front bench
Top celebrity	Top hat
Huge arse	Huge arse

THE ✦ TIMES
—— OF LONDON —— Friday, 2 August, 1804

Fury over building plans

by Our Poetry Staff **Nimby Pimby** (pronouns He/Hymn)

Top poet William Blake is under attack from the Conservative party for his reckless plans to build Jerusalem on England's mountains green.

Said one prominent Tory, "This scheme, proposing a new city on an unspecified greenfield site somewhere in England, is an assault on everything we hold dear. It's all very idealistic, but those of us who live in perfectly agreeable dark satanic mills do not want our views ruined by a supposedly perfect new town called something silly."

Said another protestor, "What Mr Blake hasn't considered, with his dreamy and impractical proposal, is the increase in traffic of chariots of fire that comes with any new build."

He continued, "I shall not rest from mental fight, nor shall my sword sleep in my hand, till we have stopped them building Jerusalem on England's green and pleasant belt."

ED DAVEY – THOSE TERRIFYING WHITE KNUCKLE RIDES IN FULL

Adrenaline rush

Weeeeeeeee!

Nemesis inferno

Wooooooooo!

Post Office inquiry

Aaaaaaaaargh!

I'm afraid seven MPs can't be with us today, as they've been removed from the group by the administrator, aka me.

Morgan McSweeney
That's pretty ruthless, boss.

Correct. And if anyone doesn't like my ruthlessness, they're out.

Morgan McSweeney
Just like those seven political dwarfs!

Dopey, Grumpy, Lefty, Stroppy, Surly, Long-Bailey and Trotsky. 😂 😂 😂

Yvette Cooper
Some would say – not me, obviously – that it's overly ruthless not to give extra benefits to people with more than two children. Because it leaves the parents with no money.

Rachel Reeves
I sympathise with them, Yvette, because we haven't got any money either. I blame the Tories.

Darren Jones
If we had a pound for every time someone says "I blame the Tories", then we might be able to abolish the benefit cap! 😜 😜 😜

Rachel Reeves
Are you sure you've properly costed that, Chief Secretary to the Treasury?

There are going to be difficult decisions...

Pat McFadden
...ie do we boot out the Corbynistas now? Or next week?

Morgan McSweeney
Steady, Pat, you're sounding more ruthless than the boss. The optics on that are not so great.

Sue Grey
It could look like in-fighting.

Morgan McSweeney
No, it couldn't.

Sue Grey
Yes, it could.

Angela Rayner
As Deputy Prime Minister, I feel I should have been consulted about the in-fighting.

Sue Grey
No, you shouldn't.

Morgan McSweeney
Yes, she should.

Sue Grey
Morgan, if you keep arguing with me, I'll have to move your desk even further away from the Prime Minister's.

Morgan McSweeney
No, you won't.

Sue Grey
Right, that's it, your desk is going from next to the stationery cupboard to just outside the toilets.

Angela Rayner
Excuse me. I just feel I'm being sidelined.

Rachel, can we go back to what you were saying about the lack of money?

Rachel Reeves
Well, it's worse than that. We've got minus money. Thanks to the Tories.

Darren Jones
Kerching! Another pound in the kitty. Soon we'll be able to pay off the junior doctors!

Wes Streeting
The NHS is broken. That's another problem we've inherited.

Rachel Reeves
Thanks to the Tories.

Darren Jones
Kerchingeroony! 35% pay rise on its way! 💰 💰

Wes Streeting
Really?

Rachel Reeves
Don't be silly. We can't afford 35%. And we can't afford 5% for the teachers and nurses.

Can I just say my mother was a nurse?

Darren Jones
And your father? 😜

Watch it, Darren. I'm ruthless and I know how to wield the axe.

Darren Jones
A chopping tool of the type your father used to make?

Angela Rayner
Can I say I'm more working class than you, Keir, and you, Wes, and all the rest of you put together, but no one's asked me about this pay dispute. Are you ignoring me, Keir?

Rachel, I think it would be good to find that 5%, even if we haven't got it.

Rachel Reeves
But we HAVEN'T got it.

Darren Jones
Is there anyone you'd like to blame for that particular financial state of affairs? 😒 😒 😒

Rachel Reeves
I suppose we could say there is a major cost to NOT settling the dispute and that in strict accounting terms we may save money by giving lots away.

Pat McFadden
But that's just giving in to the leftie unions! What kind of Labour Government are we supposed to be?

A ruthless one. One that'll make tough decisions. Rachel, don't announce anything for a while and we'll see what happens.

Rachel Reeves
There is one announcement that I've got to make. The biscuits in Cabinet are too expensive.

Wes Streeting
Lighten up, Rachel. Next you'll be telling us to bring in our lunches in Tupperware boxes, like you!

Rachel Reeves
Not yet, though that's subject to review. But I'm talking biscuits today. And the OBR, the Office for Biscuit Responsibility, has made it clear that unfunded biscuits are unacceptable, so we're going to have to cut down on the chocolatey ones and there'll be a two-biscuit cap on each individual.

Darren Jones
That's not Nice! Like the biscuit. 😈 😈

Rachel Reeves
Actually Nice biscuits do fall within the acceptable fiscal parameters. As do Rich Tea.

Morgan McSweeney
Rich Tea? No, that's terrible brand association.

What about Jaffa Cakes? I like those!

David Lammy
Keir, as Foreign Secretary and expert on all things foreign, I should point out that Jaffa Cakes are named after the ancient Levantine port of Jaffa, now part of Tel-Aviv in Israel, making it a contentious choice of teatime comestible, which could lead to boycotts, rallies and chanting outside Downing Street.

Darren Jones
"From the river to the tea!" 😂 😂 😂

I apologise. I need to be ruthless about this. And so I am immediately withdrawing the whip from myself.

Angela Rayner
Does this mean I'm in charge?

Rachel, over to you.

OLYMPIC RAIN: STARMER COMES PREPARED

"Dull and wet?"

"I prefer decisive and ruthless"

"What an anorak!"

"He certainly is!"

Team GB favourite for Seine event

by Our Environmental Staff
Sue Widge

THE British athletes taking part in the Triathlon are hotly tipped for gold medals, thanks to their superior training facilities back in the UK.

Said the Team GB captain, "Our boys and girls will have no trouble taking a dip in the heavily polluted Seine, as they've been training for years in filthy British rivers.

"They will return home covered in glory, but not as much raw sewage as they would had they been in a British river."

He continued, "We are looking for a not-so-clean sweep, where we come in First, Second and Turd.

"We're going for Gold, Silver and Brown."

The Paris Triathlon consists of the 1.5 km swim, the 100m sprint to the toilet and, finally, the three-day runs.

World unites for amazing international fireworks

by Our International Correspondent
A. Pocalypse

THE world has taken great joy in its regular ritual of seeing an extraordinary firework display, as Israel, Hezbollah, Lebanon and Iran gear up for a month of remarkable athletic feats.

With a series of "oohs" and "aarghs", the people of the contested territories – even their children – were able to join in this display, which has united the whole world yet again in agreeing how horrific it is and that someone should stop it but they have no idea who that could be.

"It's a tradition as old as time," said one witness. "This is the proud continuation of a tradition that dates back nearly 3,000 years: namely, people in the Middle East mudering each other and then launching huge retaliatory strikes. These fireworks are simply the beginning of a great summer of slaughter."

....

On other pages

■ **Double-sided cancel-your-subscription-form, which you can use to complain about us mentioning either side in this conflict**

@Vilwisrimo

What You Missed
Olympics round-up

Clare Balding: So over to Tom and Bianca for the finals of the Freestyle Street Skateboarding at Montmartre's Superdrome des Dieux.

Tom: Oh. My. God, I don't believe it, the Finnish teenager has just nailed a nolly olly dolly with a fish-face sausage roll. That's a full 540! Incredible stuff!

Bianca: He's going for a hubble double voulez-vous followed by a treble flakie fakie with a full grinder. Oh, no – he's come off on the backside griddle grab. That is a catastrophe!

Tom: He was laying down such a great wheel boogie and then, whap! No, he's up again! This is unprecedented skateboarding history. The whole of Finland is holding its breath as he goes for the soggy bottom frontside with a dogger bank... YES! YES! YES!

Balding: Thanks, Tom and Bianca, we'll be back to the Superdrome for the Underwater BMX Sailing shortly, but first an exclusive interview with Britain's newest silver medalist.

Presenter: So you've spent the last four years training 24/7 for this one event, sacrificing a normal life with your family and friends, and eating a strict diet of nuts and watercress, and you've only come second. How do you feel?

Athlete: Er…

Presenter: You must be totally gutted. You must feel like weeping. And your entire family is here to witness you losing by two microseconds.

Has it all been pointless?

Athlete: Well... Er...

Presenter: But, hey. Let's get this in perspective. You won a silver medal at the Olympics. You must be so thrilled. You've done your country proud, not to mention your family who've all travelled over here to share this moment with you. Isn't that wonderful?

Athlete: Er...

Balding *(wiping tears from her eyes)*: What a moving interview there. We'll have another silver medalist along in a minute. But first, it's over to the Jacques Cousteau Centre de Diving for the Synchronised Men's Six-inch Springboard. We join our commentator, Willy Waving. Over to you, Willy!

Willy: And the first pair are Jean Baguette and Olivier LeCoq. They will be performing a double Budgie Smuggler with a difficulty rating of 6.9, which could create problems for the American boys, Hugh Japaratus and Larry Lunchbox, who made a big splash on entry after their attempt at a manoeuvre known as the Triple Double-entendre. It's certainly looking very tight. Very, very tight indeed. And the judges are pleased to see them, or maybe they've just got starting guns in their pockets. Back to you, Clare…

CONSPIRACY UPDATE

 French pole vaulter Anthony Ammirati failed to get into the final because his penis got in the way. Really?

MAGA435 has a few compelling thoughts on his substack:

"If he had been SIRCUMBSIZED he would have triumphed. This is obviously the work of George SOROS and the Zionist cabal to turn us all into JEWS so the chanses of us not doing well at poll-vaulting will be much less."

WHO-WATCHES-THE WATCHMEN-WATCHING-THE-WATCHMEN disagrees:

"I don't believe the Olympic opening ceremony ever ended. It just went viral. This is part of French propaganda, telling the world that all French Men have huge penises."

TRUTH-IS-OUT-THERE's Facebook page reads thusly:

"I believe his penis was actually an alien, housed inside a spaceship that looks like a Frenchman and he needed to raise his ship a certain distance off the ground to contact the invasion fleet. It's only a matter of hours before the sky will be black with hordes of penis-shaped monsters."

Here's hoping they invade in the winter, so they'll be much smaller! The mystery continues...

Daily Male

WHY DO FEMALE BEACH VOLLEYBALL PLAYERS HAVE TO WEAR THESE TINY BIKINIS?

IN AN outrageous display of outdated sexism, the chauvinists of the International Olympic Committee have yet again forced some of the world's most attractive women athletes into demeaning and inappropriate sportswear that bears no relation to the demands of the professional and exacting sporting endeavour in which they are engaged.

What can be the reason for this inexcusable misogynist travesty, when all any viewer wants to do is focus on the art of the ancient sport of beach volleyball, which dates all the way back to ancient Greece? We at the Daily Male want to know why these girls are forced to dress like this:

WE SAY: *STOP THIS EXPLOITATION NOW!*

ON OTHER PAGES

■ Hundreds more pics of the women's beach volleyball, plus one dull one of the blokes in shorts.

"...but unfortunately the judges have deducted points because the tattoos aren't synchronised"

New personal best achieved

■ Accounts Manager Helen from Stevenage, has described it as "the best day of her life" after she smashed her personal best for sprinting into the kitchen and back to the sofa during the cycling and fetching a cold drink in 10.34 seconds.

"I had my sights on breaking the world record set by my husband of 10.12 seconds during the Tokyo Olympics as he raced to get a plate of fried chicken, but I am overjoyed to have set a personal best."

Her husband, James, however, admitted to underperforming when he could only get from the sofa to the fridge and back in a time of 12.7 seconds during the second night of the gymnastics.

James put this down to a minor knee injury and eating three bags of Chilli Hot Doritos before falling asleep the previous evening while watching the skeet shooting and basketball.

Obesity epidemic 'linked to sport'

■ In what's being described as a major breakthrough, doctors say they've established a clear link between the UK's current obesity epidemic and sporting activity.

"Yes, it's sporting activity on the television that's making us all fat," said the doctor leading the study.

"There has been so much amazing sport on the TV – from the Euros, to Formula 1, to Wimbledon and now the Olympics, there's been little reason to leave the sofa, other than to walk to the front door to collect your latest junk-food order from Uber Eats.

"Unless we can put a stop to this incredible glut of sport, the obesity epidemic will only get worse, as people pile on the pounds, eating crisps, nachos and cheese dips while watching the men's kayak slalom and the women's 400m backstroke.

"Furthermore, as soon as the Olympics end and people contemplate getting off the sofa, the Premier League will start."

THOSE OLYMPIC DAYS OF THE WEEK

Magic Monday	**watch-some-more-Olympics Friday**
Terrific Tuesday	
Wonderful Wednesday	Shit-I-really-need-to-prepare-for-next-week's-presentation Saturday
Think-I-should-probably-do-some-work-now Thursday	
Forget-work-I'm-going-to-	**Sod-it-I'll-just-watch-some-more-Olympics Sunday**

Royal family announces new member

by Our Royal Correspondent
Rick Spittle

FOLLOWING the closing ceremony of the Olympic Games, Prince William and the Duchess of Cambridge have proudly welcomed the newest member of the Firm – Snoop Dogg, who appeared in a video congratulating Team GB.

"We're thrilled he's joining," said one courtier of the singer of *Bitch Please* and *Drop It Like It's Hot*.

"He's got convictions for drug possession, gun charges and other felonies, has been arrested for starting fights, and he's written hundreds of lyrics which denigrate women. In short, he's an enormous improvement on Prince Andrew."

Another royal added, "With the addition of Mr Dogg, the royal family has taken a welcome step into the 21st century – or at least, into the West Coast gang wars of the 1990s. As someone who enjoys shooting, he will fit right in."

King Charles is understood to be welcoming Dogg to Buckingham Palace for his investiture as Duke of (New) York this week.

"I'm training for a marathon" *"I couldn't give a fuck"*

LAZINESS IS THE BRITISH DISEASE

by Our Productivity Staff
Phil Space

MILLIONS of people in Britain are now officially unable to work. The excuse is that they are unfit on medical grounds; the simple truth is that they are lazy and workshy.

A number of recent surveys, which I can't be bothered to look up, make this very clear: British productivity is way lower than lots of other countries, although the figures are all in foreign languages and it's too much effort to translate them.

What is the answer to this long-term malaise? I don't know really; I'm sure someone's written something about it, but it's a real effort tracking down the stats, isn't it?

Suffice to say, British people are incredibly indolent and the idleness of the workforce is now becoming a major political issue. Is this enough? *(No. Keep going. Ed.)*

Ugh. Well, there are loads of jobs about and nobody wants to fill them, I reckon. It stands to reason, probably. No, I'm done. Just put a big picture in of some young people looking bored and useless. *(Great. Thanks. Please don't resign. Ed.)*

Good news. We've arrested hundreds of people and started locking them all up.

Morgan McSweeney
Top ruthlessness, boss! 👍

This is a simple matter of criminal justice. Violent thuggery will not be tolerated.

Yvette Cooper
Can I just say that violent thuggery will not be tolerated?

Angela Rayner
I was going to say that.

Quite right, Yvette.

Angela Rayner
Are you ignoring me?

As you say, Yvette, violent thuggery will not be tolerated.

Morgan McSweeney
Great repetition of agreed messaging, boss.

Did I mention I was the Director of Public Prosecutions during the last riots, when I cracked down ruthlessly on violent thuggery?

Morgan McSweeney
You did boss. Great repetition!

Sue Gray
You've already said that, Morgan.

Morgan McSweeney
No I haven't.

Sue Gray
Don't argue with me or I'll move your desk again.

Morgan McSweeney
I'm already blocking the fire escape.

We also need to crack down on social media. I've just been very ruthless with Elon Musk.

Yvette Cooper
What action have you taken?

I told him I'm not going to respond to any more of his tweets about civil war being inevitable.

Sue Gray
You shouldn't engage with nutters online. Let me deal with it.

Morgan McSweeney
I give the media advice round here.

Sue Gray
No you don't.

Morgan McSweeney
Yes I do!

Darren Jones
Did someone say civil war was inevitable? 😈😈

Shabana Mahmood
Can I just say, as Justice Secretary, that it's great to lock everyone up ruthlessly but we haven't got anywhere to put them.

Darren Jones
How about re-opening the Bibby Stockholm? A prison ship for anti-immigrant protestors! 😌

Rachel Reeves
I don't think you have fully costed that proposal, which makes it unhelpful. However I am prepared to instigate a full review of barge fiscal feasibility.

Darren Jones
All right, let's send them all to Rwanda! 😂😂😂

Shabana Mahmood
But this is a real problem. What's the solution?

Yvette Cooper
We blame the Tories.

Angela Rayner
I was going to say that.

Good point, Yvette.

Yvette Cooper
Thanks, boss. I said it during my interview on Good Morning Britain.

Morgan McSweeney
Was that with TV's top investigative interviewer, your husband?

Yvette Cooper
He asked me all the tough questions. "Why are Labour so brilliant?" "Why are you such a great Home Secretary?" and "What would you like for supper tonight, I'll pick it up on my way home, as you've got a far more important job than me?"

And did you tell him who is to blame for the riots?

Yvette Cooper
Dangerous right-wing idiots.

Darren Jones
Yes, it's the Tories! Bingo! Another pound in the Swear-they're-to-blame Box!

Rachel Reeves
However much we collect, it won't be enough to fill the black hole.

Darren Jones
How bad are things?

Rachel Reeves
For the record, I recently took the precaution of marking the level of milk in the bottle in the fridge, clearly marked 'Rachel's – Do Not Touch', and since I last used it, the volume has gone down by 32% in real terms.

Larry the Cat
I blame the Tories!

INTRODUCING THE EX-MEN... & EX-WOMEN

THE ONCE MIGHTY SUPERHEROES HAVE LOST THEIR POWERS AND ARE IN DISARRAY...

I'M BATSHITMAN! FOLLOW ME!

NO, FOLLOW ME – BRAVERMAN!

NO, FOLLOW ME... ACTIONMAN!

LET'S FIGHT FOR UNITY!

CRASH! BANG! WALLOP!

LOOKS LIKE TOM'S THROWN HIS TUGENDHAT INTO THE RING!

THE HUMAN LETTUCE! DID SOMEONE SAY CRASH?

THE SPERMINATOR! DID SOMEONE SAY BANG?

FAGMAN! MINE'S A PINT OF WALLOP!

OH NO! NOT MORE EX-MEN! AND WOMEN! WHO WILL SAVE THE MARVILE TORYVERSE?

IF IT'S A DOWNWARD SPIRAL, LEADING TO OBLIVION YOU'RE AFTER, I'M YOUR WOMAN!

HOORAY! IT'S KEMIKAZE!

DOWN, DOWN AND AWAY!

ONE OF THE MORE OBSCURE SUPERHEROES, EH READERS?

WILL OUR EX-MEN AND EX-WOMEN STOP FIGHTING AND RESOLVE THEIR DIFFERENCES? FIND OUT NEXT WEEK IN THE NEW EPISODE: **THE FIGHT GOES ON!**

UK RIOTS: RINGLEADERS IDENTIFIED

"I'm an X-tremist!"

"I'm an elderly right-wing skinhead"

"I'm happy to offer some incite"

"I'm seeking asylum in this five-star hotel"

"We torch green bins on Tuesdays and black bins on Thursdays"

Britain 'plunged into total civil war'

by Our Social Media Correspondent **Bo Locks**

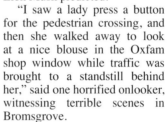

On ordinary streets the length and breadth of Britain, the country was plunged into the chaos of total civil war, just as Elon Musk predicted.

"I saw a lady press a button for the pedestrian crossing, and then she walked away to look at a nice blouse in the Oxfam shop window while traffic was brought to a standstill behind her," said one horrified onlooker, witnessing terrible scenes in Bromsgrove.

"I just came outside my house, and found the milkman had left full-fat instead of semi-skimmed, AND he had left the gate open. My dachshund could easily have got out," whimpered another shellshocked observer from Godalming.

Said a UN observer, "Elon Musk has got it bang on. All across the UK we've had reports of people leaving their umbrellas in shops, eating cream cakes messily in tea shops, and sounding a bit miffed when their train is late. It's utter carnage.

"Thank heavens Mr Musk was here to warn us of the terror that is about to unfold."

"It's really good for fanning the flames"

THE Sun SAYS

These riots are a disgrace. The overriding lesson for Britain to learn is that we must hold social media to account. Just not ourselves. (That's it. Ed.)

OPENING CEREMONY OF BRITISH RIOT OLYMPICS 'WATCHED BY MILLIONS'

What a way to not welcome people from every nation to Britain

Ironyometer victim of UK riots

THE famous ironyometer, which has served the nation so well, has become the latest unfortunate casualty of the disorder sweeping Britain.

A series of extreme spikes in irony rendered the highly sensitive measuring machine inoperative after the internal mechanism began to malfunction seriously.

The first shock came when violent right-wing protestors, chanting "Protect our kids!", attacked an asylum hostel containing children, who needed protection from people setting fire to their temporary home, threatening to assault them.

The ironyometer's needle was further jolted into the red zone at the sight of violent right-wing protestors setting fire to a library, a centre of learning for the community which, had they entered it rather than torching it, might have resulted in the kind of transformative educational process that leads to critical assessment of material content rather than kneejerk reactions to malicious disinformation.

With the library fire raging, the ironyometer was finally sent into a catastrophic meltdown, as the violent right-wing protestors cheered at the burning of books and shouted, "How dare you call us Nazis?" At this, the ironyometer exploded.

Team GBH triumphs!

AS THE Riotolympics flame burned brightly over Rotherham from the torched police van, Team GBH could look back with pride on the achievements of the past fortnight.

Said one champion rioter, "We did the team Union Jack and balaclava proud. I may not have come home with gold or silver, as I'd hoped, but I did come home with a Greggs sausage roll and a pair of Crocs, which don't actually fit me, but will come in handy for Nan at Christmas."

Pundits said this was Team GBH's biggest haul of loot since the 2011 Riotolympics.

"This year, the lads and lasses just smashed it – namely the window of the Sainsbury's Local. They were on fire – as was the migrants' Holiday Inn."

But there was heartbreak for some who failed to do themselves justice.

The tears flowed, as the judges awarded them custodial sentences and (cont. 2028)

Those events in full
- The Brick Put
- Hammered Throwing
- 100m Sprint Race-ism
- Hurling the Chair
- Synchronised Swigging
  (That's enough events. Ed.)

Future President Trump

That Republican Rally speech in full

"I'm here today to unite this beautiful country. And I'm going to unite America behind my new nicknames for Krazy Kamala. So I've called her a sick bum, a Marxist fraud and dumb as a rock – but from now on, it's no more Mr Nice Guy. I'm sick of being Kind Trump. Nasty Trump is back. So from now on I'm calling her 'Lying' Kamala. 'Cos if there's one thing I hate, it's lying. And I've got a new one. How about: "Kambalaya-crawfishpie-and-a-filé-gumbo!" No one's going to forget that. Unlike her, she's gonna be history. And how about her new running mate? Some white kid. I mean, he's only 60! What's he ever done. Okay – teacher, football coach, national guardsman. Just like me – if I hadn't had the bone spurs. The guy's called Tim Walz. You know what I call him – "Walz ice cream!" Cos he's soft and he's gonna melt and he's Flakey. We need to Build a Wall! To keep Walz out! A big beautiful wall. *(continues for several hours...)*

...Hey, so the Democrats think they're funny, calling me weird. I'll tell you what's weird – calling someone weird. I'm a normal guy. Like Hannibal Lecter – no one called him weird! JD Vance – nothing weird about him. I'll tell you who's weird. Kamalakbar – she's a Muslim. FACT! Used to be an Indian. Then turned black. Married a Jewish guy. Hates jews so much so she brought up Jewish kids. FACT! Did she buy them ice cream? I don't think so! You wouldn't believe it, but I'm not using autocue – it's all in my head! And another thing... True fact!"

(Crowd begins to disperse, thinking perhaps the once-mighty orator is past his prime...)

"It's the first US election in history where neither candidate is white"

SHOCK OVER BBC PRESENTER SACKING

by Our Celebrity Staff **Stu Pidd**

THE country has reacted with astonishment to the news that BBC TV presenter Jermaine Jenas has been sacked by the corporation over complaints about his workplace conduct.

"It's just extraordinary," said one viewer. "This sort of thing is not what should be happening at the BBC at all. When the Beeb found out, they should have told nobody for several days, hoping to suppress it, then let him go to a private sanatorium, then investigated him for a year before coming to a conclusion that it's too early to make any firm judgment, hoping everyone's forgotten about it."

Another fan of *The One Show* agreed: "This is unbelievable. One better option would have been to wait for 45 years, until he died, make a programme saying how marvellous he was, then attack the other people who were looking into him and dismiss their work, before eventually collapsing and apologising."

A senior BBC executive added, "This sort of thing sets a very bad precedent. Mr Jenas should have been given an immediate pay rise and a boost to his pension, before the BBC then suddenly decided that was a bad idea. That is normal procedure, and there has clearly been a lapse in poor standards."

Nursery Times

COW'S RETURN FROM SPACE IN DOUBT

by Our Star Reporter **Twinkle Twinkle-Little**

THE future of Nurseryland space exploration is on hold, following a glitch which has seen a cow stranded in earth's orbit with no signs of how Mission Control can bring it down.

Said a spokesman for NASA (Nurseryland Aeronautics and Space Administration), "After a successful moon leap, we were hoping the cow would return to earth, but a technical fault in the udder-carriage has seen the astro-ruminant unable to initiate suitable lactal thrust to re-enter the earth's atmosphere."

The fiddle-playing cat continued, "Although at present it remains in good spirits, spending its time in orbit, mooing and lowing, it's not much fun. Despite what that little dog thinks, it's certainly no laughing matter."

In its defence, the chuckling mutt responded, "Oh come on, it's a zero gravity situation!"

Letter to the Editor

SIR – I write with reference to the story about television personality Kirstie Allsopp's 15-year-old son, who has spent three weeks travelling Europe without adult supervision, and the shock and dismay this has caused.

It is all a long way from my own experience during the summer holidays of 1936. We were encouraged in those days to make our own fun, and consequently I and two pals travelled that summer to Central Europe, thinking it might be fun to assassinate Adolf Hitler.

We were trusted entirely by the adults to whom we suggested the plan, and experienced no mollycoddling as we put together our supplies of boat, tent, rifles, high explosives, cyanide capsules, etc.

Nobody dreamed of reporting our parents to social services.

While ultimately unsuccessful, and while my two friends sadly perished as we returned at high speed across the English Channel (I myself lost a leg due to the actions of an irritating Messerschmitt, which naturally nurse made a huge fuss about at the start of the next school term), it was a golden summer and one of which the kid-glove younger generation today could hardly conceive.

Sir Herbert Gussett
The Old Battery, Nuttsford

Results day mad scramble for places

by Our Prison Correspondent **Philippa Cell**

MANY of Britain's top criminals are not getting into their first-choice prisons, as a surge in demand has left the prison sector in crisis.

Said one violent rioter, "The lack of places is a real shame, and can only be blamed on Tory mismanagement. I just feel let down by the whole thing, to be honest. I spent ages getting my personal statement down to one word – 'guilty'."

Another felon added, "I had my eye on a category A* prison, like Belmarsh, but I was put on the waiting list – they said that they were already oversubscribed for the next few years. So, I applied through clearing and now (fingers crossed) I might be off to Wormwood Scrubs!"

Jeremy Clarkson took to X to offer some consolation to the unsuccessful prisoners: "I punched a man, and I never went to prison. Now I'm driving cool cars and have my own shows. Prison is not the be-all and end-all."

"It's one in, one out"

CLASSICAL NEWS

23 August 2024

NEW HEAD OF HYDRA APPOINTED

Following the successful decapitation of the legendary monster Hydra by the Israeli army, the ferocious creature has immediately sprouted a new head to replace the old one.

Experts had warned that merely cutting the head off a multi-headed threat may not result in the desired effect, ie the elimination of said Hydra. In fact, it may just lead to more trouble and more attacks by the Hydra.

However, a spokesman for the Israeli army said, "Our policy is to cut off all the heads and burn everything else. It's a strategy that worked for Hercules and even though we know this particular story about the Labours of Hamas is a myth, why on earth shouldn't it work in the real world?" *[cont. until 2094]*

FEARS OVER HOUSING MARKET REVIVAL

by Our Property Staff **Ivan Offer** (*subject to survey*)

AS MORTGAGE rates fall and the cost of living crisis shows signs of abating, the property market looks set for an upswing.

But there are concerns that it will have a knock-on effect up and down the land, splitting couples and rupturing friendships.

Said one potential buyer, "I'm really dreading a surge in property-price conversations at dinner parties or even when picking the kids up from school. The market's been quiet for so long – we've enjoyed several meals with friends without any mention of how much their home is now worth or the financial benefits of downsizing or moving to St Albans, which apparently is a reasonable commute and you can be in Oxford Circus by – oh my God, it's happening already!"

Another flat-hunter agreed, saying, "I'm already anxious about what the property price surge will do to friendships. I was in the middle of telling my anecdote about a viewing in Hackney when I got gazumped by Simon who had a much bigger story to tell about a two-bedroom maisonette which was available as a part-ownership but with a lease of less than – aaaaargh!"

POETRY CORNER

In Memoriam copper coins

So. Farewell
Then the 1p piece
And the 2p piece.

You are no longer
Being minted.

Is it time for change?
Well, yes,
And no.

E.J. Thribb (17½p)

BANX

"I want my country back"

CARPOOL KARAOKE REVIVED

Everybody wants to rule ♪ the world! ♬

A Tank Driver writes

Vlad 'Mad' Putin, Tank No: ZZZZ

Every week a well-known tank driver gives his opinion on a matter of topical importance.

"Oi mate, get off the road! Yeah, up yours 'n' all!... Hang on – who's driving that tank?! It's bloody Zelensky! And he's only gone and crossed the border into Russia. Not that there is a border of course, cos it's all Russia, innit?! Anyway, the bloody cheek of it! Doesn't he know this is a one-way system! I can drive to his place, but he doesn't get to drive to mine! Now look at him – his tank's flattening civilian buildings. Talk about provocative – someone could get killed! Specifically, the Russian General currently in charge of road management, ie keeping Zelensky's tanks off my patch! Tell you what, I had that Evan Gershkovich in the back of my tank the other day. Well, I say "the back", he was actually tied up in the boot. And I say "the other day", it was actually 17 months. Anyway, no hard feelings. All sorted now. He's back home in America, and my old pal Vadim Krasikov is safely back home in Russia. Old Vadim, bit of a handyman – did a nice little job for me in Berlin back in the day. He's what you might call a disposal expert – makes a killing! Except this time he got caught. Just because someone I didn't get on with was floating in the river – the Germans put zwei and zwei together and made fünf. And poor old Vaddy ended up in the slammer. Still, he's out now, so no harm done! Stay lucky!"

© *A tank driver*

Russia invaded shock

THE Ukrainian government has issued a statement in response to Russian protests about the recent "special military operation" into Russia.

A spokesman defended the decision to send its armed forces into the Kursk province, explaining, "This area has actually always been a part of Ukraine, and the Kursk people have long yearned for their freedom as part of the Greater Ukraine. Ha ha ha ha ha."

He added, "Now we're going to have a referendum, and I have a funny feeling it might just go our way. Ha ha ha ha ha."

He concluded, "Would you like to read a 20,000-word rambling historical tract explaining that this is all completely justified in the context of Kievan Rus and the reign of Yaroslav the Wise in 1015? Ha ha ha ha ha." (*Rotters*)

Eye Chess Puzzle Corner

Can you solve this conundrum? How can white secure checkmate in the next few moves?

a) Rook to d8; Rook to a8.

b) Smear mercury on board; pour Polonium all over black king; cover clock in Novichok; wait for your opponent to collapse.

Answer: a), unless you are competing in Russia, in which case it's b), as proven by grandmaster Toksik in 1934.

CULTURE BORES

by Grizelda

POETRY CORNER

**In Memoriam
Reader's Digest**

So. Farewell
Then Reader's Digest,
Famous for condensing
Great literary works
Into versions that readers
Could easily digest.

Sadly, your readers
Began to die off
And now you have,
As well.

And even your
Truncated texts
Were too long for
The modern reader.

> E.J. Thribb
> (17½ copies in the doctor's
> waiting room in the old
> days when you could
> see a doctor)

**In Memoriam
Reader's Digest –
a Reader's Digest version
of the immortal poem by
E.J. Thribb**

So. Farewell
Then Reader's Digest.

> E.J.T.

**In Memoriam
Lines on the passing of
Sven-Goran Eriksson,
football manager**

So. Farewell
Then Sven-Goran Eriksson.

You broke some hearts
As England manager
And with your colourful
Love life.

If only your team
Had scored
As often as you.

But still,
The tabloids never
Called you
A Turnip
Because you were
A Swede.

> E.J. Thribb
> (17½ years of hurt)

THE KING OF TROUBLES

A short story special by Dame Hedda Shoulders

WITHIN days of the smooth transition of His Majesty's Government, Charles' kingdom has fallen prey to civil unrest, but now the status quo has returned and the royal party has repaired to Scotland for a well-earned break. Now read on...

ZAP! "Got the buggers!" The scent of frying insect wafted across Glen Hoddle as Camilla swatted the traditional cloud of midges with "Ol' Sparky", her electronic anti-bug paddle. What a useful gift that had been, from Sheikh Mustafa Kraq-Dhown, following Charles' visit to one of Araby's most historic dungeons.

The smell of the burning winged "Scourge of the Highlands" mingled with the sweet aroma of scorched stag, as the morning's kill sizzled on the barbecue. Yes, the King's summer holiday at Balamoray Castle, nestling on the banks of Royal Jackdeeside, was finally settling into the peaceful repose that the weary monarch so urgently craved. Now, after the Summer of Discontent, Charles could at last relax, surrounded by his family, friends, flora, fauna and midges. For a while, as police vehicles burned, he had feared for the monarchy.

"It's such a relief, Camilla, that our Sceptred Isle is once again set in a becalmed silver sea," sighed the King, "albeit silver with traces of brown."

"As your predecessor, Charlie Number One, might have said, Civil War is a right royal pain in the neck!" chortled his soul-mate, while lighting a Rothsayman's Queen-sized gasper on the coals underneath the once-proud Monarch of the Glen, now destined to be a feast of deer burgers.

Charles Number Three subconsciously felt his own neck and winced at the reminder of his ancestor's untimely demise.

Thwack! The glinting blade of razor-sharp steel thudded into the chopping block and Charles shuddered as Camilla tossed the dripping slice of lemon into her glass of Ramsay Gordon's gin.

"Tonic, ma'am?" offered Sir Alan Fitztightly, the Lemon-Aide-de-Camp and Master of the Mixers, wearing his traditional porridge tartan kilt.

"Don't be daft!" she rasped thirstily, topping up her drink with another dash of her favourite 99 percent-proof elixir.

With a jewel-encrusted fork and his King-sized barbecue tongs, Charles struggled to turn the 40-stone slab of meat that Old Ghillie Cooper had only that morning culled, in the interests of eco-preservation and lunch.

The King wiped his royal brow, smearing it with Levi Roots Regal-Regal Jerk BBQ Sauce.

"What ho, bro!"

Charles' noble heart sank as Andrew, clad only in a towel, appeared dripping beside him.

"Just been for a skinny-dip with Fergie! Here's a salmon that got caught up... well, never mind where! Bon appétit!"

Andrew slapped the wet, wriggling fish alongside the sweating stag. An unappealing sight, but for Charles there was some consolation for his disgraced sibling joining the straightforward hunting, shooting and fishing weekend.

While Andrew and his dreadful ex-wife were ensconced in the Minerva McGonagall suite in the Harry Potter wing of the castle, down in Windsor the Master of Bailiffs and Changer of the Locks would be itemising their possessions in preparation for their permanent removal from the Royal Lodge.

Refusing to pay for Andrew's security detail was all part of the master game of chess that Charles was playing although, as King, it was somewhat frustrating that he had to move so slowly, whilst his Queen seemed to be free to dash around and do as she pleased. It really was... what was the word?

"I'm peeling!" cried Fergie, also betowelled, thrusting her raw, pink, freckled shoulder under Charles' nose.

Ignoring his ex-sister-in-law-but-live-in-lover-in-law, Charles attempted to stab the stag's glistening flesh with his fork, to test whether the carcass was cooked.

"Shall I stick it in for you?" Sir Alan ventured, with a lascivious grin, "As Backstairs Billy used to say to the Clerk of the Closet, in the days of your dear old..."

"Yes, thank you, Sir Alan, but perhaps it's time to start carving."

The marching band of Billie Pipers announced the arrival of the 18th-century mahogany Fish'n'Chippendale dining table, carried by four periwigged flunkeys and already laden with paper plates and cardboard cutlery, as befitted the al fresco state picnic.

In spite of all the recent challenges of his troubled reign, at this moment in time, Charles could reflect that he and his nation were, at last, at peace – and all thoughts of insurrection and rebellion could be banished to history.

Suddenly, the drone of bagpipery was drowned out by an unmistakable blast from the Donald Trumpeteers as they played a welcoming fanfare for the arrival of his new Prime Minister and weekend guest, Sir Keir Starmer, dressed in holiday-mode suit-jacket, shirt, tie and shorts.

"Good news, Your Majesty," Sir Keir bowed unctuously, "I come bearing a special gift." The PM dipped his hand into the pocket of his shorts and produced a glittering shiny object. "The first pound coins featuring Your Majesty are now in circulation."

Charles looked at the small yet significant item of currency with pride and awe.

"Oh look," burst in Camilla, "it's got your head on it! And it's been cut off at the neck, hahaha!"

Though surrounded by kinsmen, kinswomen and loyal liegemen, the latest in the Carolingian line suddenly felt the solitude of a sovereign. Charles' eyes met those of the stricken stag. As the great Bard of Avoncalling had so wisely put it, "Heavy is the head that wears the chef's hat."

(To be continued...)

SHARKS TEST POSITIVE FOR COCAINE

I've got a great idea for a movie!

Woohoo! Let's set up a production company

Royal Navy fleet review 2024

MailyEXPRESSOgraph

STARMER SLEAZE ROTS GOVERNMENT

ONLY six weeks into the new Labour Government and the stench of corruption fills the fetid air, causing Westminster insiders to gag.

Keir 'Freeloader' Starmer taunts ordinary working people with his extra pairs of glasses, handed to him by his chumocracy crony, Lord 'Backhander' Alli, as he greases the wheels of power and (*this is very thin stuff, keep going! Ed.*)

With his freebie spectacles, he really should have seen this coming.

He clearly lacks vision and (*actually, this is too thin, even for us. You're fired. Ed.*)

meet the lofty standards of sleaze reached by the Conservative Party over the past 14 years.

Said Baroness Michelle Mone, "He should be forced to return at least one pair of the glasses, which I'd have charged him £38 million for. These people are amateurs."

Starmer on brink of resignation (p94)

ONLY six weeks into the new Labour Government, the beleaguered Prime Minister was today phoning the removal men to check on their availability as he prepares to vacate Number 10, five years early – in 2034.

A Conservative spokesman said, "It's typical of the hapless 'holier than thou' Starmer that he should be embroiled in a dreary Specs Scandal, as opposed to all the Tory Sex Scandals which have cheered the nation for decades."

ON OTHER PAGES
Tories condemn Starmer sleaze (p2)

ONLY six weeks into the new Labour Government and Starmer has shown himself completely unfit for Government, as he fails to

BORIS JOHNSON ON STANDARDS IN PUBLIC LIFE

TALK about summertime and the living is sleazy! Or should I say "Starmertime and the cost of living is squeezy?!" (*This doesn't work at all, keep going! Ed.*)

Never in the history of British politics has any Prime Minister – make that CRIME Minister – shown himself to be more, corrupt, venal and in the pay of rich donors than Sir Clear Stinker. Can anyone remember a Prime Minister – or should I say PRIME SINISTER – who is more obviously on the make, amoral and utterly bent than the man wearing free glasses and a shiny suit in the Rose Garden? Or should I say POSE Garden?

Yes, friends, (*you don't have any – Ed. But never mind, this is great!*) we all know that Sir Sheer Smarmer has shown himself unfit to occupy Number 10 Downing

Street, where he "downs" beers and curries, before putting on his expensive glasses, which he clearly needs because he can't see what a staggeringly hypocritical humbug he is! (*Are you sure you want to go down this route? Ed.*)

Whatever next? Will we see Sir Barmy Starmy arranging £800,000 loans from distant relatives and taking freebie holiday while spaffing millionaires' moolah on soft furnishings and gold wallpaper? (*Boris, I think you should stop now. Even our readers might find this line of attack a little bit unconvincing, coming from you. Ed.*)

How long before Sir Complete Bummer starts holding drunken parties, breaking all the rules, not to mention the kiddies' swing in the garden? What a two-faced, lying, fraudulent scumbag and (*That's enough Boris. Really! Ed.*)

KAMALA OFFERS NEW HOPE FOR AMERICA

It's time to end the politics of division and abuse...

...and give that orange weirdo a kicking!

That Republican rally speech in full

Hello, North South Sweet Carolina. Here's the thing about the economy – I'm prettier than Kamala. Fact. That's not just me saying so, even Kamala says so, everyone says so. Except those who don't. And they're liars! I'll tell you something else, I'm brighter than she is. I'm so bright, everyone says I am, and I don't wanna be rude, but she's stupid. Really dumb. Dumbala! How's that for a name? Dumb-allah! Like Obamallah Hussein Khomeini! You gotta be smart to be president and I'm probably the smartest president who ever lived. Unlike Kamalala-land! Did I tell you she's dumb? And did you see Sleepy Joe crying like a bigly baby. "Boo-hoo-hoo. I'm no longer president!" He's not Sleepy Joe anymore, he's Weepy Joe! "Oooooh, I wanna be president!" Sorry, Weepy Joe, it's nap time! And did you see the fake crowds in that empty hall? So fake! Fake fake crowd news. Fact!

And did you see Michelle Obamalamadingdong? She wasn't there, 'cos no one was there, but you know what she said to that empty hall? She said, "Hope is back". That's so, so rude. I don't know anyone called Hope. Unless she's that stripper from Vegas? It's a witch hunt! If I paid Hope $3million to keep quiet, that's a lie. Fact! And she's not so smart. And not so pretty. Not like me. And someone else I'm prettier than? The Queen. She's dead and she's rude, so rude. I'm not rude and it's rude of her to say I'm rude. She says I looked over her shoulder to find someone more interesting. Well, she's dead. How boring is that? She had more fun with me than any other president ever. Best two weeks of her life! Better than Abe Lincoln, she told me. Better than Dopey George Washington. Cut down a cherry tree. Didn't lie about it. What a dope! (*continues for another 70 days...*)

WINIFRED ROBINSON: Every single day, harrowing news of severe physical and mental abuse on Strictly Come Dancing floods into the You and Yours offices. We've carried reports of severe bruising, broken arms, legs and ribs, concussion caused by blunt objects applied to the skull. There have also been unconfirmed reports of waterboarding conducted by the judges.

This has led to urgent calls for emergency legislation to prevent future atrocities. Campaigners seek a new Two Metre Rule to stop any professional dancer coming within two metres of their celebrity partner, and a senior police officer to be in the rehearsal room at all times, day and night. In addition, professional dancers would be required to provide urine samples before and after every session, and to be regularly assessed by a clinical psychologist. Yet the Home Secretary still refuses to give a firm date for the introduction of these laws. Do you think this is reasonable – or do you find it yet another example of the continued victimisation of the weak and defenceless by the relevant authorities? We'd like to know what you think, so contact us on Call You and Yours.

TOM BOWER: The exact number of corpses of former contestants stored in the closely guarded temperature-controlled morgue beneath the BBC's Strictly Come Dancing studios remains a closely-guarded secret, though some experts estimate the figure at anywhere between thirty and zero.

D I A R Y

STRICTLY COME DANCING: A SYMPOSIUM

The family of one former Emmerdale star have barely heard a word from her since she left home to dance on the sixth series of Strictly. When I put it to them that she may have been kicked to death by Anton du Beke after a misstep in the Cha-cha-cha and that she now lies packed in ice in the top-secret Strictly morgue, they were too traumatised to reply.

ANN WIDDECOMBE: Stuff and nonsense. That's my reaction to the so-called "stars" – nonentities, more like! – who whinge about so-called "abuse" on Strictly Come Dancing.

They clearly never fought in the Battle of the Somme, where plucky young soldiers faced the choice of death at enemy hands or drawn-out misery in filthy rat-filled trenches.

Did those soldiers whinge about it? No, they did not. They simply got on with the job in hand, ie killing Germans, and jolly good thing too.

As has been well-documented, I danced with Anton du Beke in the tenth series of Strictly. Thanks to my efforts, I pulled us through to the semi-finals. Anton did what I call the grinning-and-spinning. He left the hard graft to me. Men!

In rehearsals, he prattled on about "technique" and "rhythm" and suchlike, but I took no such nonsense. Did he "bully" me? Not that I noticed. And if he had, I'd have given him a jolly good kick in the shins. It's the only language they understand.

THE DUKE AND DUCHESS OF SUSSEX: As we watch the growing humanitarian disaster at Strictly Come Dancing, we are left heartbroken.

The world is exceptionally fragile right now. And as we feel the many layers of pain, due to the situation at Strictly, we are left speechless.

It is so easy to feel powerless in the face of the continuing crisis at Strictly Come Dancing. But, as Dr Martin Luther King said, "Whatever happens, we must keeeep dancing."

We must put our values into action –together. It is up to each and every one of us to do our best to save Strictly, and we hope to give that lead.

As beacons of light in an increasingly dark world, we want to reach out to all the courageous victims of Strictly, regardless of race, gender or sexual preference.

And by channelling our globally acclaimed powers of human empathy, help them heal.

As told to
CRAIG BROWN

WHY THE SUPERYACHT BAYESIAN SANK IN JUST 60 SECONDS THE TRUTH

The truth is, we don't know.

CUT-OUT-AND-KEEP GUIDE

Boats sinking off Italy, which don't matter

Boats sinking off Italy, which do

A Doctor Writes

AS A doctor, I am often asked by famous ex-supermodels, "Doctor, I had cancer and now I'm fine – shall I tell everyone I rejected traditional medicine and treated myself with natural holistic remedies?"

The simple answer is, "Elle, this is a terrible idea. You really should mention that you had surgery and it was successful, so on the whole it may not be a great idea to recommend to people that they should simply rely on wellness products."

This is what we doctors call "Macpherson Syndrome", "Online Influenza", or to give it its full medical name – *Celebritus Quackus Looniensis*".

If you are worried that you might be seriously ill, I would advise taking advantage of centuries of medical science and popping into a hospital for a second opinion other than Ms Macpherson's.   © *A doctor*

The Anglo-Saxon Chronicle
Danegeld payment solves strike crisis

by Our Pillage Correspondent
Vi King

FOLLOWING a series of military strikes by marauding Danes, pay levels have been raised by above-inflation amounts, which will definitely keep them away from our shores in future. Trade unions, including ASLEF (Associated Society of Longship Enforcers and Firebrands) have been demanding huge pay rises to cover the costs of their activities, saying that the cost of swords, mead and looting have all risen and their members deserve a boost to their salaries.

"I don't know why we didn't think of this earlier," said a village headman, collecting taxes from all the peasants to give them to the Danes currently floating offshore and threatening to bring vital British infrastructure to a halt.

"If we pay the Danes this one-off lump sum, they will almost certainly never come back again."

Said a Dane, "Yes, we will definitely leave you alone forever now, unless macro-economic conditions change and we are reluctantly forced to come back in three months, rather than the usual six."

ON OTHER PAGES

✣ Send The Boats Back, plead coastal locals
✣ Revolutionary new building material: thatch!
✣ World's Oldest Man turns 43

THE COMPLETE BADENOCHS

Kemi

Semi

Hemi

Demi

Angela Rayner
Happy birthday, Keir!

> No, it isn't. Now is not a time for happiness. There may be happiness in the future, but in the short term we have to be realistic about the black hole of unhappiness that we've inherited from the previous government.

Angela Rayner
Oh come on, Sir Killjoy, let's get this party started! I've got a cake and vodka shots! And I haven't slept since Friday! Whoop-whoop-whooooooooo!

Morgan McSweeney
She may have a point, boss. I think we may be overdoing the doom and gloom.

Sue Gray
I disagree. I'm very happy with doom and gloom.

Morgan McSweeney
Well, I think the doom and gloom may backfire on us.

Darren Jones
That's a bit pessimistic! Bit gloomy, Morgan. And doomy! 😂😂😂

Angela Rayner
So I should cancel the DJ, then?

> Correct. The fun stops here. It's back to work, back to school, the end of the holidays.

> Not that I had one.

Pat McFadden
Oh, I don't know – you went to Balmoral for the weekend.

> Exactly. You think *I'm* gloomy? Try spending a weekend with King Charles.

Wes Streeting
How did Camilla take it when you told her not to smoke in the garden?

Darren Jones
Bet she was fuming!

> Even worse, Balmoral was absolutely freezing.

Rachel Reeves
Good. Two wealthy pensioners who do not merit a winter fuel allowance and are therefore economising.

Morgan McSweeney
Yuh, OK, so it's *mostly* doom and gloom, obvs. But there is some good news – Oasis are back together.

David Lammy
It's like 1997 all over again. New Labour Government, Britpop!

Angela Rayner
Cool Britannia!

Darren Jones
Especially without the heating allowance!

> I'm glad you've raised Oasis, because I am absolutely scandalised by the exorbitant and exploitative ticket pricing strategy. We can't have people just naming their price and getting what they want.

Pat McFadden
Unless they're train drivers.

Rachel Reeves
I don't think that's a fair equivalence of two different complex economic models. It's like comparing chalk and the cheese that someone took from the fridge, which was in a Tupperware box clearly marked 'Property of the Chancellor of the Exchequer'.

Darren Jones
Was it Emmental? With a massive hole in the middle of it?

Rachel Reeves
I'm not sure you are treating this surge pricing scandal with the seriousness it deserves. It's profiteering on a major scale.

Angela Rayner
Talking of which, I'm scrapping the Right to Buy scheme!

Sue Gray
From which you profited on a major scale?

Darren Jones
Not so much 'Right to Buy' as 'Left to Buy', eh Angela? 🏠😊💰 £££££

Sue Gray
I wonder if perhaps it'd be better if the Deputy PM avoided policy issues and stuck to party matters?

Angela Rayner
So I'll rebook the DJ? What banging tunes do you want them to play, birthday boy?

Darren Jones
Affordable House Music? With Garage? 😂😂😂

WINDFARMS TO BE PLACED IN UK COASTAL WATERS

The shit's about to hit the fan

WHO ORDERED THE CALAMARI?

ANTI-POLLUTION BILL
WATER BOSSES THREATENED WITH JAIL OVER BREACHES OF LAW

But the prisons are overflowing!

Don't worry – we'll dump any spillover on the public

Are we the People's Front of Islington or the Islington People's Front?

Ten ants come out in defence of Labour MP landlord

by Our Housing Staff
Joanna Slumley and **Amold Rajan**

As Labour MP Jas Athwal has come under fire for the condition of his 15 rental flats, he was cheered when ten ants who had been living in one of his small properties, along with 10,000 of their mates, spoke up in his defence.

"He was an ideal landlord," said the ten ants, "and he never once threatened us with eviction. We felt perfectly secure in the knowledge that he would never try and get rid of us or any of our friends."

The ten ants continued, "As to the state of the flats, I don't know what everyone's going on about. They were in perfect condition. He provided floor-to-ceiling mould in every room, and running water down the walls.

"As for the heating system, it was in perfect working order – ie it didn't work at all."

"Our only complaint," said the ten ants, "was that there was an infestation of humans. But they never stayed long, as Mr Athwal always ensured that their rent kept rising at the same rate as the damp."

The Labour MP thanked the ten ants for their support, and declared, "I've always been on the side of the workers, particularly if they're ants."

"I live in one of those ant-infested flats over there"

Doolally Mail SPORT

New England manager in anthem snub

THERE were angry scenes when one of the most sacred traditions in the build-up to an international match was ignored and England fans refused to sing the national anthem *'You're shit and you know you are'* at the new caretaker manager, Lee Carsley.

Said one pundit, "It was a disgrace. Gratuitously attacking an England manager is an integral part of England's footballing history. To fail to insult him before the match showed a disrespect for sacred tradition."

TV replays showed fans' mouths staying shut, when they should have been hurling abuse, calling him a "Turnip", or "Wally with the Brolly".

Readers of this newspaper can rest assured that we will strive to maintain the proudest traditions of the beautiful game, by dragging the new manager's name through the mud before running lots of pieces complaining that we never fulfil our potential on the international stage.

....

LATE NEWS

■ **As England wins some matches, the whole nation asks why the man who has restored our faith in the national team has not received a knighthood. Arise, Sir Lee! Come on King Charles, show us you care!**

Maily EXPRESSO graph
Friday 13 September 2024

STOP TALKING THE COUNTRY DOWN, PM!

WITH his continual moaning about the dire state of Britain and how things are going to get worse, Sir Keir Downer has unnecessarily plunged the nation into gloom.

Based on nothing more than the fact that he inherited the worst economic situation since World War 2, Sir Fear has chosen to wallow in misery, when what a truly great leader would do is talk up our prospects, create optimism and lie to the British public.

Where are the sunlit uplands and Singapore-on-Sea that we were all looking forward to with Boris and Liz Truss? What happened to the fixed NHS, the thousands of new hospitals, the zero immigration, the Brexit bonuses and the slashing of taxes that we enjoyed imagining under Tory governments?

Unrestrained boosterism raised morale, Sir Dire, and if you can't inspire the nation with feel-good empty promises, what's the point of you?

The nation has spoken, and it wants to be told what it wants to hear – that everything's great – and if you're not up to that, then let's get a PM who is truly deluded enough to take on the job!

EYEWITNESS REPORT

*Private Eye's smoking correspondent **PHIL ASHTRAY** was in the beer garden when the news filtered through that the new government was considering banning outdoor smoking in pubs. Here is his harrowing first-hand account...*

WHEN I heard the news, my eyes filled with tears. But that's because I was smoking. I gasped, not at the authoritarian nanny state diktat issued by Labour showing its true colours – but more on account of the toxic fugg hanging over the garden.

Yes, I choked, possibly because it was my 27th fag of the afternoon – and one of my smoking companions was literally speechless – on account of his voice box having been removed, and... *(cont. p94)*

DER SPIEGEL   31 July 1932

Far-right party makes significant gains in election

NAZI leader Adolf Hitler has hailed the 1932 election results, which made his party the largest in the Reichstag for the first time, though short of an overall majority.

"These election results prove we are now a mainstream anti-immigration party which is ready for government," Hitler told cheering supporters at a victory rally. "Our vote in Berlin doubled from 15% to 29%.

"I have transformed the party from being a disreputable bunch of far-right cranks into being a highly electable bunch of right-wing cranks. We cannot simply be dismissed anymore as Nazis simply because we are the Nazis."

Hitler delighted the Nazi faithful, promising to light a fire beneath German democracy, as reports of plumes of smoke billowing from the Reichstag... *(cont. p94)*

Ghost stories
"...and then the bastard stopped replying to my texts or answering my calls, leaving me feeling depressed, empty and broken-hearted"

London Fire Inquiry finally releases report

THE long-awaited report into the causes of the Great Fire of London was finally published today, after a wait of 358 years.

The report identifies a series of failings that led to the great conflagration of 1666, and lays the blame on a wide range of institutions.

Governments have neglected their duty of care towards residents over a number of years covering both Tudor and Stuart administrations, with a very hands-off approach to building regulations.

The much delayed report identified some building materials, such as tinder-dry wood, as being largely responsible for the fast spread of the fire. A spokesman for one Stuart timber merchant insisted their materials were 100 percent safe, so long as they weren't exposed to extreme heat from, say, the hot coals of a baker's oven.

As the clamour for prosecutions intensifies, the authorities are concerned that it may take a while to secure any convictions, as those responsible for the 358-year-old fire could now prove difficult to track down. The Chairman of London's Great Fire Inquiry said, "The important thing is that we learn lessons from the tragedy of 1666 and ensure that this kind of disaster never happens again."

LATE NEWS

Great Plague Inquiry report expected soon

▨ Inquiry Chairman says: "Lessons will be learned from the 1665 pandemic, to ensure that this kind of disaster never happens again."

GRENFELL: EXCLUSIVE TO ALL NEWSPAPERS

LESSONS TO BE LEARNED ABOUT WHY LESSONS WEREN'T LEARNED FROM PREVIOUS FIRE WHERE LESSONS WEREN'T LEARNED

GRENFELL FIRE How did the truth spread so slowly?

AS THE Grenfell Inquiry publishes its report, critics have highlighted the incredible lack of speed with which the truth spread.

Said one observer, "It was unbelievable just how slowly the truth came out – in these situations, truth can move at a slow speed, but I've never seen it move that slowly.

"It was months before we saw the first signs of truth and even then it was several years before more of the truth was visible."

Many blame the building companies involved for the slow spread of the truth, but the companies deny all responsibility.

Said one executive, "We are perfectly safe and to be trusted. Furthermore," he continued as flames began to rise around his pants, "we would do nothing to stop the truth spreading – our materials are as safe as the materials used in my underwear."

It is feared that justice will be even slower to spread than the truth, and, as one legal expert pointed out, "The tower of money these companies have made will probably remain undamaged and last for a very long time."

MUSIC TELLS TRUMP 'PLEASE STOP USING ME!'

by Mo Town Our US Pop Staff

IN AN astonishing intervention from the world of the arts, Music today pleaded with Donald Trump to stop using any of its material to promote and bolster his rallies.

Said the angry art-form, "The whole MAGA campaign simply doesn't strike a chord with me.

"I feel sick every time I hear a single note being played as that orange-faced buffoon jives his way onto the stage, pointing fingers of recognition at people he's never met."

Said one semi-quaver, "I'm meant to be A sharp, but I feel A flat every time I find myself associated with that narcissistic megalomaniac. He's so tin-eared and tone deaf!"

Music has now instructed its lawyers to pursue the Trump campaign through the courts, threatening to do whatever it takes, saying, "The only problem with lawyers is, I'm bound to run out of notes."

JAMES BOND
Producers announce further postponement of the next film in the franchise

Those 2028 Bond film titles in full

- ● **Delay Another Day**
- ● Diamonds are For Never
- ● **The Wait is Not Enough**
- ● Tomorrow Never Happens
- ● **Quantum of Solong**
- ● Doctor No Script
- ● **Doctor No Actor**
- ● Doctor No Ideas
- ● **Casi-no Script**
- ● Casi-no Actor
- ● **Casi-no...**
  (We get the idea. Ed.)
- ● Don't Ex-Spectre Nother Film Anytime Soon.
  (You're fired. Ed.)

"I'll not tolerate talking at the back of class, even if you are recording a podcast"

TORY LEADERSHIP RACE LATEST
JENRICK ADMITS TO INJECTING OZEMPIC

Everyone says they want to see less of me

What's the big deal? It's just a little prick

Bohemian Times

Friday 930AD

OUTRAGE OVER SCRAPPING OF WINTER FUEL ALLOWANCE

by Our Political Staff
Carol Christmas

The reputation of "good" King Wenceslas is under attack tonight over his controversial plans to ban yonder peasant from collecting winter fuel.

The King, Good Keir Wenceslas, got the idea for his money-saving policy when he looked out on the Feast of St Stephen and saw a poor man gathering winter fuuuu-eellll, proclaiming, "Frankly, I don't care if the snow is falling deep and crisp and even and the poor man's blood is freezing coldly, there's a big black hole in the Bohemian government's finances, and I'm not having every yonder peasant who comes in sight helping themselves to free firewood."

The winter fuel ban has been dubbed "as cruel as the frost that night", but Good Keir Wenceslas is unrepentant and blaming the previous king for creating an enormous deficit of tinder.

Yonder peasant said, "I used to think he was 'Good', but I'm beginning to think he's a bit of a bastard. The cost of flesh and wine has gone up hugely under the Wenceslas administration and I'm thinking, frankly, of not following in his footsteps."

According to one political commentator, "This has gone down very badly in the polls and Good King Wenceslas really needs to look out!"

(Cont. Good My Page 94)

Pensioners 'mean' testing fury

by Our Winter Allowance Staff
Jack Frost and **Peter Snow**

PENSIONERS throughout the home counties have expressed their anger at not being given free money this winter – instead being subjected to means testing.

Said one, "The fact that I'm sitting in a £2 million house with a triple lock pension and £100k savings in the bank, shows how mean I am, and this policy is testing that meanness to the limit."

Another old-timer agreed, saying, "I've saved my large amounts of money for a rainy day, and I've checked outside and it's not raining, it's snowing, so give me my free money immediately!"

"It is typical of Labour to target the comfortably off when they could so easily charge students double to go to university. None of the pensioners I meet on the cruises I take every year are made of money – as they've spent it all on themselves." *(Cont. 2094)*

POETRY CORNER

Lines on the nuptials of Sir Alan Bates on the island of Necker

So. Congratulations
Then Sir Alan and
Lady Bates.

You were married by
Richard Branson.

What a shame
You could not find
A proper priest to
Conduct the ceremony.

Like the Reverend
Paula Vennels.

E.J Thribbute (17½ years
waiting for compensation)

"This country's going to the cats"

Nursery Times

Friday, Once-upon-a-time

FEUDING BROTHERS IN TICKET NIGHTMARE

by Our Music Staff **Alison Wonderwall**

THERE was frustration throughout Wonderland today as residents scrambled to get hold of tickets for the reunion of the two warring brothers, Tweedle Liam and Tweedle Noel.

Famous for their fights and musical differences, which usually involved squabbling over a rattle, the infamous Tweedle brothers haven't spoken for years, but news that they had forgotten their quarrel and were planning a comeback created enormous excitement.

Said one Bucket Hatter, "I'm Mad fer it, me!" However, even the Cheshire Cat stopped smiling when it tried to get

hold of tickets only to find the system severely overloaded and prices soaring.

Another fan, Alice, said, "I got hold of a ticket saying 'Buy Me' on it and either I got very, very small or the price got very, very big."

The short-tempered Queen of Hearts got so furious at the prices that she shouted "They're off their heads!"

When contacted for comment, Tweedle Liam said something which cannot be repeated in a Nurseryland family paper, whilst Tweedle Noel simply called his brother "a total C*ntrariwise".

Post Office compensation row continues

■ The Post Office today refused to back down over its payment of £250 million to its lawyers.

Said a spokesman, "Yes, we know it's considerably more than the payout to the sub-postmaster victims, but we've checked the computer and it has confirmed that the sub-postmasters aren't lawyers and therefore are not entitled to exorbitant multi-million pound payouts."

He continued, "The sub-postmasters have clearly made a serious error in not going to law school and qualifying as greedy solicitors and barristers."

Pressed as to the ethical fairness of Post Office policy, he concluded, "We have taken legal advice from our lawyers and they confirm that they should have as much money as possible."

The View from The Shard and Three-Course Meal with Cock...
Groupon

Asian hornets that can kill in minutes attack 10 people with squads using Henry Hoovers
Mirror

I found a condom wrapper on my 19-year-old son's floor and told my friends about it - people say I've invaded his privacy, but others say it's normal to offload
Mail Online

Explainer Joe Biden meets Xi Jinping: seven key takeaways
Guardian

Pet owners may be paying too much for vets, says watchdog
Business · 1h
BBC News

Morrisons
Unsmoked Horse…   **• • •**
🏷 Buy 3 for £10
Morrisons website

Edward ReformUK Penis...
@EdwardDUK
Twitter/X page for Reform candidate Edward Dillingham

Disney offers something that streaming competitors 'are not offering,' anal...
Yahoo finance

Share a love of beavers this Valentine's Day
Dorset Wildlife Trust email

Water firms forced to pay back customers for poo...
BBC News (via Apple News)

Uninformed - Essex Police said uniformed foot patrols help them engage with residents and acquire local intelligence *(Image: Essex Police)*
Maldon and Burnham Standard

A grave error saw a man buried in the wrong cemetery plot meaning his body had to be exhumed and reinterred weeks later.
Great Yarmouth Mercury

New events planned to boost tourism in Dorchester
3rd February
CULTURAL ATTRACTIONS EVENTS FESTIVALS LEISURE DORCHESTER

Dorset Echo

Robotic arm development aims to help stroke patients
BBC News

HEARING SCREENING CLINIC PATIENTS
PLEASE SIT HERE AND WAIT TO BE CALLED
Cannock Chase Hospital, Staffordshire

Herring Achieves World Swimming Rankings
Sherringham Independent

Food giant Kraft Heinz wants to build a £40m green-powered hydrogen plant at its Wigan baked bean factory that could generate more than half of the gas it uses.
Manchester Evening News

Best Western Plus Intercourse Village Inn
£162.00
Booking.com

DUE TO UNFORSEEN CIRCUMSTANCES THIS EVENT IS CANCELLED
Psychic Night
Facebook post from Ludworth Community Association

PLANS for the annual Summer Fair in Windsor and Eton have been revealed.
    The event, which usually includes a fair and fuck race, will be including the Royal Borough's Armed forces day
Slough and South Bucks Observer

commiserations to those sex acts who did not make it through.
Eurovision, BBC1

This event has passed.

🗐 Event Series: Bereavement Friendship Café – Drop In
Longfield Community Hospice event

Esther McVey claimed Rishi Sunk would win a confidence vote 'by a country mile'
GB News

CK Group are recruiting for a Senior Chemist to join a leading provider of waste management services on a full time, permanent basis in Liverpool. This is a shit role, 6am-3pm, 11am-8pm, alternating each week.
LinkedIn job listing

The public toilets here are now closed.
We apologise for any inconvenience.
Bath, Somerset

Airbnb   11:22
Master the art of the long wee...
Airbnb email

Labour's 'vow to nationalise rail' and school stabbing
BBC News

British Naturism, while a much smaller organisation than its German equivalent, had a big rise in members during the pandemic.
Times

According to Dr Fanny Leboulanger, who specialises in gynaecology, my ancestors
i Newspaper

West Yorkshire railway station cat dies from terminal illness
Rail Advent

Conservative
Lib Dims
Telegraph

Key features
- Sought After Location
- Four Bedroom Detached
- Grade II Listed World War II Pillock
Rightmove property listing

𝕿𝖍𝖊 𝕿𝖊𝖑𝖊𝖌𝖗𝖆𝖕𝖍
MUST END SOON
Telegraph

Harry Wentworth-Stanley, an associate director at estate agents Savills, is the son of Nick Wentworth-Stanley, a debonair Old Etonian, and Clare, now the Marchioness of Milf...
Daily Mail